MW00855942

Laws for Life

Laws for Life

by

Keith Keyser

PRECIOUS SEED PUBLICATIONS

© Precious Seed Publications 2016
Picot Farm, Pitcot Lane, Stratton-on-the-Fosse, Radstock, BA3 4SX

Printed in the United Kingdom

Contents

List of Major Bible Translations Used

ASV = *American Standard Version*, Logos, 1995.
ESV = *English Standard Version*, Standard Bible Society, 2001.
HCSB = *Holman Christian Standard Version*, Holman Publishers, 2009.
JND = JOHN NELSON DARBY, *The Holy Scriptures: A New Translation from the Original Languages*, Logos, 1996.
LEB = W. HALL HARRIS, III, ELLIOT RITZEMA, RICK BRANNAN, DOUGLAS MANGUM, JOHN DUNHAM, JEFFREY A. REIMER, AND MICAH WIERENGA, eds, *The Lexham English Bible*, Lexham Press, 2012.
NASB = *New American Standard Bible: 1995 Update*, The Lockman Foundation, 1995.
NET = Biblical Studies Press, *The NET Bible First Edition; Bible. English.NET Bible; The NET Bible*, Biblical Studies Press, 2006.
NIV = *New International Version*, Zondervan, 1984.
NKJV = *The New King James Version*, Thomas Nelson, 1982.
NLT = *New Living Translation,* Tyndale House Publishers, 2013.
NRSV = *New Revised Standard Version*, Thomas Nelson, 1989.
RSV = *The Revised Standard Version*, Logos, 1971.

Foreword

For many Christians, the Old Testament is a 'clean' part of their Bible, remaining untouched and unread. Indeed, some have suggested that the Old Testament has little value for believers today. Either by design or default, both positions are dangerous, as they challenge the integrity of the scriptures and the obvious connection between the Testaments.

Any thoughtful reader would notice that so much of the New Testament is linked with the Old. The Lord quoted and referred to many passages and events that had been faithfully recorded in the Old Testament. The same could be said of His disciples. That thesis of gospel truth, the Epistle to the Romans, draws from a number of books, including Exodus, Numbers, Deuteronomy, and the Psalms, and relies upon illustrations from the life of Abraham and David. Any study of the Epistle to the Hebrews would prove baffling without some appreciation of the books covered here. The richness of that which Christ has accomplished and fulfilled becomes all the more precious when considered in the light of the truth of Leviticus alone.

In this particular volume, Keith Keyser provides us with an overview of the books that reveal the divine expectations in relation to a redeemed people. It is important that we, as redeemed believers, should understand what God expects of us. Leviticus commences with the offerings, emphasizing the children of Israel's and our primary responsibility – approach to, and worship of, God. The book continues to set out a manner of life for God's people that is both distinctive as well as separate. Whilst New Testament believers are not bound by this extensive system of regulation, it is interesting to pause and consider why God sought adherence to these things. What do these chapters tell us about the character of our God – His holiness, and righteousness, as well as His care for His people?

Clearly, New Testament believers needed to be reminded that, though they were not subject to Jewish ritual, God had not changed. What God condemned in regard to Baal-Peor, Numbers chapter 25, He condemns today! Hence, Paul wrote, 'Be not unequally yoked together with unbelievers . . . what concord hath Christ with Belial . . . Wherefore come out from among them, and be ye separate, saith the Lord', 2 Cor. 6. 14-17. Indeed, a few verses later, there is a reminder of aspects of truth covered in the books under consideration here: 'let us cleanse ourselves from all filthiness of the flesh and spirit, perfecting holiness in the fear of God', 7. 1.

It is the prayerful desire of the trustees that this volume and those that follow it in the series may whet the appetite of the reader to spend more time in these neglected areas of the Bible and, as a consequence, find that which will be a blessing to their souls.

On behalf of the Precious Seed Trust,

John Bennett
General Editor

Leviticus

1. Introduction

The Name of the Book: Like the other books of the Pentateuch, the English Bible follows the ancient Greek translation *The Septuagint* – as transliterated in Latin by *The Vulgate* – in titling it 'Leviticus'. Some have objected that this is something of a misnomer because Leviticus is mostly about the priests; in contrast, Numbers deals more with the subject of the Levites. But this complaint is based on a misunderstanding of ancient people's use of the term. The priesthood is levitical; hence they used the term *Leviticus.*[1] In keeping with its standard practice of using early words in the book, the Hebrew Bible calls it *vayiqra*, meaning 'And He called' after the opening statement: 'And the Lord called unto Moses', Lev. 1. 1. The place of this calling is interesting: in Exodus chapter 19 God called from Mount Sinai with dramatic signs that said 'stay away' to the Israelites, cf. Heb. 12. 18-29. But Leviticus chapter 1 verse 1 opens with Him calling Moses from the tabernacle – the dwelling place that He pitched in the midst of His people. It is a book of grace that inspires the believer with the confidence that the Lord wants a relationship with His people.[2]

---

[1] W. H. GISPEN, 'Leviticus, Book of', ed. D. R. W. WOOD ET AL., *New Bible Dictionary*, InterVarsity Press, 1996, pg. 683.

[2] Two gifted brothers of the past tease out the implications of this setting: 'Now, the tabernacle was God's dwelling-place in grace. He could take up His abode there, because He was surrounded on all sides by that which vividly set forth the ground of His relationship with the people. Had He come into their midst in the full display of the character revealed upon Mount Sinai, it could only have been to "consume them in a moment," as "a stiff-necked people"; but He retired within the veil – type of Christ's flesh, Heb. 10. 20, and took His place on the mercy-seat, where the blood of atonement, and not the "stiff-neckedness" of Israel, was that which met His view and satisfied the claims of His nature. The blood which was brought into the sanctuary by the high-priest was the type of that precious blood which cleanses from all sin; and although Israel after the flesh saw nothing of this,

Some prefer the rabbinic Talmudic title of the book, 'the priests' law'.[3] All of these are good descriptions of the contents of the book; it is God who speaks in Leviticus regarding the priestly offerings and the law that they taught concerning His holiness. He calls people to know, worship, and serve Him in a holy manner.

---

it nevertheless justified God in abiding amongst them – it "sanctified to the purifying of the flesh", Heb. 9. 13. Thus much as to Jehovah's position in this book, which must be taken into account in order to a proper understanding of the communications made therein. In them we shall find inflexible holiness united with the purest grace. God is holy, no matter from whence He speaks. He was holy on Mount Sinai, and holy above the mercy-seat; but in the former case, His holiness stood connected with "a devouring fire", in the latter, it was connected with patient grace. Now the connection of perfect holiness with perfect grace is that which characterizes the redemption which is in Christ Jesus, which redemption is, in various ways, shadowed forth in the book of Leviticus. God must be holy, even though it should be in the eternal condemnation of impenitent sinners; but the full display of His holiness in the salvation of sinners calls forth Heaven's loudest and loftiest note of praise – "Glory to God in the highest, and on earth peace, good-will toward men", Luke 2. 14. This doxology could not have been sung in connection with "the fiery law". No doubt there was "glory to God in the highest", but there was no "peace on earth" nor "good pleasure in men"'. C. H. MACKINTOSH, *Genesis to Deuteronomy: Notes on the Pentateuch*, Loizeaux Brothers, 1972, pg. 281. 'The first words from Sinai had been the holy law, forbidding sin with threatening of wrath: the first words from the tent of meeting are words of grace, concerning fellowship with the Holy One maintained through sacrifice, and atonement for sin by the shedding of blood. A contrast this which is itself a Gospel!' S. H. KELLOGG, *The Expositor's Bible: Leviticus*, A. C. Armstrong & Son, 1903, pg. 29.
[3] A. T. CHAPMAN, *An Introduction to the Pentateuch*, The Cambridge Bible for Schools and Colleges, Cambridge University Press, 1911, pp. 4-5.

2. The Purpose of the Book

Historically, the book of Leviticus provided teaching to Israel regarding the divinely ordained Aaronic priesthood and the proper way of approaching the holy God. In this postmodern age, these lessons are also important for contemporary people to learn. People think that there are many ways to God and that it does not matter how one approaches Him. Nor is one's lifestyle of much consequence in the grand scheme of the universe, they assert. Nevertheless, Leviticus declares that there is only one God, who is perfectly holy and demands holiness in His human creation. Holiness is not only negative – separation from what is common or impure – it is also positive – being devoted to the Lord for His purposes and glory. It entails both separation and consecration. This book teaches God's people in every age the importance of holiness in all of its aspects.[4]

R. LAIRD HARRIS recounts the context of the book in Israel's history, putting it alongside Exodus, Numbers, and Deuteronomy:

'The Israelites thus encamped before Mount Sinai just short of a year. During that time Moses spent eighty days on the mountain with God. Then the people of Israel, at Moses' instruction, built the wilderness tabernacle. During this year Moses organized the nation, built up the army, established courts and laws, and ordered formal worship. It was a busy year. Although most of the laws – both secular and profane – that Moses drew up at that time are found in Exodus and Numbers, Leviticus is the law book par excellence. Its laws, however, mainly emphasize Israel's worship of God and the instructions for the priests. For this reason,

---

[4] 'Leviticus speaks forevermore: Of the awfulness of sin in the light of the holiness of God, Of the plenteous redemption springing from the love of God, and Of the possibility of holiness of life, created by communion with God'. G. CAMPBELL MORGAN, *Living Messages of the Books of the Bible*, Baker, 1982, pg. 14.

doubtless, the LXX called the book Levitikon ("pertaining to the Levites"). Leviticus therefore does not include numerous prescriptions for secular court procedures and penalties. Such laws are concentrated more in Exodus 20-23. Deuteronomy, being a summary of both history and law, repeats some of the laws of both Exodus and Leviticus and gives other details'.[5]

Teaching His people ethical behaviour and holiness

Israel was a people who were called to be the Lord's possession – a direct theocracy meant to be a light to the surrounding pagan nations. As COATES remarks: 'The Book of Leviticus has in view a people in covenant relations with God, in whose midst God dwells, and who have movements of heart Godward . . . Here we see the manner and order of that service – the service of a free and willing people; and we learn that every outgoing of heart in the service of God is concerning Christ. Blessed service!'[6] In a sense, therefore, Leviticus has missionary intentions, for it provides a roadmap for the theocracy of Israel to live differently in this world and thereby draw the Gentiles to faith in Him. One of the ablest commentators on Leviticus, S. H. KELLOGG points this out:

> '[Leviticus] was given to direct them how they might live as a holy nation in fellowship with God. The keynote of the book is "Holiness to Jehovah". More particularly, the object of the book was to furnish for the theocracy set up in Israel a code of law which should secure their physical, moral, and spiritual well being. But the establishment of the theocracy in Israel was itself only a means to an end; namely, to make Israel a blessing to all nations, in mediating to the Gentiles the redemption of God.

---

[5] R. LAIRD HARRIS, 'Leviticus', in *The Expositors Bible Commentary*, ed. FRANK GAEBELEIN, Zondervan, 1990, electronic edition, no pagination.
[6] C. A. COATES, *An Outline of the Book of Leviticus*, Stow Hill Bible & Tract Depot, n.d., pg. 1.

Hence: the Levitical laws were all intended and adapted to train and prepare the nation for this special historic mission to which God had chosen them'.[7]

Although they never achieved this in the Old Testament era, in a future day Christ will reign over them and draw many peoples to Himself, Zech. 2. 10-12; Isa. 2. 2-4.

Why should one study an ancient book of rituals and laws?

With its seemingly arcane sacrificial and legal details, Leviticus is admittedly difficult for the modern reader. Nevertheless, it is part of the inspired word of God and is 'profitable', 2 Tim. 3. 16-17. A classic nineteenth-century commentary reminds one of this truth: 'There is no book, in the whole compass of that inspired Volume which the Holy Ghost has given us, that contains more of the very words of God than *Leviticus*. It is God that is the direct speaker in almost every page; his gracious words are recorded in the form wherein they were uttered. This consideration cannot fail to send us to the study of it with singular interest and attention'.[8] Studying Leviticus is recommended for the following reasons:

---

[7] KELLOGG, pg. 20 [brackets mine].

[8] ANDREW A. BONAR, *A Commentary on the Book of Leviticus, Expository and Practical*, Robert Carter & Brothers, 1851, pg. vii [italics original]. Another writer agrees in these words: 'No other book in the Bible affirms divine inspiration so frequently as Leviticus. Under the heading of the verb *to speak* (*dibbēr*) alone, the concordance lists no less than thirty-eight occurrences of the statement that Jehovah spoke to Moses or to Aaron. Nothing could be clearer than that this entire sacrificial system was no invention of the Hebrew people (either in Moses' day or in the course of later centuries) but a direct revelation of God. Otherwise no affirmation of divine origin is to be trusted for any statement in the rest of Scripture. While there may be some general resemblances or analogies which can be pointed out between these Levitical regulations and the cultus practiced by other ancient Semites, there is a complete absence of the degrading and

1. It is a tremendously theological book,[9] discussing God's essential being and His requirements for humanity. More than any other single book it teaches the concept of holiness. WIERSBE deploys impressive statistics to make this point: 'The word *holy* is used 91 times in Leviticus, and words connected with *cleansing* are used 71 times. References to *uncleanness* number 128. There's no question what this book is all about':[10] God's uniqueness and separation from anything

---

superstitious elements characterizing the worship of the idolatrous nations during the Old Testament age. A remarkable authentication of the divine origin of this Mosaic code is to be found in the semiprophetic twenty-sixth chapter. Here there is a preview of the subsequent history of Israel, with its progressive decline from faith to apostasy, and a clear intimation of the Babylonian Exile, vv. 32-39, and the subsequent restoration, vv. 40-45'. GLEASON ARCHER JR., 'Leviticus', in *A Survey of Old Testament Introduction*, 3rd ed., Moody Press, 1994, pg. 258 [italics original].

[9] '[T]his is one of the most theologically oriented books in Scripture. After all, it covers in some detail how the holy God defines sin, forgives sin and helps people avoid sin. It discusses how God's will is revealed and how God's presence can be assured. Leviticus also describes how God's people may be declared holy or how they may be what God envisioned from their origin (cf. Ex 19:5-6)'. PAUL R. HOUSE, *Old Testament Theology*, InterVarsity Press, 1998, pg. 126. AVERBECK makes a similar point, concisely: 'Overall, therefore, the theology of the Book of Leviticus focuses on the presence of God in the tabernacle, but that presence was to effect everyone and everything in ancient Israel'. RICHARD E. AVERBECK, 'Leviticus, The Theology', in Walter A. Elwell, *Evangelical Dictionary of Biblical Theology*, Baker Reference Library; Logos Library System, Baker Book House, 1996 [italics original]. Another lists its primary theological themes: 'Four themes are very important in the theology of Leviticus: (1) the presence of God, (2) holiness, (3) sacrifice, and (4) the Sinai covenant'. GORDON J. WENHAM, 'Leviticus', in WALTER A. ELWELL AND BARRY J. BEITZEL, *Baker Encyclopedia of the Bible*, Baker Book House, 1988, pg. 1329.

[10] WARREN W. WIERSBE, *Be Holy*, 'Be' Commentary Series, Victor Books, 1996, pg. 9 [italics original]. He goes on to write: 'The Hebrew word for "holy" that Moses used in Leviticus means "that which is set apart and marked off, that which is different". The Sabbath was holy because God set it apart for His people, Exod. 16. 23. The priests were holy because they were set apart to

evil, dark, or defiling. He is the exact opposite of anything base or impure. Moreover, He is supremely beautiful and is to be worshipped in 'the beauty of holiness', Ps. 29. 2. Thus, in Leviticus He demonstrates that He wants to commune with His people, but in order to do this He must deal with their sin and make them holy.[11] Another states it this way:

> 'The book of Leviticus communicates real and timeless truths about the God of Israel. He is holy and radically independent, yet intentionally joined to His people . . . His redemptive act requires that His redeemed people act redeemed. Many years later, the ultimate sacrifice of God's Son would not diminish these characteristics but bring the holiness of God, the sinfulness of man, and God's willingness to intentionally attach Himself to man into sharper focus'.[12]

Contrary to popular belief, the Almighty's holiness is a reflection of His love, because sin mars and destroys His creation. His love is jealous in the purest sense of that word. He wants to preserve His beloved creatures from the impurity, pain, and separation from Himself that sin causes. Thus, even though Leviticus only uses the actual word 'love' twice – both times horizontally, Lev. 19. 18, 34 – the concept of God's love is the foundation of the sacrificial system

---

minister to the Lord, Lev. 21. 7-8. Their garments were holy and could not be duplicated for common use, Exod. 28. 2. The tithe that the people brought was holy, Lev. 27. 30. Anything that God said was holy had to be treated differently from the common things of life in the Hebrew camp. In fact, the camp of Israel was holy, because the Lord dwelt there with His people, Deut. 23. 14'. WIERSBE, pg. 10.

[11] On God's distinct holiness this may be said: 'Paradoxically, the near, revealing, holy God is also the separate, distinct, other-than-human deity as well. God may come near to Israel, but God never shares Israel's need to repent of sins committed against self or others'. HOUSE, pg. 128.

[12] D. JEFFREY MOONEY, 'Leviticus, Book of', ed. JOHN D. BARRY ET AL., *The Lexham Bible Dictionary*, Lexham Press, 2012, 2013, 2014.

that provides people access to His presence.[13] Commenting on the burnt offering, ANDREW BONAR exclaims: 'What love is here! The heart of our God, in the midst of all his own joy, yearning to pour itself out to man'![14]

2. The holy life of the redeemed is depicted in the historical injunctions given to the Israelites; these have value as examples for modern believers. R. V. COURT speaks of this emphasis on holy living: 'For Israel, God's requirements were obedience and faith, and a reflection of God's own holy character in their daily life. The standard of the New Testament is the same, 1 Pet. 1. 16'.[15] Leviticus reminds

---

[13] 'Contrary to what you may hear today in some sermons and popular religious songs, the emphasis in the Bible is on the *holiness of God* and not on the love of God. "Love is central in God," wrote American theologian Augustus H. Strong, "but holiness is central in love".[2] God's love is a *holy* love, for the Bible states that "God is light", 1 John 1. 5, as well as "God is love", 4. 8, 16. Love without holiness would be a monstrous thing that could destroy God's perfect law, while holiness without love would leave no hope for the lost sinner. Both are perfectly balanced in the divine nature and works of God'. [Fn.2: AUGUSTUS H. STRONG, *Systematic Theology*, The Judson Press, 1949, pg. 271. WIERSBE, pp. 9-10.] G. CAMPBELL MORGAN eloquently concurs: '. . . [I]n this book of Leviticus there is most evidently present, though unnamed, a recognition of the love out of which the work of redemption proceeds. It is unnamed, for the word love does not occur in the book; but it is present, for the whole economy is evidence thereof. The only sufficient reason for redemption, and the only sufficient impulse for suffering, is love. I am aware that this is a theological question, and that other reasons have been assigned for God's work of redemption. I am only able to state that which is the profound conviction of my own heart, that the final explanation of the Divine provision of redemption is to be found in the all-inclusive statement of the New Testament, "God is love"'. MORGAN, pp. 12-13.

[14] BONAR, pg. 18.

[15] R. V. COURT, 'Introducing Leviticus', in *Day by Day through the Old Testament*, ed. C. E. HOCKING AND M. HORLOCK, Day by Day Series, Precious Seed, 1982, pg. 64.

Christians that our lives should be theocentric, revolving around God and His word.

3. The nature of sin is minutely described and the divine remedy through redemption is explicitly explored. As MORGAN cogently explains: 'There are two supreme values. First, a recognition of sin, and a revelation of its nature; and second, a recognition of redemption, and a revelation of its nature. Or, more briefly, sin and redemption, the fundamental matters concerning man and his need, and God and His provision'.[16]

4. A basic knowledge of the book is absolutely necessary to understand the teaching of many New Testament books, such as Hebrews, 1 Corinthians, Romans, 1 Peter, and the four gospels.

5. It is filled with types and shadows of the person and work of the Lord Jesus Christ. A careful reading of the book will repay one with beautiful pictures of Christ, as well as many principles stemming from God's holy character. The five offerings and the Feasts of Jehovah are particularly rich sources of truth regarding the Lord's redemptive work and plan for this world.[17]

---

[16] MORGAN, pp. 10-11.

[17] KELLOGG describes this typical purpose of Leviticus: 'And this leads to the observation that this law was further adapted to the training of Israel for its world mission, in that to every thoughtful man it must have suggested a secret of redeeming mercy yet to be revealed. Every such one must have often said in his heart that it was "not possible that the blood of bulls and of goats should take away sin;" and that as a substitute for human life, when forfeited by sin, more precious blood than this must be required; even though he might not have been able to imagine whence God should provide such a Lamb for an offering. And so it was that the law was fitted, in the highest degree, to prepare Israel for the reception of Him to whom all these sacrifices pointed, the High Priest greater than Aaron, the Lamb of God which should "take away the sins of the world", in whose person and work Israel's mission should at last receive its fullest realisation. But the law of

6. Leviticus affirms the exclusivity of Jehovah as the true and living God in contrast to the idols of the nations. HOUSE unpacks this teaching well:

'Throughout Leviticus the one God continues to command fidelity to himself. Israel must avoid idols at all cost and must reject the worship practices of the Egyptians and Canaanites. Only one God can save. Only one God makes a covenant with human beings. Only one God reveals concrete, understandable, holy standards to the people. Only one God lifts Israel out of harmful and shameful activities to make them a holy people. Only one God forgives

---

Leviticus was not only intended to prepare Israel for the Messiah by thus awakening a sense of sin and need, it was so ordered as to be in many ways directly typical and prophetic of Christ and His great redemption, in its future historical development'. KELLOGG, pp. 22-24. Elsewhere he writes: 'Finally, and for this same reason, Leviticus is still of use to us as embodying in type and figure prophecies of things yet to come, pertaining to Messiah's kingdom. We must not imagine with some that because many of its types are long ago fulfilled, therefore all have been fulfilled. Many, according to the hints of the New Testament, await their fulfilment in a bright day that is coming. Some, for instance, of the feasts of the Lord have been fulfilled; as passover, and the feast of Pentecost. But how about the day of atonement for the sin of corporate Israel? We have seen the type of the day of atonement fulfilled in the entering into heaven of our great High Priest; but in the type He came out again to bless the people: has that been fulfilled? Has He yet proclaimed absolution of sin to guilty Israel? How, again, about the feast of trumpets, and that of the ingathering at full harvest? How about the Sabbatic year, and that most consummate type of all, the year of jubilee? History records nothing which could be held a fulfilment of any of these; and thus Leviticus bids us look forward to a glorious future yet to come, when the great redemption shall at last be accomplished, and "Holiness to Jehovah" shall, as Zechariah puts it, Zechariah 14. 20, be written even "on the bells of the horses"'. KELLOGG, pp. 27-28.

unreservedly and judges fairly. Only one God stands ready to give Israel a land of its own'.[18]

3.   The Plan of the Book

Like other books of the Bible, Leviticus may be divided in several ways. Whichever approach one chooses, the book obviously begins with the Lord speaking and inviting His people to approach Him, Lev. 1. 1. The sacrifices and priesthood explain that this is not a lightly undertaken invitation. Something must be done to permit humans to come into their Creator's presence without holy wrath consuming them. Therefore, the book opens with redemption (sacrifice) and mediatorship (priesthood).

4.   Content Outlines of the Book

a) Chapters 1-7: Sacrifices.
b) Chapters 8-10: Priesthood.
c) Chapters 11-15: Personal purity and impurity.
d) Chapter 16: The Day of Atonement.
e) Chapters 17-22: Laws concerning individual holiness.
f) Chapter 23: Feasts of the Lord.
g) Chapter 24: Tabernacle function (lampstand and shewbread) and the penalty for blasphemy.
h) Chapter 25: The effects of the Year of Jubilee.
i) Chapter 26: Blessings and cursings pertaining to performance.
j) Chapter 27: Vows and dedication of things to the Lord.

> 'Theme: The holiness of God – "Be holy, for I am holy"
> Theme verses: Leviticus 11. 44-45
> I. Holy Offerings – chapters 1 – 7
>   1. Laws for the worshipers: 1. 1 – 6. 7
>   2. Laws for the priests: 6. 8 – 7. 38

---

[18] HOUSE, pg. 152.

II. A Holy Priesthood – chapters 8 – 10, 21 – 22
    1. Consecration: 8 – 9
    2. Admonition: 10
    3. Qualification: 21 – 22
III. A Holy Nation – chapters 11 – 17
    1. Clean and unclean food: 11
    2. Childbirth: 12
    3. Diseases and defilement: 13 – 15
    4. The Day of Atonement: 16 – 17
IV. A Holy Land – chapters 18 – 20, 23 – 27
    1. Immorality: 18
    2. Idolatry: 19
    3. Capital offenses: 20
    4. Annual feasts: 23
    5. Blasphemy: 24
    6. Sabbatical Year: 25
    7. Blessings and cursings: 26 – 27'.[19]

Others favour a two part outline:
Chapters 1-16: Worship (Doctrine)
Chapters 17-27: Walk (Practice)

  '1. Access, chs. 1 – 10
    (a) The five offerings, 1. 1 – 6. 7,
    (b) The law of the offerings, 6. 8 – 7. 38,
    (c) The priesthood, chs. 8 – 10.
  2. Holiness, chs. 11 – 27
    (a) Purity;
        (i) Pure Food, ch. 11,
        (ii) Pure Bodies, 12:1 – 14:32,
        (iii) Pure Homes, 14:33-57,
        (iv) Pure Habits, ch. 15,
        (v) Constant resort to Blood, ch. 16

---

[19] WIERSBE, pg. 8.

(*b*) Sundry Laws, chs. 17 – 27'.[20]

ROOKER points out that Leviticus' literary approach is similar to Romans and Ephesians:

'Doctrine	Application
Leviticus 1-16	Leviticus 17-27
Romans 1-11	Romans 12-16
Ephesians 1-3	Ephesians 4-6'.[21]

Others see the book as a collection of six manuals that give direction to Israel's collective spiritual life:

'I. The Manual of Sacrifice: Enjoying God's Presence, chs. 1 – 7
    A. The Offerings from the People's Perspective, 1. 1 – 6. 7 [HB, 1. 1 – 5. 26]
    B. The Offerings from the Priest's Perspective, 6. 8 [HB, 6. 1] – 7. 38
II. The Manual of Priesthood: Entering God's Service, chs. 8 – 10
    A. The Ordination of the Priests, ch. 8
    B. The Beginning of Priestly Ministry, ch. 9
    C. The Violation of Priestly Ministry, ch. 10
III. The Manual of Purity: Encountering God's Design, chs. 11 – 15
    A. Holiness and Daily Food: Clean and Unclean Animals, ch. 11
    B. Holiness and the Physical Life: Childbirth, ch. 12
    C. Holiness and Disease: Discerning and Cleansing of Disease, chs. 13 – 14
    D. Holiness and the Body: Cleansing after Discharges, ch. 15
IV. The Manual of Atonement: Ensuring God's Forgiveness, ch. 16
V. The Manual of Holiness: Enacting God's Word, chs. 17 – 26
    A. The Laws, chs. 17 – 25

---

[20] R. V. COURT, 'Introducing Leviticus', in *Day by Day through the Old Testament*, ed. C. E. HOCKING AND M. HORLOCK, Precious Seed, 1982, pg. 64.
[21] MARK F. ROOKER, 'The Best-Known Verse in Leviticus', in *Faith and Mission* 21:1, Spring, 2004, pg. 4.

1. The Sanctity of Blood, ch. 17
2. The Sanctity of Intimacy, ch. 18
3. Sanctity of Interpersonal Relationships, ch. 19
4. Punishment for Holiness Violations, ch. 20
5. Worship and Holiness, chs. 21 – 22
6. The Worship Calendar, ch. 23
7. Holiness at the Sanctuary, ch. 24
8. Holiness of the Land: Sabbatical Year and the Year of Jubilee, ch. 25

   B. The Cursings and Blessings, ch. 26
VI. The Manual of Dedication: Enamoured by God's Grace, ch. 27'.[22]

5.   The Author and Date of the Book

Moses' authorship of Leviticus does not appear to have been seriously challenged until the rise of the nineteenth-century sceptical critics. Nonetheless, we prefer to side with the remainder of the Old and New Testaments that clearly view him as the author of Leviticus. The other Old Testament books frequently refer to the Torah or Pentateuch 'the law of Moses'.[23]

The infallible Son of God implied Mosaic authorship when He gave instructions based on the commands delivered through Moses, as one sees when He quotes from Leviticus chapter 14 in Matthew chapter 8 verse 4: 'And Jesus saith unto him, See thou tell no man; but go thy way, shew thyself to the priest, and offer the gift that Moses commanded for a testimony unto them'. Elsewhere, the Lord referred to part of the Pentateuch as 'the book of Moses', Mark 12. 26.

[22] MICHAEL GRISANTI, 'Leviticus', in EUGENE H. MERRILL ET AL., *The World and the Word: An Introduction to the Old Testament*, B&H, 2011. He cites the major points as coming from DEREK TIDBALL, *The Message of Leviticus*, IVP Academic, 2005, pp. 5-6.
[23] See 2 Chr. 23. 18; 30. 16; 35. 12; Josh. 8. 31; Judg. 4. 11; 1 Kgs. 2. 3; 2 Kgs. 14. 6; Ezra 3. 2; 7. 6; Neh. 8. 1; Dan. 9. 11, 13; Mal. 4. 4, etc.

He recognized the well-known Jewish division of the Old Testament as '. . . Moses and all the prophets', Luke 24. 27, and in verse 44 describing it as: 'the law of Moses . . . the prophets . . . and the psalms'. Other instances of His verification of Mosaic authorship abound in the gospels, e.g., John 5. 46; 7. 19; and Matt. 19. 7-8. His apostles also believed this truth.[24] On one occasion even Abraham spoke from beyond the grave to authenticate the Pentateuch as genuinely Mosaic, Luke 16. 29!

Clearly, the Bible attests that Moses wrote the book of Leviticus and the other four books of the Pentateuch. To borrow the Welsh poet WILLIAM COWPER'S lines: 'Blind unbelief is sure to err And scan His work in vain; God is His own interpreter, And He will make it plain'.[25] As for its date, it was written in approximately 1445 B.C.[26] WENHAM explains the chronology of the book this way:

'God revealed some of the laws in Leviticus by speaking to Moses from the tent of meeting, or tabernacle, Lev. 1. 1. Other laws were revealed on Mount Sinai, 26. 46. Such statements show that Moses learned the contents of Leviticus after the tabernacle had been built, but before the Israelites left Mount Sinai. This fits in with Exodus chapter 40 verse 17, which says that the tabernacle was erected exactly a year after the Israelites left Egypt. They then spent another month at Sinai, during which time the laws in Leviticus were given to Moses. Then, one month later, Num. 1. 1,

---

[24] See, for example: Luke 2. 22; John 1. 17, 45; Acts 3. 22; 7. 37; 13. 39; 15. 21; 26. 22; 28. 23; Rom. 10. 5, 19; 1 Cor. 9. 9; 2 Cor. 3. 15; Heb. 10. 28; Rev. 15. 3.

[25] WILLIAM COWPER, Hymn 'God moves in a mysterious way', in JOHN NEWTON AND WILLIAM COWPER, *Olney Hymns*, Oxford: The University Press, 1783, pg. 294.

[26] JOHN MACARTHUR, JR., ed., *The MacArthur Study Bible*, electronic edition, Word Publishing, 1997, pg. 153.

Moses was commanded to prepare the people to leave Sinai to conquer the Promised Land of Canaan'.[27]

6.   Important Themes in the Book

A) God's holiness.
B) Personal holiness.
C) Christ's redemptive work – His multifaceted sacrifice.
D) Priesthood/mediatorship.
E) Israel as God's special people, separated to Himself.
F) The nature of sin and defilement.
G) The danger of bringing God what He does not ask for/the proper approach to God.
H) The uniqueness of Jehovah against the pluralism of the ancient near east (i.e., against idols).
I) Sexual morality based on divine teaching.
J) Freedom from indebtedness (Jubilee).

7.   The Contents of the Book

The instructions regarding the offerings – chapters 1-7

The five levitical offerings present a comprehensive and multifaceted view of the Lord Jesus Christ's person and redemptive work. Just as there is one gospel told from four vantage points in Matthew, Mark, Luke, and John, so there is one perfect sacrifice typically described in these five forms of sacrifice. The offerings themselves were offered at different times by different people.[28] The opening chapters of

---

[27] WENHAM, 'Leviticus, Book of', in ELWELL AND BEITZEL, *Baker Encyclopedia of the Bible*, pp. 1328–1329.

[28] For example, consider the NETmg.'s fn.3 on the burnt offering at Lev. 1. 3: 'It could serve as a votive or freewill offering, e.g. Lev. 22. 18-20, an accompaniment of prayer and supplication, e.g. 1 Sam. 7. 9-10, part of the regular daily, weekly, monthly, and festival cultic pattern, e.g. Num. 28-29,

Leviticus view them as voluntary offerings presented by individuals. Later, the offerings reoccur in differing combinations for individuals – such as the healed leper, Lev. 14 – and the nation as a whole, e.g., in the feasts of the Lord, ch. 23. A basic familiarity with the offerings is needed to understand much of the teaching of the book of Hebrews. What is more, the New Testament clearly understands them as pointing to Christ's saving work, calling it 'an offering and sacrifice to God for a sweet-smelling savour', Eph. 5. 2.

The order in which the offerings are presented is significant: one sees Christ's work from the divine vantage point (see the chart below). As sinners, humans usually think of the trespass and sin offering first – the former speaking of sin's damage and the latter emphasizing the principle of sin at work in fallen beings. Man immediately thinks of his guilt and the penalty that his sins merit. But God looks first at absolute devotion, which is the special theme of the first two offerings. He wants people to love him with the entirety of their person: heart, soul, and might, Deut. 6. 5. Only one man ever did this 100% of the time. Only one loved His Father perfectly every moment, as doing what pleased Him, John 8. 29, and never acting contrary to or independently of Him, Matt. 4. 1-11. It was the impeccable and incarnate Son of God who so devoted Himself to God the Father, offered up by the Holy Spirit, Heb. 9. 14.

Chart on the order of the sacrifices in Leviticus 1. 1 – 6. 7

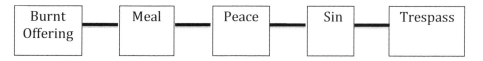

The offerings also may be categorized in different ways. For instance, the first three are 'sweet savour' offerings that do not emphasize

---

or to make atonement either alone, e.g. Lev. 1. 4; 16. 24, or in combination with the grain offering, e.g. Lev. 14. 20, or sin offering, e.g. Lev. 5. 7; 9. 7.'

25

Christ's sin-bearing or payment for the consequences of sin. The sin and trespass offerings deal with this aspect of the Lord's work and so they do not emit a sweet savour – or 'soothing aroma' as the *New American Standard Bible* renders the phrase. Nothing connected with sin – even representatively – is sweet to the Almighty.

The offerings may also be grouped according to whether or not they involve blood. Four of them are animal sacrifices and manifest the truth of life given in death by the shedding of blood. The meal offering is the exception, being a bloodless grain offering made of the finest ingredients. Therefore, the burnt, peace, sin, and trespass offerings all offer different views of Christ's work in His death; in contrast, the meal offering presents His work in His life as a perfect man.[29]

---

[29] MR. DARBY observes this distinction in his comments on the burnt and meal offerings: 'This devotedness to the Father's glory could, and indeed did, show itself in two ways: it might be in service, and of every faculty of a living man here, in absolute devotedness to God, tested by fire even unto death; or in the giving up of life itself, giving up Himself – His life unto death, for the divine glory, sin being there. Of this latter the burnt-offering speaks; of the former, I judge, the meat-offering: while both are the same in principle as entire devotedness of human existence to God – one of the living acting man, the other the giving up of life unto death'. J. N. DARBY, *Synopsis of the Books of the Bible: Genesis to 2 Chronicles,* Logos Research Systems, Inc., 2008, pg. 157. One of his friends agrees in this way: 'Neither in the burnt-offering nor in the meat-offering have we Christ as a sin-bearer. In the latter, we see Him *living*; and in the former, we see Him *dying*; but in neither is there a question of the imputation of sin, nor of enduring the wrath of God on account of sin. In short, to present Christ as the sinner's substitute any where else save on the cross, is to rob His life of all its divine beauty and excellency, and to displace the cross altogether'. MACKINTOSH, pg. 295 [italics original].

The burnt offering[30] – Leviticus 1; 6. 8-13

The Hebrew word for 'burnt offering' occurs 287[31] times in the Old Testament and refers to that which ascends in the flames of the altar.[32] With the exception of its skin, Lev. 7. 8, all of the animal was offered on the altar to God. It speaks of Christ offering every part of His being to God the Father on the cross. Nothing was held back. His utter devotion is prophetically depicted in graphic terms: 'He trusted on the Lord that he would deliver him: Let him deliver him, seeing he delighted in him. But thou art he that took me out of the womb: Thou didst make me hope when I was upon my mother's breasts. I was cast upon thee from the womb: Thou art my God from my mother's belly'. As Philippians chapter 2 verse 8 declares: 'And being found in appearance as a man, He humbled Himself and became obedient to the point of death, even the death of the cross', NKJV. Hebrews chapter 9 verse 14 succinctly states that He 'offered Himself'. The universal testimony of God's word is that the Lord Jesus offered up all of Himself to His Father on the cross.

The burnt offering presents the Saviour's complete consecration, which forms the basis of the believer's acceptance before God. Symbolically, the offerer identified himself with the sacrifice by

---

[30] Like the meal offering, Gen. 4. 4, the burnt offering predates the levitical system, Gen. 8. 20.

[31] G. WEHMEIER, עלה (olah), in ERNST JENNI AND CLAUS WESTERMANN, *Theological Lexicon of the Old Testament,* Hendrickson Publishers, 1997, pg. 885.

[32] FRANCIS BROWN, SAMUEL ROLLES DRIVER, AND CHARLES AUGUSTUS BRIGGS, *Enhanced Brown-Driver-Briggs Hebrew and English Lexicon,* Logos Research Systems, 2000, pg. 750. Another adds: 'The Hebrew term 'ôlâ, 'holocaust', expresses the manner of offering that sacrifice. Its aromatic smoke 'ascends' heavenward (the Hebrew verb 'ālâ) and is inhaled by the deity, in acceptance of the offering (Gen. 8. 21)'. A. LEVINE, 'Leviticus, Book of', ed. DAVID NOEL FREEDMAN, *The Anchor Yale Bible Dictionary,* Doubleday, 1992, pg. 312.

laying his hand on its head, Lev. 1. 4.[33] Ephesians chapter 1 verses 5-6 describe this blessed position that believers possess 'in Christ': 'Having predestinated us unto the adoption of children by Jesus Christ to himself, according to the good pleasure of his will, To the praise of the glory of his grace, wherein he hath made us accepted in the beloved'. IRONSIDE grasps this truth, saying:

> 'The offerer when he presented his unblemished burnt sacrifice was practically saying, "I have no worthiness in myself. I am full of sin and failure, but I bring to God that which is without blemish, that which speaks of the worthiness of His own blessed Son" . . . Observe, not according to our faithfulness, nor according to the measure of our zeal, nor yet according to the measure of our devotedness, but according to His own thoughts of His beloved Son. We who have been brought through grace divine to see that we have no worthiness in ourselves, have all our worthiness in Christ'.[34]

Even better is COATES' comment: '[I]n the burnt-offering we see that infinite perfection was there, and that the fire brought out the sweet odour of it. Everything in Him was found, even in that place of supreme testing, perfectly responsive to God in obedience, devotedness, and love, and though all was offered to God it was for us. How wondrous the privilege to bring the memorial of it to God for His delight, and for our conscious acceptance'![35]

---

[33] BONAR remarks: 'The happy Israelite who saw this truth might go home, saying, "I have put my hand on its head; it shall be accepted as an atonement". Faith in the Lord's testimony was the ground of an Israelite's peace of conscience, nothing of it rested on his own frame of mind, character, or conduct'. BONAR, pg. 22.

[34] H. A. IRONSIDE, *Lectures on the Levitical Offerings*, Loizeaux Brothers, 1929, pg. 17.

[35] COATES, pp. 13-14.

The burnt offering also presents an example of perfect devotion for our imitation, Rom. 12. 1-2. A 'living sacrifice' must be presented in the totality of our being. Every thought, word, attitude, and action ought to be presented to God for His good pleasure. Though we fail in this, the standard is still set by the Son of God who voluntarily offered His all to the Father on the cross.

The different types of animals offered indicate differing values and therefore represent various degrees of appreciation of Christ in His person and work. Happily, whether it was from the herd, flock, or birds, it was accepted by the Almighty. Our thoughts of Christ ought to be increasing in quality as we grow in the Lord. Yet despite our lack of complete knowledge, our acceptance rests in Him.[36] The chart below lays out pictorially the classes of burnt offering:

---

[36] Again DARBY captures the idea: 'loved as Christ is loved; it brings into fellowship and communion with God, as to the value of Christ's place. I know He takes perfect delight in me – a worthless creature in myself – and the more I know it, the better; but there is no condemnation for them that are in Christ Jesus. I go to God in Him, in the perfect sweet savour of Christ. It is not a question of any particular sin, but I go to God with the consciousness of being received and delighted in; I go, as the fruit of the travail of His soul. God sees in me, the perfection of Christ's work, and it is *for ever and ever*; but it rests upon our hearts *now*'. JOHN NELSON DARBY, 'The Burnt Offering, The Meal Offering, The Peace Offering' in *Notes of Addresses* [1880], pg. 244; electronic edition.

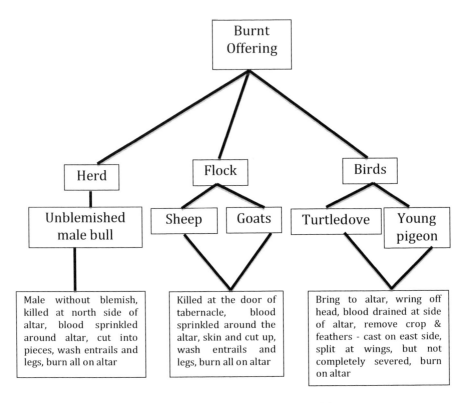

The meat/meal/grain offering – Leviticus 2; 6. 14-23

The above title reflects different translations of the *minchah*, the bloodless – that is, non-animal – sacrifice of Leviticus chapter 2. 'Meat' is the *King James Version's* translation of the word, reflecting the seventeenth-century use of the word 'meat' to connote food in general.[37] The British *Revised Version of 1881* and its cousin translation, the *American Standard Version of 1901*, use 'meal' in keeping with the flour base of this offering. More modern versions

---

[37] *Webster's Dictionary* (1913), definition #1; electronic edition accessed here: http://www.webster-dictionary.org/definition/meat.

prefer 'grain', describing the raw form of its basic ingredient, e.g., NKJV, NAS, ESV, NIV, NET, and HCSB.[38] The word originally meant an offering of any type – sometimes in the Bible it even denotes a non-religious 'present' for someone, Ps. 45. 12.[39] In Leviticus it has the technical sense of a food offering.

Given its composition of bloodless matter, the meal offering speaks of Christ's life rather than His death. Collectively, all of the types express His perfections, but this one particularly stresses His perfect and impeccable manhood. It was made of fine flour with no admixture of anything else. It was also unleavened, for 'leaven' – yeast as it is known today – is the biblical picture of moral or doctrinal evil.[40] It is unadulterated and represents purity in its composition. Oil – a term frequently associated with the Holy Spirit in scripture – was poured on it, and it was also anointed with frankincense, Lev. 2. 1-2. This last ingredient emits a sweet smell and is conspicuously absent from sin and trespass offerings, cf. 5. 11 and Num. 5. 15.

'The Word became flesh and dwelt among us', John 1. 14, and the angelic proclamation explained that His incarnation brought this holy one into a virgin womb and from thence into the world, Luke 1. 35. 'God was manifest in the flesh', 1 Tim. 3. 16, and elsewhere we are told that He was 'without sin', Heb. 4. 15.[41]

His manhood was absolutely real, Gal. 4. 4; Heb. 2. 14, 17, but it was not like fallen humanity, as Philippians chapter 2 verse 7 reminds us: 'But made himself of no reputation, and took upon him the form of a

---

[38] Less compelling are the *Revised Standard Version's* 'cereal offering' and 'oblation' of DARBY'S *New Translation*.

[39] The word occurs 211 times in the Hebrew Old Testament. WILLIAM D. MOUNCE, *Mounce's Complete Expository Dictionary of Old & New Testament Words,* Zondervan, 2006, pp. 304–305.

[40] Matt. 16. 12; 13. 33-35; 1 Cor. 5. 6; Gal. 5. 9.

[41] 'Sin apart', JND.

servant, and was made in the likeness of men'. On this last description, the noted Greek scholar GORDON FEE explains:

'. . . the troubling word *likeness* (*homoiōma*), which is most likely used because of Paul's belief (in common with the rest of the early church) that in becoming human Christ did not cease to be divine. This word allows for the ambiguity, emphasizing that he is similar to our humanity in some respects and dissimilar in others. The similarity lies with his full humanity; in his incarnation he was "like" in the sense of "the same as." The dissimilarity lies with his never ceasing to be "equal with God"; while "like" us in being fully identified with us, he was not "human" only. He was God living out a truly human life, all of which is safeguarded by this expression'.[42]

Another adds:

'The two phrases, "in the likeness of men" and "in fashion as a man", might seem to suggest an unreal, docetic view of Christ's humanity if we were dependent upon these alone for our doctrine of the Incarnation. Fortunately we have the whole testimony of the Gospel records to guide us in the interpretation of these expressions, and this testimony affirms that the humanity of our Lord was real. The Apostle's reason for speaking as he does in this text is not to insinuate that Christ was not true man, but probably to remind his readers that there is after all a difference between the man Jesus and man who is a sinner. Sinfulness is not a *necessary* characteristic of humanity, though it happens to be a *universal* characteristic of the humanity that we know. Because this last is so, men are in the habit of regarding sinfulness and humanity as correlative terms. Who has not heard that hoary-headed excuse for the sinner, "Well, he is only human"? We have

---

[42] GORDON D. FEE, *Philippians*, The IVP New Testament Commentary Series, Vol. 11, InterVarsity Press, 1999, pg. 96.

here, I think, a sufficient explanation of Paul's use of such terms as "likeness" and "fashion" in his reference to Christ's humanity; it is the guarded language of inspiration upon a theme where a misstep may invite confusion. (Compare the careful phrase in Rom 8. 3.) To the New Testament writers Christ is a real man made "in all things like unto his brethren", yet we are not to forget there is a difference; we are sinners, but He is "holy, guileless, undefiled, separated from sinners'".[43]

So the Lord Jesus is fully God and fully man, without sin or imperfection. Throughout His ministry on earth, He displayed total loyalty to God the Father. He is the one whom the Spirit abode upon like a dove, Matt. 3. 16; [44] there was nothing in Him to grieve, Eph. 4. 30, or quench the Spirit, 1 Thess. 5. 19. Moreover, there was no traitor within for Satan to exploit as a fifth column for making Him fall, John 14. 30;[45] Matt. 4. 1-11; Heb. 2. 14-15.[46]

---

[43] ALVA J. McCLAIN, 'The Doctrine of the Kenosis in Philippians 2. 5-8', *Master's Seminary Journal* 9:1, 1998, pg. 93. This article is a reprint; it was originally published in *The Biblical Review* 13:4, October 1928, pp. 506-527.

[44] Compare Genesis chapter 8 verses 8-12, where the dove finds no place to rest – it would not abide on carrion, for instance. But at His baptism, the dove readily abides on the One who is incorruptible and without moral spot or taint.

[45] 'There is no sense of indwelling sin. He could not describe his religious experience as his apostle does and his people do: "The flesh lusts against the spirit, and the spirit against the flesh", Gal. 5. 17'. WILLIAM GREENOUGH THAYER SHEDD, *Dogmatic Theology*, ed. Alan W. Gomes, 3rd ed., P&R Pub., 2003, pg. 662.

[46] Two quotations from the *Precious Seed* magazine's archives sum up Christ's perfect humanity well: 'This Bearer of holy humanity had no principle or root of sin within Him, did not commit sins, nor could because He was God incarnate. His holy humanity was and is impeccable and unassailable'. CYRIL CANN, 'Thoughts on the Humanity of Christ', *Precious Seed*, Vol. 52, Issue 2, 1997; electronic edition accessed here: http://www.preciousseed.org/article_detail.cfm?articleID=2562&keyword= impeccable; 'Sinless beyond argument; sinless in nature, sinless in act and

Christ's humanity was repeatedly tested and always came forth as completely pure and sweet. The various forms of baking the meal offering in an oven or in a pan, Lev. 2. 5-7, demonstrate the multiple ways that He suffered as a man, sometimes out of the public eye and other times in full view of men. The priest burned a memorial portion of the meal offering on the altar, showing that His perfectly obedient manhood and its attendant ordeals were a sweet smelling savour to His Father, John 8. 29. What remained of the meal offering was given to Aaron and his sons, Lev. 2. 10; thus men fed on that which spoke of Christ's perfect life on earth. Similarly, modern believers feed on the accounts of His life in the Gospels. We delight in the One in whom the Father has found all of His delight, Matt. 3. 17.

The last ingredient to be added was salt, Lev. 2. 13, which has the characteristics of preservation and permanence. Salt is indestructible and is also a common preservative for food. This pointed to the durability of the sacrifices' effects and its abiding value to God.[47] Jesus' salt-like speech, Col. 4. 6, is detailed by MACKINTOSH:

---

thought. He was incapable, by inherent perfection, of sin whatsoever. His purity therefore is fundamental to His mission of salvation. Only a sinless Saviour can offer Himself as a sacrifice for guilty, sinful men, Heb. 7. 26-27. The teaching of a sinless Saviour is absolutely fundamental to the Christian gospel'. MICHAEL BROWNE, 'Fundamentalism and the Gospel', *Precious Seed*, Vol. 40 Issue 6, 1989; electronic edition accessed here: http://www.preciousseed.org/article_detail.cfm?articleID=1387&keyword= impeccability.

[47] DARBY defines it as: 'the stability, the durability, the preservative energy of that which was divine, not always perhaps to us sweet and agreeable, was there – the seal, on the part of God, that it was no passing savour, no momentary delight, but eternal. For all that is of man passes; all that is of God is eternal; the life, the charity, the nature, and the grace continues. This holy separating power, which keeps us apart from corruption, is of God, partaking of the stability of the divine nature, and binding unto Him, not by what we are in will, but by the security of divine grace. It is active, pure, sanctifying to us, but it is of grace, and the energy of the divine will, and the obligation of the divine promise binds us indeed to Him, but binds by His

'The whole conversation of the Perfect Man exhibited the power of this principle. His words were not merely words of grace, but words of pungent power – words divinely adapted to preserve from all taint and corrupting influence. He never uttered a word which was not redolent with "frankincense", and "seasoned with salt". The former was most acceptable to God; the latter, most profitable for man. Sometimes, alas! man's corrupt heart and vitiated taste could not tolerate the pungency of the divinely-salted meat-offering. Witness, for example, the scene in the synagogue of Nazareth, Luke 4. 16-29. The people could "bear Him witness, and wonder at the *gracious* words which proceeded out of His mouth"; but when He proceeded to season those words with *salt*, which was so needful in order to preserve them from the corrupting influence of their national pride, they would fain have cast Him over the brow of the hill whereon their city was built . . . Grace is attractive; but "salt is good". Gracious discourse may be popular; but salted discourse never will. The pure gospel of the grace of God may, at certain times, and under certain circumstances, be run after by "the multitude" for awhile; but when the "salt" of a fervid and faithful application is introduced, it will soon thin the benches of all save such as are brought under the power of the Word'.[48]

The chart below demonstrates the different methods of preparation for the meal offering.

---

energy and fidelity, not ours - energy which is mingled with and founded on the sacrifice of Christ, in which the covenant of God is sealed and assured infallibly, or Christ is not honoured. It is the covenant of God. Leaven and honey, our sin and natural affections, cannot find a place in the sacrifice of God, but the energy of His grace (not sparing the evil, but securing the good) is there to seal our infallible enjoyment of its effects and fruits. Salt did not form the offering, but it was never to be wanting in any - could not be in what was of God; it was indeed in every offering'. DARBY, *Synopsis of the Books of the Bible: Genesis to 2 Chronicles*, pg. 183.
[48] MACKINTOSH, pg. 299.

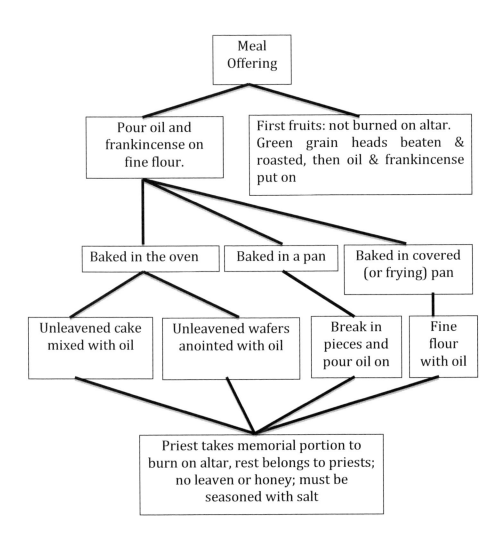

Meal Offering

Pour oil and frankincense on fine flour.

First fruits: not burned on altar. Green grain heads beaten & roasted, then oil & frankincense put on

Baked in the oven

Baked in a pan

Baked in covered (or frying) pan

Unleavened cake mixed with oil

Unleavened wafers anointed with oil

Break in pieces and pour oil on

Fine flour with oil

Priest takes memorial portion to burn on altar, rest belongs to priests; no leaven or honey; must be seasoned with salt

The peace offering – Leviticus 3; 7. 11-21, 28-35.

The peace offering[49] – a related word to the well-known Hebrew greeting 'shalom'[50] – brings the offerer, the priest, and the Lord together at the festive table. Each of these three participants was given a portion of the offering:

1. The Lord received the blood which was sprinkled around the altar, Lev. 3. 3, and the fatty portions, vv. 14-17[51] – including the kidneys and lobe of the liver, v. 4, which were burned on the altar atop the burnt offering, v. 5.

2. The offerer received the meat, Lev. 7. 15-16.

3. The priest received the breast and right thigh of the sacrifice, vv. 31-32, along with a heave offering of 'unleavened cakes mixed with oil, unleavened wafers anointed with oil, or cakes of blended flour

---

[49] The KJV's 'peace offering' is the best English translation as adopted by the most reliable modern translations, e.g., NKJV, JND, ESV, RSV, and NET. Following the Hebrew with exact literalness, the ASV and NAS have the plural rendering 'peace offerings'. A few of the more 'dynamic equivalence' style versions have alternative suggestions such as 'sacrifice of well-bring', NRSV, and 'fellowship offering', NIV, HCSB, NCV, GW, and LEB. MOUNCE defines it as 'fellowship (offering)'. MOUNCE, pg. 1056.

[50] 'Shelem' is from the same Hebrew root as shalom, and occurs 87 times in the Hebrew Old Testament.

[51] On the fat, DARBY writes: '. . . [T]he fat, the sign of the energy of nature, all given to God – no thought with Christ, no act, no object, but His Father. It was for us, thank God! But still absolutely to God: no infirmity, no listlessness of heart, but all given to God entirely, all the inward fat burned to God. Mark, not bearing our sins – that is never called a sweet savour except in one particular case. He was made sin, and that was not a sweet savour, though He was never so holy and perfect as then'. DARBY, 'The Burnt Offering, The Meal Offering, The Peace Offering', in *Notes of Addresses*, pg. 255 [brackets mine].

mixed with oil', v. 12 NKJV, plus leavened bread, v. 13. This last is surprising given leaven's association with sin in typology; nevertheless, two observations may be made: (1) It is offered as a heave offering – thus, it is not offered on the altar in keeping with Leviticus chapter 2 verse 11.[52] (2) It is an appropriate component in the offering, because one party of the festal meal – namely the offerer – has sin which must be dealt with by the blood sacrifices that make up the other parts of the offering. As 1 John chapter 1 verse 7 says: 'the blood of Jesus Christ his Son, cleanseth us from all sin'.

Three different reasons for offering this sacrifice were:

1. Thanksgiving, Lev. 7. 12.

2. Votive – i.e., from a vow, v. 16.

3. Voluntary, v. 16.

The peace offering provided the believing Israelite the opportunity to thank the Lord for making peace. Through the Almighty's gracious work – this sacrifice is based on the burnt offering, 3. 5 – he is able to approach God and fellowship around the one that reconciled him to his Maker, 7. 15-21. KINGSCOTE concurs with this assessment in these words:

> 'It is really a communion sacrifice, and thanksgiving and praise naturally flow from communion. Consequently, we have that expression, "If he offer it for a thanksgiving", Lev. 7. 12. Praise and worship necessarily flow from communion. The ground of it all is the value of the work of Christ in the sight of God. That, no doubt,

---

[52] See also Exod. 23. 18; 34. 25; Lev. 6. 17; 10. 12. Compare Amos chapter 4 verse 5 for a description of Israel's disobedience in this matter.

is why we find in chapter 3 that the peace offering is founded, as it were, upon the burnt offering'.[53]

The inclusion of the festal meal is reminiscent of peace-making and covenant ratification meals like the one that Jacob and Laban participated in, Gen. 31. 54-55. In that passage, one sees two parties who were previously antagonistic forming a peace treaty for mutual protection. Moreover, when God ratified the Mosaic covenant with Israel a peace offering with its corresponding meal was celebrated, Exod. 24. 1-11. Thus, the peace offering assures believers of the abiding faithfulness and everlasting love of the Almighty based on the redemptive work of His unique Son.

Truly, the Lord Jesus is 'the prince of peace', Isa. 9. 6, who makes peace for us with God through His sacrificial death on the cross, Rom. 5. 1; Col. 1. 20. Having this objective peace with our Creator opens the way for the enjoyment of subjective peace during life's trials and vicissitudes, Phil. 4. 7 (compare v. 9). Ephesians chapter 2 verses 14-15 demonstrate that 'he is our peace', and that this blessed state unites believing Jews and Gentiles in the one body. As the classic hymn declares: *'Peace, perfect peace, in this dark world of sin? The blood of Jesus whispers peace within'.*[54] Another poetically affirms:
'A mind at perfect peace with God:
Oh, what a word is this!
A sinner reconciled through blood:
This, this indeed is peace'.[55]

---

[53] R. F. KINGSCOTE, *Christ as Seen in the Offerings*, electronic edition accessed here:
http://www.stempublishing.com/authors/RF_Kingscote/RFK_Christ_Offeri ngs3.html.

[54] EDWARD HENRY BICKERSTETH, Hymn: 'Peace, perfect peace'; lyrics from http://www.hymnary.org/text/peace_perfect_peace_in_this_dark_world_of_ sin.

[55] CATESBY PAGET, Hymn: 'A mind at perfect peace with God', lyrics and a cappella version accessed here: http://saintsserving.net/song.php?id=1.

The chart below shows the different kinds of peace offering:

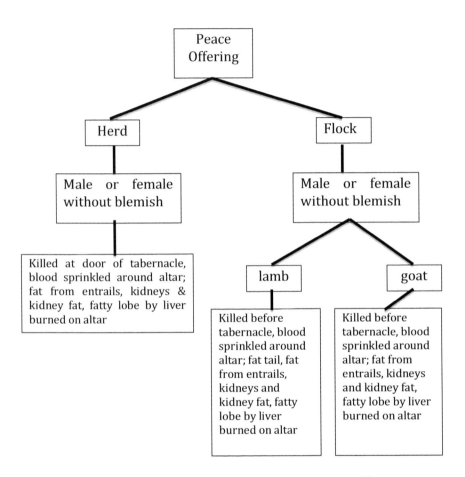

The sin offering – Leviticus 4; 6. 24-30 and the trespass offering – Leviticus 5. 1-6. 7; 7. 1-7

As previously mentioned, the first three offerings are sweet savour sacrifices that speak of Christ's worth and the Father's delight in Him, cf. Eph. 5. 2. The believer's acceptance and positive personal standing before God flow from this part of the Lord's work. By contrast, the sin and trespass offerings speak of God's abhorrence of sin and the high cost of forgiving the sinner. GIRDLESTONE relates the difference between the burnt and sin offerings in these words:

> '[T]he 'Olah, which was an offering of devotion, went *upwards*, both the blood and the flesh being lifted on the altar and turned to vapour, the sin-offering, which was mystically identified with sin, went *downwards* – the blood was poured down at the side of the altar, the animal, if not eaten by the priest, was burnt up on the ground, and as there was nothing pleasing to God in the sin which it represented, the smoke is not described as rising up to God as a sweet odour'.[56]

Since all of the offerings speak of the Lord Jesus, it is not surprising that the burnt and sin and trespass offerings are connected by where they are slain, Lev. 4. 24; 7. 2. The burnt offering holds the whole framework together. If Christ did not offer Himself without spot to God then the payment-for-sin side of the work would be useless. As KINGSCOTE describes it:

> 'So there are the two sides of the work of Christ. He gave Himself for our sins, in order to put them all away, never to be remembered anymore before God. But in the same place where He bore our sins, He was a "sacrifice to God for a sweet-smelling savour". The fire of God's judgment consumed our sin, and now, instead of there being judgment for us, the judgment is all past, and there is nothing left but the sweet savour of that sacrifice in which we are accepted. Compare Ephesians 5. 2: Christ loved us

---

[56] ROBERT BAKER GIRDLESTONE, *Synonyms of the Old Testament: Their Bearing on Christian Doctrine,* Logos Research Systems, Inc., 1998, pp. 200–201 [italics original; brackets mine].

and gave Himself for us – our side; "an offering and a sacrifice to God for a sweet-smelling savour" – what that work was to God'.[57]

Although their blood was shed at the altar and their fatty portions were offered thereon, the sin offerings were burned outside the camp, 4. 12. For sin offerings on behalf of a ruler or the common people some of the blood was put on the corners of the altar and the rest was poured out at its base, vv. 25, 34; if the blood was carried into the tent of meeting for atonement, then no part of the animal could be eaten, 6. 30. The Lord Jesus likewise suffered outside the camp of official Judaism – literally, outside of Jerusalem, Heb. 13. 11.

The high cost of sin[58]

The sin offering emphasizes sin's culpability before the Almighty; meanwhile, the trespass offering[59] has in view sin's injury.[60]

---

[57] KINGSCOTE, accessed here:
http://www.stempublishing.com/authors/RF_Kingscote/RFK_Christ_Offeri ngs4.html.

[58] 'By reading Leviticus one realizes the depth and pervasiveness of sin, the chasm between God and man and the absolute necessity for atonement to make mankind right with God. While the sacrificial system demonstrates these things, it also manifests its own insufficiency to meet these needs. Indeed, it points to something greater to come, and that is the fulfilment of the sacrificial system in the person and work of Jesus Christ'. JOHN D. CURRID, *A Study Commentary on Leviticus*, EP Study Commentary, Evangelical Press, 2004, pg. 24.

[59] Some prefer to translate it 'compensation' ESV. The ESV margin says: 'Hebrew *his guilt penalty*; so throughout Leviticus'. The NAS and RSV have 'guilt offering'; others have 'penalty for guilt', NET.

[60] 'Trespass' means '**sin**, disobedience, i.e., a violation of a standard and so incurring guilt, with a focus on not being steadfast and faithful to a person in a committed relationship, Lev 5. 15, 21[EB 6. 2]'. JAMES SWANSON, *Dictionary of Biblical Languages with Semantic Domains: Hebrew (Old Testament)*, Logos Research Systems, Inc., 1997 [boldface original]. See also WIERSBE, pg. 25.

Interestingly, the value of the offering was linked to the station of the one committing the sin – a 'missing the mark' like its New Testament counterpart, *hamartia*.[61] Priests, Lev. 4. 3, the congregation, v. 13, a ruler, v. 22, or a common person, v. 27, all had different instructions. So often the privileged get away with things in human society. In God's community, however, greater position brought greater responsibility.[62]

See Sin Offering Chart/Table on page 44.

---

[61] MOUNCE, pg. 654.

[62] The spiritual principle is noted here: 'There is a principle here that is well for us all to remember: The more light we have on the truth of God and the greater the privileges which we enjoy in this scene, the more responsible God holds us; we shall be called to account in accordance with the truth He has made known to us. Alas, my brethren, is it not a lamentable fact that should bow us in shame before God that many of us who pride ourselves upon a wonderful unfolding of truth are ofttimes most careless in our behaviour, and become stumbling-blocks to those who have less light than we? How we need to have recourse to the great Sin Offering, to remember as we bow in confession of our failures before God that all our sins were dealt with on the Cross of Christ'! IRONSIDE, pp. 56-57.

Sin Offering

Anointed Priest sins	Whole congregation of Israel sins	Ruler sins	Common People		If a person sins — Concerning an oath, touching an unclean thing, swearing		
			Female kid	Female lamb	Female lamb or kid	Two young pigeons or two turtledoves	Fine flour
Young bull without blemish	Young bull	Male kid of the goats					
Killed at door of tabernacle. Priest dips finger in blood and sprinkles 7 times before veil, blood on altar of incense, rest of blood poured at base of bronze altar. Fat (as listed in peace offering) burned on altar, rest of bull taken outside the camp to clean place and burned.	Elders lay hands on bull, killed before the Lord. Priest dips finger in blood and sprinkles 7 times before veil, blood on altar of incense, rest of blood poured at base of bronze altar. Fat (as listed in peace offering) burned on altar, rest of bull taken outside the camp to clean place and burned.	Ruler lays hands on goat, kills. Priest dips finger in blood and puts on horns of bronze altar. Pours rest of blood at base of altar. Fat burned on altar.	Lay hands on head, kills. Priest dips finger in blood and puts on horns of bronze altar. Pours rest of blood at base of altar. Fat burned on altar.			One as sin offering, one as burnt offering. Sin: wring off neck, sprinkle blood on side of altar, rest drained at base. Burnt: according to prescribed manner.	1/10th ephah: no oil, no frankincense; memorial portion burned on altar, rest is priest's.

44

No trespassing

Restitution is an intrinsic part of the trespass offering. C. F. KEIL explains: 'No crime against the property of a neighbour was to remain without expiation in the congregation of Israel, which was encamped or dwelt around the sanctuary of Jehovah; and the wrong committed was not to remain without restitution, because such crimes involved unfaithfulness . . . towards Jehovah'.[63] The Lord Jesus is the fulfilment of the trespass offering. He not only died for our sins, Gal. 1. 4; 1 Cor. 15. 3, He also 'restored that which He took not away', Ps. 69. 4. The idea behind the trespass offering's 'fifth part', Lev. 5. 16 – 20% in modern terms – is to make the one harmed better off than they were initially. Not only is the damage repaired, there is an added element to assuage the pain of the trespass. This principle is seen in the Lord's redemptive work. Many Bible students note that in His death, resurrection, and ascension the last Adam regained more than the first Adam lost, Rom. 8. 16-30; 1 Cor. 15. 20-28, 42-57.

See Trespass Offering Chart on page 46

[63] CARL FRIEDRICH KEIL and FRANZ DELITZSCH, *Commentary on the Old Testament*, Vol. 1, Hendrickson, 1996, pg. 668.

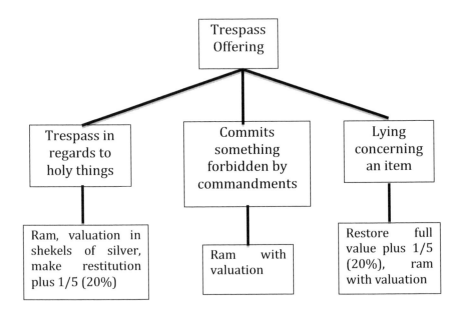

The consecration and beginnings of the Aaronic Priesthood – Leviticus chapters 8-10

These three chapters concern the inauguration of the Aaronic priests' office and ministry, as well as an early instance of their failure. Chapter 8 describes the divine order for putting them into this sacred position; chapter 9 details their sacrificial work; and chapter 10 recounts Aaron's two eldest sons' disobedience in their worship and the divine judgement that followed. WIERSBE summarizes the priestly responsibilities in these chapters in these words:

Chapter 8: 'Submitting to God's authority'
Chapter 9: 'Revealing God's glory'

Chapter 10: 'Accepting God's discipline'.[64]

Chapter 8 follows a literary parallelism known as a 'chiastic' structure:[65]

'A   Introduction at doorway to Tent of Meeting, 8. 1-5
B   Anointing of Aaron and his garments, 8. 6-13
C   Bull of the sin offering, 8. 14-17
D   Ram of the burnt offering, 8. 18-21
C[1] Ram of installation, 8. 22-29
B[1] Anointing of Aaron and his garments, 8. 30
A[1] Conclusion at doorway to Tent of Meeting, 8. 31-36'.[66]

The elaborate ordination of these priests employed sacrifices that were previously revealed in Leviticus chapters 1-7. Chapters 8-9 are the fulfilment of the instructions in Exodus chapter 29 – see also the description of the holy garments in Exodus chapter 28. The burnt, sin, and meal offerings all play a part on the outfitting of Aaron and his sons for their new ministry.[67] The chart below depicts the various sacrifices and their recipients:

---

[64] WIERSBE, pg. 31.
[65] Or 'chiasmus' from the Greek letter 'chi' whose shape the structure resembles.
[66] CURRID, pg. 103.
[67] COATES is reminded of the New Testament assembly as he reads the injunction for Aaron and his sons to stay at the Tent of meeting's door for seven days, Lev. 8. 33, and the subsequent reception of their ministry, 9. 24. See COATES, pp. 106-107.

Leviticus 8: Consecration of Aaron and sons

Take: v. 2

Garments
Anointing oil
Bull as sin offering
Two rams
Basket of unleavened bread

Place: v. 3

Door of tent of meeting

1.   Wash (by Moses) v. 6
2.   Aaron clothed (by Moses) vv. 7-9
3.   Anointed
(a) Tabernacle and furniture vv. 10-11
(b) Aaron's head v. 12
4.   Sons clothed v. 13
5.   Sin offering (bull) vv. 14-17
(a) Purified altar v. 15
(b) Poured at base v. 15
(c) Fat, lobe of liver, kidneys & fat offered on altar, v. 16
(d) Bull burned outside camp, v. 17
6.   Burnt offering (ram), vv. 18-21
7.   Ram of consecration, vv. 22-32
(a) Blood on right ear, thumb, and big toe, vv. 23-24: (i) Aaron; (ii) Sons
(b) Fat and right thigh, v. 25
(c) Offered with the thigh, v. 26: (i) Unleavened cake; (ii) Cake anointed with oil; (iii) One wafer
(d) Hands filled with these, wave offering, then burned on the burnt offering, vv. 27-28
(e) Breast wave offering, then given to Moses, v. 29
(f) Flesh boiled and eaten with unleavened bread, v. 31: (i) At door of tent of meeting, v. 31; (ii) Leftovers burned with fire, v. 32

		Seven days – stay at door of tent of meeting, vv. 33-36 'For seven days he shall consecrate you', v. 33	

Chapter 9 describes the beginning of their official work as priests, offering for themselves and their nation.[68] The table below shows their activities:

I			On the 8th day, v. 1
	A		For Aaron, v. 2
		1.	Young bull = sin offering
		2.	Ram = burnt offering
	B		For the children of Israel, vv. 3-4
		1.	Kid of goats = sin offering
		2.	1st year calf and 1st year lamb = burnt offering
		3.	Bull and ram = peace offering
		4.	Grain offering mixed with oil
	C		Obedience to this and further instructions
II			Carrying out instructions from verses 1-4:
	A		Aaron sacrifices, vv. 8-11
		1.	Aaron kills calf of sin offering for himself
		2.	Puts blood on altars' horns and pours out the rest
		3.	Fat & portions burned on altar
		4.	Flesh & hide burned with fire outside the camp
	B		Offered burnt offering, vv. 12-14
	C		People's offering, vv. 15-21
		1.	Goat = sin offering

---

[68] As marvellous as this system was for the Old Testament believers affording them tremendous access to God's presence, New Testament believers' privileges are far superior. COATES describes it this way: 'These precious types are full of instruction, but Christianity transcends even what is so wondrously pictured here'. COATES, pg. 107.

II	C	2.	Burnt offering
		3.	Part of grain offering burned on burnt offering
		4.	Bull & ram = peace offering
		5.	Breast & right thigh = wave offering
	D		Conclusion, vv. 22-24
		1.	Priestly blessing
		2.	Glory of the Lord with fire = awe of the people

Playing with fire

The Lord manifested His reception of the Aaronic priesthood and their offerings by consuming the burnt offering and fat on the altar through a dramatic display of divine fire. Chapter 10 speaks of a second incident where His fire came forth, but this time it was wrath not grace that motivated the burning. Nadab and Abihu offered 'strange fire' – 'profane fire' as some render it[69] – from their own censers, and discovered to their cost that God requires obedience[70] in worship, not human innovation. Despite their privileged position of nearness to the Almighty, they failed to sanctify Him by following His

---

[69] As it is in the NKJV; the NIV, ESV, and HCSB have 'unauthorized fire'; the LEB has 'illegitimate fire'; the RSV has 'unholy fire'.

[70] 'Nothing was needed on man's part save a spirit of implicit obedience to the divine command. But herein they failed. Man has always proved himself ill-disposed to walk in the narrow path of strict adherence to the plain Word of God. The bypath has ever seemed to present resistless charms to the poor human heart. "Stolen waters are sweet, and bread eaten in secret is pleasant", Prov. 9. 17. Such is the enemy's language; but the lowly, obedient heart knows full well that the path of subjection to the Word of God is the only one that leads to "waters" that are really "sweet", or to "bread" that can be rightly called "pleasant". Nadab and Abihu might have deemed one kind of "fire" as good as another, but it was not their province to decide as to that. They should have acted according to the word of the Lord; but instead of this, they took their own way and reaped the awful fruits thereof. "He knoweth not that the dead are there; and that her guests are in the depths of hell"'. MACKINTOSH, pg. 344.

word. Fire in the tabernacle sacrifices was to come from the brazen altar; to bring in incendiary material from a foreign source violated God's holy standards. Privilege does not guarantee faithfulness.[71] This is a principle that repeatedly appears in the Bible from man's fall in the garden, Gen. 3, to the failure of apostate churches, Rev. 3. 14-21.[72] Worship is meant to focus the attention on the Lord, not on man's talents or ideas.

---

[71] WIERSBE'S enumeration of their failures is devastating: 'Everything that these two men did was wrong. To begin with, they were *the wrong people* to be handling the incense and presenting it to the Lord. This was the task of their father, the high priest, Exod. 30. 7-10. They also used *the wrong instruments*, their own censers instead of the censer of the high priest, sanctified by the special anointing oil, 40. 9. They acted at *the wrong time*, for it was only on the annual Day of Atonement that the high priest was permitted to take incense into the holy of holies, and even then he had to submit to a special ritual, Lev. 16. 1ff. They acted under *the wrong authority*. They didn't consult with Moses or their father, nor did they seek to follow the Word of God, which Moses had received. In burning the incense, they used *the wrong fire* . . . The high priest was commanded to burn the incense on coals taken from the brazen altar, 16. 12, but Nadab and Abihu supplied their own fire, and God rejected it. They acted from *the wrong motive* and didn't seek to glorify God alone, 10. 3 . . . Finally, they depended on *the wrong energy*; for verses 9-10 imply that they were under the influence of alcohol. This reminds us of Ephesians 5. 18, "And be not drunk with wine . . . but be filled with the Spirit". If every child of God were killed who substituted fleshly energy for the power of the Spirit, not many would be left'! WIERSBE, pp. 38-39 [italics original].

[72] MACKINTOSH'S comments on this phenomenon are outstanding: 'The page of human history has ever been a sadly blotted one. It is a record of failure from first to last. Amid all the delights of Eden, man hearkened to the tempter's lie, Gen. 3; when preserved from judgment by the hand of electing love, and introduced into a restored earth, he was guilty of the sin of intemperance, Gen. 9; when conducted, by Jehovah's out-stretched arm, into the land of Canaan, he "forsook the Lord, and served Baal and Ashtaroth", Judges 2. 13; when placed at the very summit of earthly power and glory, with untold wealth at his feet, and all the resources of the world at his command, he gave his heart to the uncircumcised stranger, 1 Kings 11. No

True priesthood entails reverent submission and appreciation of God's uniquely holy character, as Leviticus chapter 10 verse 3 says: 'This is it that the LORD spake, saying, I will be sanctified in them that come nigh me, and before all the people I will be glorified. And Aaron held his peace'. The high priest's silence stemmed from his awe of the Lord's righteous judgement. The same Hebrew expression occurs in Exodus chapter 15 verse 16, referring to the Canaanite enemies who would be frozen with fear during Israel's conquest: 'They will be as still as a stone'. His reaction was one of devastated acceptance. Throughout the passage, Aaron puts God's honour ahead of his family loyalty. His sons sinned against the Lord; he sides with his Creator over his own offspring. The New Testament bids every believer to show the same kind of allegiance to Christ, Matt. 10. 34-39; 19. 29-30.

God forbids any public display of mourning by Aaron and his surviving sons due to their consecrated status. Instead, the nation grieves on behalf of their spiritual representatives, Lev. 10. 6-7, their kinsmen remove them to the unclean place 'outside the camp'. Verses 8-11 explain why priests are forbidden to drink 'wine nor strong drink' when attending to their spiritual duties. Such things could impair their judgement, and so they must be left to the domestic scene. Jewish tradition and some Christian commentators believe that this exhortation alludes to the fact that Nadab and Abihu's

---

sooner had the blessings of the gospel been promulgated than it became needful for the Holy Ghost to prophesy concerning "grievous wolves", "apostasy", and all manner of failure, Acts 20. 29; 1 Tim. 4. 1-3; 2 Tim. 3. 1-5; 2 Pet. 2; Jude. And, to crown all, we have the prophetic record of human apostasy from amid all the splendours of millennial glory, Rev. 20. 7-10. Thus, man spoils everything. Place him in a position of highest dignity, and he will degrade himself; endow him with the most ample privileges, and he will abuse them; scatter blessings around him in richest profusion, and he will prove ungrateful, place him in the midst of the most impressive institutions, and he will corrupt them. Such is man! Such is nature in its fairest forms and under the most favourable circumstances'! MACKINTOSH, pg. 343.

intemperate behaviour flowed from inebriation. The scriptures do not directly say this, however, so it seems best to remain silent on that point. Obviously, discernment and clear minds for teaching the Lord's commandments are paramount in priestly service, as verses 10-11 explain: 'And that ye may put difference between holy and unholy, and between unclean and clean; And that ye may teach the children of Israel all the statutes which the Lord hath spoken unto them by the hand of Moses'. Holy and royal priests in this age need the same clear-headed ability in worship and preaching, 1 Pet. 2. 5, 9; Eph. 5. 18.

The remainder of the chapter speaks of Moses' instructions for the newly ordained priests to eat the grain and sin offerings. He diligently investigated the priests' activities, doubtless not wanting any further instance of wrath to break for any failure on their part.[73] When he discovered that Eleazar and Ithamar had not eaten the sin offering – the second one which was offered for the people – he believed this to be a violation of the instructions in chapter 6 verse 30. Actually, Aaron's defence reveals that their action was prompted out of the fear of the Lord, Lev. 10. 19-20. Grief, and a reluctance to offend any further, led to their fasting on this occasion. Moses accepted that explanation for their behaviour in the knowledge that it was pious and natural under the circumstances.

Leviticus 10 content outline

Nadab and Abihu's strange fire and the Lord's wrath, vv. 1-3.
Burial by their kin, vv. 4-5.
Aaron and sons forbidden to grieve or leave tent, vv. 6-7.

---

[73] The NKJV renders the KJV's 'diligently sought' in Leviticus chapter 10 verse 16 as 'he made careful inquiry'. The Hebrew phrase says 'looking, he looked', laying emphasis grammatically on his serious efforts at arriving at the true state of things. See CURRID, 'fn.56', pg. 136.

Admonition to sobriety so that they may discern and teach statutes, vv. 8-11.

Moses instructions regarding eating the offerings.
Grain offering, vv. 12-13.
Breast of wave offering and thigh of heave offering for you, sons, and daughters, vv. 14-15.
Moses angry that grain offering not eaten and blood not brought into Holy place, vv. 16-18.
Aaron's defence and Moses' acceptance, vv. 19-20.

Purity and separation in the camp, Leviticus chapters 11-15

The elaborate laws of the next section of Leviticus focused all of daily Israelite life around ceremonial purity and separation from defilement.[74] God's standard for His people is holiness, like His own character, Lev. 11. 44-45; 1 Pet. 1. 15-16. As HARRISON writes: 'God's people must be seen to be distinctive in their way of life, and as free as possible from any evil pollution of body or spirit'.[75] MACKINTOSH goes further in grounding the reason for personal holiness in their relationship with the Lord:

> 'It is well to see that the personal holiness of God's people – their entire separation from all manner of uncleanness, flows out of

---

[74] As a contemporary author notes: 'So the next time you read through Leviticus 11-15, slow down. Read the details. Contemplate how deeply sin affected the ordinary life of the ancient Israelite. From that, be reminded how deeply, and how thoroughly, sin affects your life. Give thanks that you do not live under the burden of the shadow of the law, with its washings and its sacrifices. Rejoice that you live under the easy yoke of Christ, whose blood has cleansed your conscience from dead works and enables you to serve, from the heart, the living God'. BENJAMIN SHAW, 'Clean and Unclean', in *Tabletalk*, October 2014, pg. 16.

[75] R. K. HARRISON, *Leviticus: An Introduction and Commentary*, Tyndale Old Testament Commentaries, Vol. 3. InterVarsity Press, 1980, pg. 136.

their relationship to Him. It is not upon the principle of "Stand by thyself: I am holier than thou"; but simply this: "God is holy", and therefore all who are brought into association with Him must be holy likewise. It is in every way worthy of God that *His* people should be holy . . . If anyone had asked an Israelite of old, Why do you shrink so from that reptile which crawls along the path? He would have replied, Jehovah is holy, and I belong to Him. He has said, "Touch not". So also now, if a Christian be asked why he walks apart from the ten thousand things in which the men of this world participate, his answer is simply to be, *My Father is holy.* This is the true foundation of personal holiness. The more we contemplate the divine character, and enter into the power of our relationship to God, in Christ, by the energy of the Holy Ghost, the holier we must, of necessity, be'.[76]

Separation in the normal activities of daily life emphasized that Israelites must be clean in what they imbibed and how they walked. Their diet was different, and, therefore, would aid them in being separate from their pagan neighbours. The dangers of eating with unbelievers are seen in the idolatrous feast at Baal Peor, Num. 25, which led to spiritual and physical adultery. By eating differently the Israelites also created opportunities to testify to unbelievers about the true and living God.

Some suggest that since the first command in the Bible is diet related, Gen. 2. 16-17, Leviticus chapter 11 is a deliberate reminder that God sets the boundaries for His people.[77] Older commentators[78] see a picture of a separated walk in the cloven hooves of the clean animals. Following the Lord leads to a holy lifestyle. Ruminating animals'

---

[76] MACKINTOSH, pp. 356-357 [italics original].
[77] MARK F. ROOKER, *Leviticus*, The New American Commentary, Vol. 3A. Broadman and Holman, 2000, pp. 174-175.
[78] For example, see MACKINTOSH, pp. 353-354.

practice of chewing the cud reminded them of careful meditation on the word of God – a vital discipline for all believers at all times.

Chapter 11 breaks down into six sections which are demarcated by the words 'this', vv. 2, 9, 29, 46, or 'these', vv. 13, 24. More broadly, the chapter divides into two sections:

1. Clean and unclean foods, vv. 1-23.
2. Defilement by contact, vv. 24-47.[79]

The following list depicts the different categories of clean and unclean foods, as well as the ceremonially defiling entities:

Leviticus 11: Clean and unclean animals for food and ceremonial defilement

A. Permitted
    i.   Divides hoof and chews cud (both, not one or the other), vv. 2-3
    ii.   Water: fins and scales

B. Not permitted, vv. 4-8, 10-20, 23, 29-30, 41-43
    i.   Chews the cud only, vv. 4-6
        a)   Camel
        b)   Rock hyrax
        c)   Hare
    ii.   Cloven hooves only, v. 7
        a)   Swine
    iii.   Anything in water that does not have fins or scales, vv. 10-12
    iv.   Specific birds, vv. 13-19
        a)   Eagle, vulture, buzzard
        b)   Kite and falcon, raven, ostrich, sea gull, hawk

---

[79] The literary breakdown here presented is originally found in ROOKER, pg. 169.

  c) Various owls, jackdaw, and carrion vulture
  d) Stork, heron, hoopoe, and bat
 v. Four footed insects that fly, v. 23
 vi. Exceptions: jointed legs above feet for leaping, vv. 21-22
  a) Locusts
  b) Destroying locusts
  c) Crickets
  d) Grasshoppers
 vii. Creeping things / rodents and reptiles
  a) Mole, mouse
  b) Large lizard, gecko, monitor lizard, sand reptile, sand lizard, chameleon
 viii. Whatever crawls on its belly, v. 42

C. Unclean
 i. Carcass of unclean insects, v. 24-25
 ii. Carcass of animal with divided foot, but *not* cloven-hooved or chews cud, v. 26
 iii. Carcass of animal that goes on paws, vv. 27-28

D. Response to uncleanness from unclean animals
 i. If carry carcass, wash clothes and be unclean until evening, v. 28
 ii. If touch when dead, unclean until evening, v. 31
 iii. Anything on which it falls when dead is unclean, put in water and unclean until evening, v. 32
  a) Wood
  b) Clothing or skin or sack
 iv. Earthen vessel into which it falls you shall break (what is inside is unclean), vv. 33-34
 v. Oven or cooking stove shall be broken down, v. 35
 vi. Exception: spring or cistern in which is plenty of water, planting seed to be sown, vv. 36-37
 vii. Clean animal that dies, if touch carcass, unclean until evening, vv. 39-40

a)   If eat carcass, wash clothes and be unclean until evening
b)   If carry carcass, wash clothes and be unclean until evening

The chapter concludes with a summary, vv. 44-47, that reminds the reader that the Lord is holy and demands holiness of those who are in a relationship with Him. His people are called 'to make a difference between the unclean and the clean, and between the beast that may be eaten and the beast that may not be eaten', v. 47. The word translated as 'make a difference' – 'distinguish' NKJV – is the same word used in the Lord's charge to the priests in Leviticus chapter 10 verse 10. Part of their job included 'making a distinction',[80] NAS, ESV, between holy and common things, as well as the purity and impurity of things. Not only were these differences important in public worship, Leviticus chapter 11 demonstrates that they were vital in the Israelite's everyday life as well.

The New Testament teaching of Christ rescinded these food laws in order to focus on human internal defilement by sin, Mark 7. 17-23, as well as paving the way for evangelizing the Gentiles and receiving them into the church, Acts 10.

Leviticus chapters 12-15 – laws of purity

From one's daily bread to other aspects of everyday life, Leviticus chapters 12-15 deal with childbirth, skin diseases, contamination of houses and garments and bodily discharges. Purity among God's people is comprehensive, touching every aspect of life. This section

---

[80] The Lord Himself leads in making distinctions, as one sees from His method of creation, Gen. 1. 4, 6, 7, 14, 18, where He uses the same word – rendered 'divide' in the KJV – to separate between light and darkness, waters from waters, water from land, and day from night. He makes distinctions between animals and humans, gender distinctions within humanity, as well as moral and ethical distinctions. For the New Testament parallel, see 2 Corinthians chapter 6.

begins with something coming from the body – a child and all of the blood associated with childbirth, ch. 12 – and ends with various types of defiling emissions, ch. 15.

Content outline for chapters 12-15

Chapter 12	
Having a male or female child, v. 5	vv. 1-5
Sacrifices for purification	vv. 6-8
Chapter 13	
Identification of various types of personal leprosy	vv. 1-46
Leprosy in a garment	vv. 47-59
Chapter 14	
Law of the leper for cleansing	vv. 1-32
Law of leprosy in houses	vv. 33-53
Summary of the Law of leprosy	vv. 54-57
Chapter 15	
Male discharge and its varied contamination	vv. 1-12
Cleansing from male discharge	vv. 13-18
Female discharge and its varied contamination	vv. 19-27
Cleansing from female discharge	vv. 28-30
Summary of Israelite purity and cleansing from discharge	vv. 31-33

Observations on chapter 12

Two main things stand out in this passage:

1. The doubled length of time for ceremonial impurity after the birth of a female versus a male baby.
2. The connection between the provision for the poor and the offering made by Jesus' mother, Mary.

Regarding the first matter, it should be noted that God's word does not denigrate women in either the Old or New Testaments. They have different roles, but are not unequal in value, Gen. 1. 26-27. This passage implies as much when it affirms that the same sacrifice was needed for purification after the birth of a boy or a girl, Lev. 12. 6. As to why the time of impurity is doubled, some suggest that the female baby's potential to eventually menstruate and give birth lengthens the time. Other interpretations have been put forth but none are clear-cut from the text.

The Lord's grace is seen in His provision for the poor in verse 8: 'And if she be not able to bring a lamb, then she shall bring two turtles, or two young pigeons; the one for the burnt offering, and the other for a sin offering: and the priest shall make an atonement for her, and she shall be clean'. This lovely exception clause came into play in Joseph and Mary's case after Christ's birth, Luke 2. 22-24. It is a tangible reminder of the poverty into which the Creator of the world entered at the incarnation. As 2 Corinthians chapter 8 verse 9 declares: 'For ye know the grace of our Lord Jesus Christ, that, though he was rich, yet for your sakes he became poor, that ye through his poverty might be rich'.

Observations on chapters 13-14

Chapter 13 focuses on diagnosis, while the following chapter discusses the cure. Most of the modern translations follow the King James Version is using the term 'leprosy', though the word seems to cover a range of infectious skin conditions – and even mildew in the case of inanimate objects.[81] The chapter deals with three categories of possible leprosy in a person's skin:

---

[81] For example, the NKJV margin has this note: 'Heb. *saraath*, disfiguring skin diseases, including leprosy, and so in vv. 2-46 and 14. 2-32'. Some Hebrew scholars vigorously reject 'leprosy', arguing that the biblical maladies bear little resemblance to the modern Leprosy, which is medically known as

1. 'a rising';
2. 'a scab';
3. 'bright spot'.

Verses 2, 9, 24,[82] 29, 38, 42, and 47 all mark separate sections by using 'when'.[83] Subsidiary clauses are demarcated by the word 'if',[84] vv. 4, 7, 12, 21, 22, 23, 26, 27, 28, 35, 37, 41, 53, 56, 57. ROOKER notes seven distinct cases of personal leprosy in chapter 13:

'Case 1, vv. 1-8
Case 2, vv. 9-17
Case 3, vv. 18-23
Case 4, vv. 24-28
Case 5, vv. 29-37
Case 6, vv. 38-39
Case 7, vv. 40-44'.[85]

A picture of sin and cleansing

With its insidiously contagious and corrupting qualities, leprosy is an outstanding picture of sin and its corrosive effects on a person's entire being. Many believers recognize this, but the nineteenth-

---

Hansen's Disease. See K. P. C. A. GRAMBERG, 'Leprosy and the Bible', in *The Bible Translator*, Vol. 11. The American Bible Society, 1960, pp. 10-23; electronic edition accessed here:
http://www.ubs-translations.org/tbt/1960/01/TBT196001.html?num=10&x=0&y=0&num1=.

[82] Rendered 'if' in the KJV and NKJV in this verse; likewise, verses 29, 38, 42, and 47. It is translated 'as' in verse 40, NKJV, but this is not a distinct section like the others. The KJV leaves it untranslated in that verse.

[83] 'When' translates the Hebrew word *ki*, Strong's number 3588.

[84] 'If' translates the Hebrew word *im*, Strong's number 518. The insight into the literary function of *ki* and *im* in the chapter comes from ROOKER, pg. 186.

[85] ROOKER, pp. 186-191.

century 'Prince of preachers' describes it more eloquently than most in these words: 'Every man by nature is like a leper; loathsome in his person, infected in all his actions and in all that he does; he is incapable of fellowship with God's people, and he is shut out utterly and entirely by his sin from the presence and acceptance of God'.[86] Thankfully, Leviticus chapters 13 and 14 hold forth the prospect of healing, cleansing, and restoration. Even though the Old Testament instances of Israelites being healed of leprosy are lacking,[87] the instructions looked forward to the day when the Lord Jesus Christ would heal bodies and souls of physical and spiritual leprosy, Mark 1. 40-45. What a testimony it would have been to the priests of His day if the cleansed leper had appeared at the temple to offer the sacrifices described in Leviticus chapter 14!

The offering of the two birds is a beautiful picture of the Lord Jesus' saving work, Lev. 14. 5. Of the living bird, the missionary G. C. WILLIS writes:

'The heavens are the home of the bird – the heavens are its native air – but it comes down and enters into a vessel of earth. It leaves its native air, it leaves its home above, for this poor sad earth. And in that earthen vessel it is killed. What a picture of our Lord and Saviour Jesus Christ. He leaves His home in the heavens, He leaves His throne above, He comes down to this sad world and takes a body of earth. For truly our bodies are but "earthen vessels". You know "Adam" means "earthy" or "red earth". So our Lord took an earthy body. How we love to watch that heavenly Man walking this world in His body of earth! And in that same body He was killed. Wicked men nailed that body to the cross, and His precious

---

[86] C. H. SPURGEON, 'The Cleansing of the Leper', in *The Metropolitan Tabernacle Pulpit Sermons*, Vol. 7, Passmore & Alabaster, 1861, pg. 43.
[87] 2 Kings chapter 5 recounts the most famous instance of healing in the Old Testament – that of Naaman, the Syrian general – but he was a Gentile. Compare the Lord Jesus' sermon in Luke chapter 4 verse 27.

blood was poured out. But the bird was killed in an earthen vessel over running, or living, water. Running water has life and power in it . . . Water in the Bible very often speaks of the Word of God (see Psalm 119. 9; Ephesians 5. 26). And the running, or living, water tells us of the living Word of God, applied by the Spirit of God to our hearts. That Word is "living and powerful", Hebrews 4. 12 . . . It takes the death of Christ, and tells me in the living power of the Spirit that the Lord Jesus Christ died for *me*, that it was for *my sins* that He suffered'.[88]

On the other hand, the living bird reminds one that Christ is no longer dead; He has risen in triumph. Collectively the two birds speak of Christ's death, resurrection, and ascension – the core elements of the gospel. The blood was sprinkled on the leper, symbolically expressing the real basis of his cleansing, 1 John 1. 7. Leviticus chapter 14 verse 8 declares that water was also used in his cleansing – a detail reminiscent of 'the washing of regeneration', Titus 3. 5, and the sanctifying ministry of God's word, Eph. 5. 26. The leper was to wash his clothes, shave his hair, and wash himself in water, Lev. 14. 8-9, portraying the new life that was opening up for him, 2 Cor. 5. 17.

On the eighth day, the cleansed leper offered two male lambs and a first-year ewe lamb as a trespass offering, Lev. 14. 12, a sin offering, v. 19, and a burnt offering, v. 20, respectively. A grain offering – three-tenths of an ephah of fine flour mixed with oil – was also offered in conjunction with the burnt offering. The former leper was first anointed with some of the trespass offering's blood on the tip of his right ear, thumb of his right hand, and big toe of his right foot, v.

_____

88 G. C. WILLIS, *The Law of the Leper: Leviticus 13-14*, electronic edition accessed here:
http://www.stempublishing.com/authors/GC_Willis/GCW_Leper.html#a5 [italics original].

14; compare Lev. 8. 24. He was then anointed on the same areas with oil. After the oil was sprinkled seven times before the Lord, v. 16, he was also anointed on his head with oil, v. 18. Verses 21-32 offer the substitution of two turtledoves or two young pigeons in place of lambs for the poor man's offering. Symbolically, all of this suggests the redemptive work of Christ and ensuing gift of the Holy Spirit for the purification and salvation of repentant sinners.

Domestic impurity

Of course, Leviticus also maintains that leprosy affects garments and houses in these passages. The New Testament reminds believers that they are to put off the flesh like an old garment, and put on the new man in Christ.[89] Conduct in their personal houses, 1 Tim. 3. 4-5, 12, and in 'the house of God', v. 15, must be pure, ridding oneself of sin's every appearance.

One notable linguistic feature in Leviticus chapter 14 is found in verse 42, where 'plaster' is referenced in repairing damage from leprosy. The same word is used in a figure of speech in Ezekiel chapter 13 verses 10-12, 14-15 and chapter 22 verse 28, condemning the wayward prophets who were rampant in sixth century BC Israel and gave false comfort to their people when chastising judgement was falling on the nation. Sin covered over will continue to fester and ultimately corrode a nation. Only by exposing and removing it may one safely be pronounced healed, 1 John 1. 9.

Leviticus chapter 15

In keeping with this section of Leviticus' emphasis on purity, chapter 15 concerns male and female bodily discharges. Various scholars notice the literary symmetry of the passage; CURRID outlines it clearly:

---

[89] Rom. 13. 12, 14; Eph. 4. 22-24; Col. 3. 9-10.

'A   long-term male discharges, vv. 2-15
B   short-term male discharges, vv. 16-17
C   male and female together, v. 18
B₁   short-term female discharges, vv. 19-24
A₁   long-term female discharges, vv. 25-30'.[90]

From a typological point of view, it is interesting that something proceeding from men and women defiles them. Human religions assume that their devotees' main problems are external. They focus on 'touch not, taste not, handle not', Col. 2. 21, rather than worshipping God 'in spirit and in truth', John 4. 24. But the Lord Jesus revealed that man's problem is actually internal, saying:

> 'Do ye not perceive, that whatsoever thing from without entereth into the man, it cannot defile him; Because it entereth not into his heart, but into the belly, and goeth out into the draught, purging all meats? And he said, That which cometh out of the man, that defileth the man. For from within, out of the heart of men, proceed evil thoughts, adulteries, fornications, murders, Thefts, covetousness, wickedness, deceit, lasciviousness, an evil eye, blasphemy, pride, foolishness: All these evil things come from within, and defile the man', Mark 7. 18-23.

The only solution for indwelling sin is the saving work of the Lord Jesus Christ!

One incident from the Lord's ministry highlights the terrible suffering and pathos of the contaminating effect of a bodily emission on one's life: the woman with the flow of blood, Mark 5. 25-34. This desperate woman was afflicted for twelve years with this embarrassing and defiling malady; by the instructions of Leviticus chapter 15 she would be barred from public worship and anything she touched would also

---

[90] CURRID, pg. 210.

be ceremonially unclean. Thus, she must have been extremely lonely – a virtual pariah in her community. How beautiful to see that the Lord purified her through His gracious power.

The Day of Atonement, Leviticus chapter 16

Chapter 16 is the thematic centre of Leviticus, providing the theological basis for Israel's approach to the Lord.[91] Since He is holy, His people must be pure to come near to Him. This can only be accomplished by His atoning work. The ceremonies and offerings of this passage point forward to the Lord Jesus' cross, resurrection, and ascension. Hebrews chapter 9 is the divine commentary on the Day of Atonement.[92] For example, consider these verses:

---

[91] 'Although structurally chapter 16 is the conclusion to the first major section of the book, it also functions as the theological center of the book and binds the two halves together. On the Day of Atonement the holiness and purity of both the tabernacle and the nation were in view. There were actually five offerings on that day: the two blood atonement sin offerings for the priests and the people, vv. 3, 5, and esp. vv. 11-19, the single scapegoat sin offering for the whole congregation (including the priests and the people, vv. 20-22, and the two burnt offerings for the priests and the people, vv. 23-24. All of these offerings are specifically said to have "made atonement"'. AVERBECK, 'Leviticus, The Theology', electronic edition, no pagination. See also JOHN E. HARTLEY, *Leviticus*, Word Biblical Commentary, Vol. 4, Word, 1998, pg. xxxv and HOUSE, pg. 137. Mackintosh notes its significance in the context of the entire Bible, writing: 'This chapter unfolds some of the weightiest principles of truth which can possibly engage the renewed mind. It presents the doctrine of atonement with uncommon fullness and power. In short, we must rank the sixteenth chapter of Leviticus amongst the most precious and important sections of inspiration, if indeed it be allowable to make comparisons where all is divine'. MACKINTOSH, pg. 379.

[92] As HOUSE observes: 'Hebrews 9. 7-12 makes the most extensive use of the Day of Atonement in the Scriptures. There the author says that the problem with the Day of Atonement was that it had to occur annually, which meant that the consciences of the worshipers could not be cleared permanently, Heb. 9. 7-9. Therefore these rules applied only until Christ's death atoned

'But Christ being come an high priest of good things to come, by a greater and more perfect tabernacle, not made with hands, that is to say, not of this building; Neither by the blood of goats and calves, but by his own blood he entered in once into the holy place, having obtained eternal redemption for us. For if the blood of bulls and of goats, and the ashes of an heifer sprinkling the unclean, sanctifieth to the purifying of the flesh: How much more shall the blood of Christ, who through the eternal Spirit offered himself without spot to God, purge your conscience from dead works to serve the living God? And for this cause he is the mediator of the new testament, that by means of death, for the redemption of the transgressions that were under the first testament, they which are called might receive the promise of eternal inheritance', Heb. 9. 11-15.

The pageantry of atonement

The high priest began by ceremonially washing himself with water. Instead of being clothed in glorious garments, the high priest wore fine white linen – the garb of holy, but humble service, Lev. 16. 3-4.[93] Then he needed to offer a bull as a sin offering for his own sins as

---

for all sins committed by God's people, Heb. 9. 10-12. Before the permanent atonement unfolded the Leviticus system atoned for sins on an annual basis and presented a picture of a greater sacrifice to come, Heb. 9. 6-8. Presumably the Day of Atonement helped instill in faithful Israelites a strong desire for a permanent forgiveness of sin . . . After the cross, however, the Day of Atonement, like the other sacrifices, is subsumed under Jesus' one comprehensive payment for sins on the cross'. HOUSE, pg. 141.

[93] Seeing a picture of Christ's condescension in the incarnation, SPURGEON, in inimitable fashion, exults: 'But, men, ye can scarce tell how glorious is your High Priest now, and ye can scarce tell how glorious he was before. But oh! adore him, for on that day it was the simple clean linen of his own body, of his own humanity, in which he made atonement for your sins'. C. H. SPURGEON, 'The Day of Atonement', in *The New Park Street Pulpit Sermons, Vol. II.* Passmore & Alabaster, 1856, pg. 330.

well as those of his family, v. 6; Heb. 7. 27. This was also offered in conjunction with a ram as a burnt offering, Lev. 16. 3. The sin offering's blood was carried into the holy of holies and was sprinkled in front of and on the mercy seat – the lid of the ark of the covenant – seven times, v. 14. This spoke of perfect atonement before God's holy presence.[94] In entering the place of divine glory, Aaron also needed a censer of incense to shield him from wrath, vv. 12-13, for God's intrinsic being is 'light unapproachable', 1 Tim. 6. 15.

During the Day of Atonement the high priest purified the tabernacle itself, because anything connected with humans requires cleansing, v. 20. Finally, two goats were offered as a collective sin offering:

1. The first one was killed and his blood was carried into the holy of holies for sprinkling before and on the mercy seat.
2. The high priest placed both hands on the head of the second one in identification and symbolically transferred the guilt of the nation onto this 'scapegoat'. It was then led off into the desert by a suitable man and it was thus removed from sight, vv. 21-22.

Verse 22 says that this goat would 'bear upon him all their iniquities'. The same Hebrew word is used in Isaiah's majestic description of Christ's vicarious sufferings: 'Surely he hath borne our griefs', Isa. 53. 4; likewise in verse 12 where it says: 'he bore the sin of many'. Typically, this represents the removal of sin in the Almighty's eyes – He promises to remove our transgressions as far as the east is from the west, Ps. 103. 12.

On the Day of Atonement the people of Israel were told to 'afflict' themselves, Lev. 16. 29 – generally understood as an expression

---

[94] Other scriptures indicate that the mercy seat was the Lord's symbolical throne, e.g., Ps. 80. 1 ESV: 'you who are enthroned upon the cherubim'; 1 Sam. 4. 4, ESV: 'who is enthroned on cherubim'.

meaning to humble oneself, usually by fasting.[95] It is also declared 'a Sabbath of rest', Lev. 16. 31, more literally, by way of emphasis, 'a sabbath of sabbaths'. Even in typology the Holy Spirit highlights the truth that putting away sin and cleansing mankind has nothing to do with man's works. It is entirely the redemptive work of God Himself, Eph. 2. 8-10.

What a blessing it is to know that on this side of Calvary, the work of propitiation is finished, Heb. 9. 26. In the Old Testament ceremony the high priest entered the holy of holies multiple times; year after year the same sacrifices needed to be offered, Heb. 10. 1, 11. The work was never completed. Yet now the Lord Jesus has perfected the work and is seated in heaven. As brother GOODING comments: 'He entered the Most Holy Place in heaven once and for all, Heb. 9. 12. He did not have to keep entering and coming out and re-entering. His great sufficient sacrifice obtained for us eternal redemption and was already complete when he entered heaven. So having entered, he has remained there in the immediate presence of God as our representative these two thousand years'.[96] When He returns, there will be no need to make any more offering for sin. Hebrews chapter 9 verse 28 puts it this way: 'So Christ was once offered to bear the sins

---

[95] Thus, ESV margin. The translator's note from the *New English Translation* offers this definition: '*Heb* "you shall humble your souls". The verb "to humble" here refers to various forms of self-denial, including but not limited to fasting, cf. Ps. 35. 13 and Isa. 58. 3, 10. The Mishnah (*m. Yoma* 8:1) lists abstentions from food and drink, bathing, using oil as an unguent to moisten the skin, wearing leather sandals, and sexual intercourse, cf. 2 Sam. 12. 16-17, 20; see the remarks in J. MILGROM, *Leviticus* [AB], 1. 1054; B. A. LEVINE, *Leviticus* [JPSTC], pg. 109; and J. E. HARTLEY, *Leviticus* [WBC], pg. 242)'. The instruction to afflict oneself also occurs with the instructions concerning this feast in Leviticus chapter 23 verse 27 and in Numbers chapter 29 verse 7.

[96] DAVID W. GOODING, *An Unshakeable Kingdom: The Letter to the Hebrews for Today*, Myrtlefield House, 2013, electronic edition, pg. 174.

of many; and unto them that look for him shall he appear the second time without sin unto salvation'.[97]

Holy people in the Holy Land, Leviticus chapters 17-22

Having established the sacrificial basis for Israel's relationship with Himself, the Lord now devotes the next six chapters to the holy lifestyle that flows from their life with Him.

Content outline, Leviticus chapters 17-22

Leviticus 17: Blood and the killing of animals in sacrificial and non-sacrificial contexts.
Leviticus 18: Sexual Purity.[98]

---

[97] Note the three 'appearings' in Hebrews chapter 9 verses 24-28, as MACDONALD writes: 'Verse 24: He *now* appears. This is a reference to His present ministry in the presence of God to save us from the power of sin (the *present* tense of salvation). Verse 28: He *will* appear. This speaks of His imminent Return when He will save us from the presence of sin (the *future* tense of salvation)'. WILLIAM MACDONALD, *Believer's Bible Commentary: Old and New Testaments*, ed. Arthur Farstad, comment on Heb. 9. 28, Thomas Nelson, 1995, electronic edition, no pagination [italics original].

[98] There is a literary parallelism in chapters 18-20, as ROOKER shows: 'In the introduction to chapter 18 in verse 3, one finds an allusion to the evil statutes of the Canaanite and Egyptian gods. Chapters 18 and 20 contain two amazingly similar, matching sets of prohibitions addressing these illicit practices. The focus of the laws in the two framing chapters (18 and 20) is upon sexual offenses, as seen in the following table.

Chapter 18	Chapter 20
Laws of incest (6-18)	Laws of incest (11-21)
Menstrual uncleanness (18)	Menstrual uncleanness (19)
Adultery (20)	Adultery (10)
Devoting to Molech (21)	Devoting to Molech (2-5)
Male homosexuality (22)	Male homosexuality (13)
Bestiality (23)	Bestiality (15-16)
	Mediums and wizards (6-8)

Leviticus 19: Assorted laws against idolatry and for governing agricultural and business pursuits.
Leviticus 20: Crimes that warrant divine cursing.
Leviticus 21-22: Laws concerning the priesthood and sacrifices.

Perhaps modern readers are in danger of thinking that this legislation possesses only antiquarian interest for lovers of all things ancient; nevertheless, some abiding principles are established for God's people of all ages. Consider the following:

The sanctity of life. 'For the life of the flesh is in the blood', Lev. 17. 11. Blood is essential for physical life in this scene; thus the

---

Land will vomit you out (24-30)	Land will vomit you out (22)

These symmetrical chapters function as outer frames for Leviticus 19, which is sandwiched between them. These framing blocks separate and enclose the laws of chapter 19. Because of this structural arrangement, many argue that Leviticus 19 should be considered the focal point of the subsection. [According to MARY DOUGLAS in her article, 'Justice as the Cornerstone': 'There could hardly be a stronger framing of the *central* chapter' than the arrangement one finds in Leviticus chapters 18-20.7.]

Another point of structural interest that contributes to the literary unity of Leviticus 19 is the phraseology repeated in the first half of the chapter (vv. 1-18) and in the last seven verses (vv. 30-36). Notice the repetition of the subjects in the first half of the chapter and in the content of verses 30-36:

Symmetry in Leviticus 19

19:3a	Reverence	19:30b
19:3b	Sabbath	19:30
19:4a	Do not turn to idolatry/mediums	19:31
19:14c	Revere your God	19:32c
19:15a	Do no injustice	19:35a
19:18c	Love neighbour as yourself	19:34b
19:19a	Keep My statutes	19:37a

All these observations provide incontrovertible evidence that Leviticus 19 is a well-defined, self-contained literary unit'. ROOKER, 'The Best-Known Verse in Leviticus', in *Faith and Mission* 21:1. (Spring, 2004), pp. 4-5.

disposition of this vital substance determines life and death. As the Creator, God insists on the sacredness of blood. It is not to be shed lightly or haphazardly. When life is taken, the claims of the Giver of all life must be remembered. What is more, offering blood to anyone besides the Lord is absolutely forbidden; this ruled out the common idolatrous practices of the nations around them and the people that they would drive out of Canaan, v. 7. The must offer their sacrifices at the tabernacle, not in whatever place which they found to be convenient, vv. 3-4. This understanding of the blood is fundamental to the Bible's teaching on redemption, propitiation, and the other aspects of salvation, Eph. 1. 7; 1 John 1. 7-9.

Sexual morality is not a personal matter. Right and wrong intimate behaviour is determined by the Creator, who is also the ultimate arbiter of truth. It is not a matter of human preference, but of divine will. To defy His teaching on sexual morality is to incur divine judgement, as chapters 18 and 20 declare. The modern notion of sexual liberation is actually quite ancient, and – if not repented of – always brings about the Almighty's wrath, Rom. 1. 18-32. Incest, Lev. 18. 11-17, adultery, v. 20, homosexuality, v. 22, and bestiality, v. 23, are all forbidden by God. Their heinous nature is seen in their classification with child sacrifice to idols, v. 21. These sins were also so serious that the Lord affirmed He would cast them out of the land if they practised them – just as He was evicting the Canaanite nations for their addiction to such barbarous customs, vv. 24-30.[99]

---

[99] WIERSBE remarks about the land and the defilement of sin, saying: 'The people belonged to the Lord, because He had redeemed them from Egypt to be His very own; and the land belonged to the Lord, and He gave it to Israel with the stipulation that they do nothing to defile it. A holy God wants His holy people to live in a holy land. In Leviticus 18-27, the word "land" is used sixty-eight times. In these chapters, Moses named the sins that defile the land and invite divine judgment: immorality, chap. 18; idolatry, chap. 19; capital crimes, chap. 20; blasphemy, chap. 23; and refusing to give the land its rest, chap. 25. Unfortunately, the Jewish people committed all these sins and more; and God had to chasten them by allowing Babylon to destroy

Ethical behaviour in Israel flowed from God's character and is encapsulated in the axiom 'Love thy neighbour as thyself', Lev. 19. 18. Sexual rules, agricultural and business practices, treatment of the elderly all proceeded from this distinctive principle, ch. 19. Even 'strangers', vv. 33-34, were afforded this protection because the Israelites knew what it was to be in that vulnerable position based on their past Egyptian sojourn. Even in the present dispensation the Lord extends tremendous grace towards 'strangers', Eph. 2. 12, 19. Christians are also instructed to show hospitality to strangers, 3 John 5.

Leviticus chapter 21 to chapter 22 verse 16 reminds one that due to their privileged access to God's presence the priests are held to high standards of behaviour. In the church, all believers are priests, Rev. 1. 6, and are therefore called to holy living, 1 Pet. 2. 5-17, eschewing anything that would take them away from their priestly work of worship and service. Offerings were also to be untainted, Lev. 22. 17-30: (a) because they typologically spoke of Christ; (b) because God demands the best in worship. These verses provide an interesting background to the Jews' errors in the book of Malachi.

Leviticus chapter 22 verses 31-33 form a fitting conclusion to these chapters on holy living: 'Therefore shall ye keep my commandments, and do them: I am the Lord. Neither shall ye profane my holy name; but I will be hallowed among the children of Israel: I am the Lord which hallow you, That brought you out of the land of Egypt, to be your God: I am the Lord'.

The Feasts of Jehovah – Leviticus chapter 23

As the previous section of Leviticus demonstrates, every aspect of life was to revolve around the Israelites' relationship with the Lord.

Jerusalem and take the people captive, 2 Chron. 36. 14-21'. WIERSBE, pg. 15.

Food, clothing, family behaviour, relationships within the community, work, marriage, and childbirth were all governed by His character and will. Their economy was agrarian and therefore centred on the harvest calendar of the major crops in Israel. Accordingly, the Lord gave them 'set feasts',[100] Lev. 23. 2 JND, ASV, to accompany their agricultural pursuits. These were also called 'holy convocations', v. 2 – festive gatherings of rejoicing before Jehovah.[101] Putting these two concepts together it is evident that He wanted the rhythms of their lives to focus their attention on Him.[102]

---

[100] Others translate it 'appointed feasts' RSV, ESV; 'appointed festivals' NIV, NRSV, NLT; 'appointed seasons' YLT. SWANSON defines it: '**feast**, i.e., a festival of celebration and/or worship, with a focus that this is a time appointed by an authority, which may include festive meals and offerings to God, Hos. 9. 5'. SWANSON, *Dictionary of Biblical Languages with Semantic Domains: Hebrew (Old Testament)*, electronic edition, no pagination [boldface original]. MOUNCE adds: 'In places, it also denotes the appointed times of Israel's pilgrimage feasts, Exod. 13. 10; Lev. 23. 2, 4, 44; Num. 9. 2; 10. 10; 29. 39. These religious festivals occur yearly and are designed to nurture community and fellowship, to educate and communicate the faith to each generation, and to establish a standard in the practice and performance of the nation's religious faith'. MOUNCE, pg. 446.

[101] 'A gathering of people who have been called for the purpose of celebrating a religious festival'. DEREK LEIGH DAVIS, 'Assembly, Religious', ed. DOUGLAS MANGUM ET AL., *Lexham Theological Wordbook*, electronic edition, no pagination. '[These were] special religious days, and on them no work was to be done . . . The setting apart of these holy days did not indicate that other days were not important, but they did serve as a reminder that all time belonged to God. The unifying theme that acts as a thread tying all these occasions together was the mighty acts of God on Israel's behalf'. ROOKER, *Leviticus*, pg. 282 [brackets mine].

[102] Of course it was possible to observe these festivals as mere holidays denuded of religious significance. By the first century A.D. they were known as the feasts 'of the Jews', John 5. 1; 6. 4, rather than 'feasts of the Lord'; see also 7. 2: 'the Jews' feast of tabernacles'. Likewise, the sacrifices could become meaningless ceremonies if they were not offered in faith, Ps. 51. 16-17; 40. 6-7. Isaiah chapter 1 verses 13-14 combines these ideas, showing that eighth century B.C. Israel was a place of unspiritual formalism, robbing

Besides the seven annual feasts that occurred in the first, third, and seventh months, there was a weekly 'feast': the sabbath. This was mandated by the fourth commandment, Exod. 20. 8, and gave them an opportunity to rest and worship the Lord. All of the annual feasts incorporated the idea of rest in some sense. Every week their thoughts and activities turned from work to appreciate God and His goodness towards them.[103] The concept of sabbath rest also pointed forward to a greater rest that is fulfilled in Christ, Heb. 4. 6-11.[104]

---

both the sacrifices and set feasts of their true meaning. The history of Christendom has been no better on this score, with baptism and the Lord's Supper turned into empty rituals that bear little resemblance to the divine intention for instituting them. Believers must guard their hearts as they practice the symbolic parts of their faith, lest they become mere theatrical performances.

[103] On the significance of the sabbath and the number seven in Leviticus, KELLOGG remarks: 'These so-called harvest feasts in fact form part of an elaborate system of sacred times, – a system which is based upon the Sabbath, and into which the sacred number seven, the number of the covenant, enters throughout as a formative element. The weekly Sabbath, first of all, was the seventh day; the length of the great festivals of unleavened bread and of tabernacles was also, in each case, seven days. Not only so, but the entire series of sacred times mentioned in this chapter and in chapter 25 constitutes an ascending series of sacred septenaries, in which the ruling thought is this: that the seventh is holy unto the Lord, as the number symbolic of rest and redemption; and that the eighth, as the first of a new week, is symbolic of the new creation. Thus we have the seventh day, the weekly Sabbath, constantly recurring, the type of each of the series; then, counting from the feast of unleavened bread, – the first of the sacred year, – the fiftieth day, at the end of the seventh week, is signalised as sacred by the feast of firstfruits or of "weeks"; the seventh month, again, is the sabbatic month, of special sanctity, containing as it does three of the annual seasons of holy convocation, – the feast of trumpets on its first day, the great day of atonement on the tenth, and the last of the three great annual feasts, that of tabernacles or ingathering, for seven days from the fifteenth day of the month. Beyond this series of sacred festivals recurring annually, in chapter 25, the seventh year is appointed to be a sabbatic year of rest to the

75

See Feasts of Jehovah Chart on page 77

land, and the series at last culminates at the expiration of seven sevens of years, in the fiftieth year, – the eighth following the seventh seven, – the great year of jubilee, the supreme year of rest, restoration, and release. All these sacred times, differing in the details of their observance, are alike distinguished by their connection with the sacred number seven, by the informing presence of the idea of the Sabbath, and therewith always a new and fuller revelation of God as in covenant with Israel for their redemption'. KELLOGG, pg. 305.

[104] KELLOGG beautifully explains it this way: 'For this sanctity of the Sabbath two reasons are elsewhere given. The first of these, which is assigned in the fourth commandment, makes it a memorial of the rest of God, when having created man in Eden, He saw His work which He had finished, that it was very good, and rested from all His work. As created, man was participant in this rest of God. He was indeed to work in tilling the garden in which he had been placed; but from such labour as involves unremunerative toil and exhaustion he was exempt. But this sabbatic rest of the creation was interrupted by sin; God's work, which He had declared "good", was marred; man fell into a condition of wearying toil and unrest of body and soul, and with him the whole creation also was "subjected to vanity", Genesis 3. 17, 18; Romans 8. 20. But in this state of things the God of love could not rest; it thus involved for Him a work of new creation, which should have for its object the complete restoration, both as regards man and nature, of that sabbatic state of things on earth which had been broken up by sin. And thus it came to pass that the weekly Sabbath looked not only backward, but forward; and spoke not only of the rest that was, but of the great sabbatism of the future, to be brought in through a promised redemption'. KELLOGG, pp. 305-306.

Feasts of Jehovah

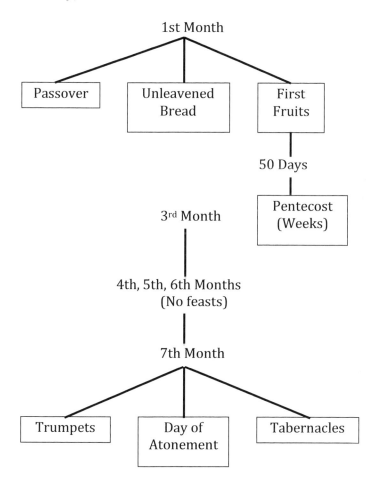

The feasts of the first month – Leviticus chapter 23 verses 5-14.

Feast:	Passover[105]
Hebrew Name:	*Pesach*
Date:	14th of Nisan[106]
Duration:	1 day.
Historical Setting:	Israel's deliverance from divine wrath and Egyptian slavery (national independence to serve the Lord)
Key Feature:	Slain lamb
Key Truth:	Redemption, 1 Cor. 5. 7

Feast:	Unleavened Bread
Hebrew Name:	*Matzot*
Date:	15th to 21st of Nisan
Duration:	7 days
Historical Setting:	Because of the Passover, Israel left Egypt without having time for their dough to be leavened and rise
Key Feature:	No leaven during the feast
Key Truth:	Sanctification and pilgrim character of the saints, 1 Pet. 1. 15-16; 1 Cor. 5. 6-8

---

[105] Sometimes Passover is referred to as 'Unleavened bread' since those feasts ran consecutively, Exod. 23. 15; Matt. 26. 17; Mark 14. 1, 12; Luke 22. 1, 7.

[106] This month is also known as 'Abib', Exod. 12. 1-3; 13. 4; 23. 15.

Feast:	Firstfruits
Hebrew name:	*Bikkurim*
Date:	16th of Nisan
Duration:	1 day
Historical Setting:	Entering the land of their inheritance and enjoying the beginning of the harvest – barley in this case
Key Feature:	Uplifted barley sheaf of the firstfruits as a wave offering[107]
Key Truth:	Resurrection, 1 Cor. 15. 20

Feast of the third month – Leviticus chapter 23 verses 15-21

Feast:	Weeks/Pentecost, Acts 2. 1/'Harvest', Exod. 23. 16.
Hebrew name:	*Shavuot*
Date:	6th of Sivan
Duration:	1 day
Historical Setting:	Further enjoyment of the harvest; another feast of firstfruits – wheat is the crop this time[108]
Key Feature:	Two leavened loaves offered as a single grain offering, Eph. 2. 11-22
Key Truth:	The coming of the Holy Spirit, Acts 2; Rom. 8. 23

There are no feasts in months 4, 5, and 6.

---

[107] Historically, Christ was crucified on the Passover and rose on Firstfruits.
[108] Jewish rabbinic tradition claims that God gave the law on this date, but I know of no biblical evidence to back up this assertion. For the Jewish tradition see the article 'Torah' from *The Jewish Encyclopedia* (1906), accessed here: http://jewishencyclopedia.com/articles/14446-torah.

Feasts of the seventh month – Leviticus chapter 23 verses 23-43

Feast:	Trumpets
Hebrew Name:	*Yom Teruah*[109]
Date:	1st of Tishri
Duration:	1 day
Historical Setting:	The Jews gathered afresh to Jerusalem; trumpets were used to direct their movements during the wilderness journey, Num. 10. 1-10
Key Feature:	Blowing the trumpets, Matt. 24. 31[110]
Key truth:	The future regathering of Israel in the Promised Land, Zeph. 3. 20

Feast:	Day of Atonement
Hebrew Name:	*Yom Kippor*
Date:	10th of Tishri
Duration:	1 day
Historical Setting:	National mourning over sin, and sacrifices and ceremonies performed to make atonement, Lev. 16. The only day of the year that the high priest entered God's immediate presence in the holy of holies
Key Feature:	The two goats: one for a sin offering whose blood was sprinkled in the holy of holies; the other – the scapegoat – sent away symbolically bearing away Israel's sins
Key Truth:	Propitiation, the basis for God's righteous forgiveness and justification of sinners, Rom. 3.

---

[109] Often called Rosh Hashanah – literally 'the head of the year' – by modern Jews; it is their new year celebration for the beginning of the civil calendar. Passover takes place in the first month of their religious calendar.

[110] This trumpet refers to Israel, but the symbol of a gathering trumpet is also used to describe the Rapture of the Church, 1 Thes. 4. 16, prior to the Tribulation.

	21-26; specifically, it looks forward to the future cleansing and restoration of the nation of Israel, Zech. 12. 10-13. 1; Rom. 11. 25-27

Feast:	Tabernacles/'Ingathering', Exod. 23. 16
Hebrew Name:	*Succoth* - sometimes spelled 'Sukkot'
Date:	15th to 21st of Tishri
Duration:	7 days
Historical Setting:	Commemorates the Israelites' sojourn in tents – also known as 'booths'[111] – in the wilderness
Key Feature:	Dwelling in booths/tents.
Key Truth:	The millennial reign of Christ, dwelling in the midst of Israel, Isa. 2; Zech. 2. 10-13; 14. 11, 16-21; Rev. 20. 1-10

Some observations on the annual feasts

Typologically, the seven feasts tell the story of the Lord's redemptive purposes for the world. There is a special emphasis on His dealings with Israel, which was the nation that He wanted to use to bless the entire world, Gen. 12. 2-3. Their national history begins in earnest with the Passover, when the Almighty purchased them by blood; thus, saving them from wrath and bondage. The manner of their deliverance naturally flows into the next feast – which is connected on the calendar with the first feast – and spells out the ongoing character of their lifestyle.[112] Firstfruits is also connected with the first two feasts on the calendar, and thematically relates to them. The redeemed and holy lives of God's people flow out of the power of His resurrection, Eph. 1. 19-23; Phil. 3. 10. The Feast of Weeks in the

---

[111] The Hebrew is 'succoth'; hence the name of the feast.

[112] Only two of the feasts take place over multiple days: Unleavened Bread and Tabernacles. Both speak of an ongoing condition: 1. Unleavened Bread speaks of the holy life that believers are to live; 2. Tabernacles speaks of their kingdom rest with the enthroned Christ in the future millennium.

third month is also connected to the first three because it occurs fifty days after the waving of the first sheaf, Lev. 23. 15-16. This is not surprising, for the coming of the Holy Spirit – and the beginning of the church – only takes place fifty days after Christ's resurrection, John 16. 7.

There are no national activities in the fourth, fifth, and sixth months, but that does not mean that the Lord ceases to work. Israel as a nation rejected their Messiah and so they are set aside for a time, Rom. 11. 11-32, but the feasts of the seventh month look forward to their restoration. Meanwhile, the Lord brings Gentiles – and a remnant of Jews – to faith in Himself. The book of Ruth takes place over the course of the early feasts into the summertime, Ruth 1. 22; 2. 23. Interestingly, it tells the story of a Gentile who was brought to faith and inheritance in the living God; she even prospers under the teaching of Leviticus chapter 23, cf. 23. 22 with Ruth chapter 2. These feast-less months anticipate the present church age.

The first four feasts represent past events, but the last three look forward to Israel's future blessings from the Lord. Despite their dispersion throughout the world, Trumpets assures one that God will regather Israel and restore a believing remnant of them to Himself. The Day of Atonement affirms that they will repent nationally for piercing their Messiah – who was also smitten for Gentile sins, 1 John 2. 2. They will be nationally restored and cleansed, leading up to the fulfilment of the Davidic, 2 Sam. 7, and New Covenants, Jer. 31. 31, in Christ's earthly reign.[113]

The feasts in the New Testament

Three of the feasts – Passover-Unleavened Bread, Weeks, and Tabernacles – were mandatory for pilgrimage to the place where the

---

[113] Numbers chapter 28 verse 16 to chapter 29 verse 39 gives information on the sacrifices that were offered during these feasts.

Lord put His name, Exod. 23. 14-19; Deut. 16. 16-17. Initially, this sacred place was the tabernacle, but was transferred later to the temple in Jerusalem. In addition to being tremendously important in the lives of Israelites, each of these feasts figure prominently in the Lord Jesus' ministry.[114] It is worthwhile studying His activities in the gospels regarding the details of these feasts.

Various applications of holiness, Leviticus chapters 24-27

Miscellaneous parts of Israelite life are described in these chapters. The first two chapters emphasize God's holiness (the arrangement of the lampstand and shewbread and law concerning blasphemy, ch. 24) and grace (the sabbatical year and the year of Jubilee, ch. 25). Chapter 26 concerns the consequences of obedience or disobedience towards the Lord – with the serious threat of expulsion from the land; for the fulfilment of this principle see 2 Chr. 36. 15-21.[115] If His grace is spurned and His holy law is flouted, then the Almighty will take severe – if measured – action. Chapter 27 concludes with regulations concerning human vows. The previous chapter asserts God's fidelity, and this chapter shows that He expects the same conduct from His people.[116]

---

[114] John 2. 23; 7. 2; Matt. 27. 15; Mark 14. 1-2; and Acts 2. 1.

[115] HOUSE points out the repercussions of Israel's historic unfaithfulness towards the Lord: 'Finally, Leviticus 26 and its companion text, Deuteronomy 27-28, set the standard for Israel's potential success and failure in the promised land. As has already been stated, Israel's obedience or disobedience to the covenant stipulations determined whether they "lived", 18. 5, were holy, 19. 2, loved their neighbor, 19. 18, or were blessed, 26. 1-13, or cursed, 26. 14-45, in their homeland. Those who assessed Israel's history in the Former Prophets, e.g., 2 Kings 17, the Latter Prophets, e.g., Ezek. 20, and the Writings, e.g., Ps. 78-79, were convinced that Israel's sin, not God's unfaithfulness, cost the chosen people the promised land', HOUSE, pg. 152.

[116] HOUSE, pg. 149.

The lampstand and shewbread, Lev. 24. 1-9, speak of God's light and provision, which were ultimately fulfilled in Christ.[117] The execution of the blasphemer demonstrates the principle of the punishment fitting the crime, Lev. 24. 15-23. Justice, not vengeance, is the operating principle in God's government. As the Psalmist writes: 'righteousness and justice are the foundation of His throne', Ps. 97. 2 NKJV. Attacking God's name is an assault on His character; it is high treason against one's Creator and necessitates capital punishment. Only by sanctifying His place in the community will righteous ethics prevail among its citizens. Throughout Israel's history when they turn from the Lord, they are reduced to barbarity and all manner of cruelties against one another.

The year of Jubilee – Leviticus chapter 25

MACKINTOSH notes the thematic connection between chapters 24 and 25, writing that:

'The intelligent reader will discern a strong moral link between this and the preceding chapter. In chapter 24 we learn that the house of Israel is preserved for the land of Canaan; in chapter 25, we learn that the land of Canaan is preserved for the house of Israel. Taking both together, we have the record of a truth which no power of earth or hell can obliterate – "All Israel shall be saved", and "the land shall not be sold forever". The former of these statements enunciates a principle which has stood like a rock amid the ocean of conflicting interpretations, while the latter declares a fact which many nations of the uncircumcised have sought in vain to ignore'.[118]

---

[117] John 1. 4; 6. 35; 8. 12.
[118] MACKINTOSH, pg. 409.

The year of Jubilee[119] manifests the Lord's gracious heart of forgiveness for the unworthy and protection of the vulnerable.[120] The modern environmental movement worships and serves the creature rather than the Creator – to borrow a phrase from Romans chapter 1 verse 25. The Creator Himself cares for His people and the land. He demands proper stewardship of His territory; the Israelites are tenants, not owners. God expects them not to defile the land, and to let the land enjoy the Sabbath – true rest under the generous and fruitful working of the Almighty. Every seven years the land was left

---

[119] BAUR explains the definition of the term 'Jubilee' here: 'The Heb. word *yōbhēl* stands for *ḳeren ha-yōbhēl*, meaning the horn of a ram. Now, such a horn can be made into a trumpet, and thus the word *yōbhēl* came to be used as a synonym of trumpet. According to Lev. 25:9 a loud trumpet should proclaim liberty throughout the country on the 10th day of the 7th month (the Day of Atonement), after the lapse of 7 sabbaths of years = 49 years. In this manner, every 50th year was to be announced as a jubilee year'. WILLIAM BAUR, 'Jubilee Year', ed. JAMES ORR ET AL., *The International Standard Bible Encyclopaedia*, The Howard-Severance Co., 1915, pg. 1756.

[120] A modern song poetically describes the fulfilment of this type in Christ in these lyrics:

'The word provided for a time for the slaves to be set free
For the debts to all be cancelled so His chosen one could see
His deep desire was for forgiveness
He longed to see their liberty
And His yearning was embodied in the year of Jubilee

Jubilee, Jubilee
Jesus is the Jubilee
Debts forgiven, slaves set free
Jesus is our Jubilee

At the Lord's appointed time His deep desire became a man
The heart of all true jubilation and with joy we understand
In His voice we hear a trumpet sound that tells us we are free
He is the incarnation of the year of Jubilee'
MICHAEL CARD, 'Jubilee', from the album *The Beginning*.

fallow and when seven sabbatical years had passed in the fiftieth year 'Jubilee' was proclaimed, Lev. 25. 8-17, ethnic Israelite slaves were freed and land reverted to owners who leased it to others.[121] Business transactions were conducted and valued with reference to the proximity to the year of Jubilee, vv. 14-17. Modern believers would do well to value things and work in the light of Christ's coming and the judgement seat to follow.[122]

CHRISTOPHER J. H. WRIGHT outlines Leviticus chapter 25 as follows:

'A	The law of the sabbatical year on the land.	vv. 1-7
B	Introduction to the jubilee with the ideas of liberty and return.	vv. 8-12
C	The financial implications of a recurring jubilee.	vv. 13-17
D	Promotion of God's provision while the sabbath year is observed.	vv. 18-22
E	The economic redemption of land and persons, interwoven with the jubilee.	vv. 23-24
F	Practical details of redemption and jubilee: 3 stages of poverty with required responses, interrupted by parenthetic sections dealing with houses in cities, and Levite properties, vv. 29-34, and non-Israelite slaves, vv. 44-46. The stages are marked off by the introductory phrase, 'If your brother becomes poor', vv. 25, 35, 39, 47'.[123]	vv. 25-55

---

[121] The 'rest' of the sabbath year and the lands provision of food apart from toil, Lev. 25. 18-22, is reminiscent of man's situation in Genesis 2 where man laboured without the curse and fatiguing toil that has been humanity's lot since Adam's fall, Gen. 3. 19. It also looks forward to the fruitfulness of the earth in the future millennial kingdom of Christ, e.g. Isa. 35. 1-10.

[122] Eph. 6. 5-9; Col. 3. 17; 4. 1.

[123] CHRISTOPHER J. H. WRIGHT, 'Jubilee, Year of', in *The Anchor Yale Bible Dictionary*, ed. DAVID NOEL FREEDMAN, Doubleday, 1992, pp. 1026-1027. I have summarized and adapted his outline for this publication.

In addition to the emancipation of the Jubilee year, the kinsman-redeemer could buy back one's inheritance at any time, e.g., Lev. 25. 25; Ruth 4. This is a beautiful picture of the reason behind the Lord Jesus' incarnation, as BELLETT demonstrates:

> '[D]uring forty-nine years, the alienated possession of an Israelite might have been purchased by the kinsman of the heir, and thus redeemed or brought back to the family to which, under God, it had belonged; but if that were not done, it would return to the heir in the fiftieth year, or the Jubilee, without purchase. These two ordinances, again, I say, seem to set forth the mystery I am speaking of redemption by money and redemption by power. The kinsman might redeem with money, the Jubilee would redeem without money, by virtue of its own title, by virtue of that force or authority imparted to it by Him who was the God of Israel and the Lord of the soil'.[124]

The Son of God took on humanity in order to identify with humanity's need, and offer the exact payment on the cross that their sin required, Heb. 2. 5-16; Phil. 2. 6-8; 2 Cor. 5. 21; 8. 9.[125] He was truly divine, yet truly human without sin, 1 Tim. 3. 16. As our nearest relative He purchased our lost inheritance and us.[126]

---

[124] JOHN GIFFORD BELLETT, 'The Redemption of the Purchased Possession', electronic edition accessed here:
http://www.stempublishing.com/authors/bellett/PURCHASD.html
[brackets mine].

[125] Anselm of Canterbury also commented on this almost a millennium ago: 'It could not have been done unless man paid what was owing to God for sin. But the debt was so great that while man alone owed it, only God could pay it, so that the same person must be both man and God. Thus it was necessary for God to take manhood into the unity of his person, so that he who in his own nature ought to pay and could not should be in a person who could'. ANSELM OF CANTERBURY, quoted by RICHARD D. PHILLIPS in *Hebrews: Reformed Expository Commentary*, P&R Publishing, 2006, pg. 79.

[126] Luke 19. 10; 1 Cor. 6. 20.

Covenant blessings and cursings – Leviticus chapter 26

Many Bible students note that this chapter resembles the blessings and imprecations that were commonly attached to ancient covenants or treaties. Under the Mosaic covenant, Israel prospered by trusting in the Lord; whenever they departed from Him, divine chastening ensued – never more spectacularly demonstrated than when the ten tribes were carried into Assyrian captivity and the two remaining tribes departed into the seventy-year Babylonian captivity. The reader may see the blessings and cursings explicitly spelled out in the chapter.[127]

Leviticus 26 Content Outline

Warning against disloyalty to the Lord through idolatry or sabbath violation, vv. 1-2.
Promised blessing of the land, vv. 3-5.
Protection from animals and enemies, vv. 6-8.
Promise of God's presence among them, vv. 9-13.
Cursing if they depart from the Lord and His word, vv. 14-39.
Promise of God's faithfulness to the covenant and promise of restoration after repentance, vv. 40-46.

ROOKER highlights the parallel structure of the blessings and cursings:

'Blessings	Cursings
Fertile land (vv. 4–5, 10)	Unproductive land (vv. 16, 19–20, 26)
Live in safety (v. 5)	Live in foreign nation (v. 33)
Savage beasts removed (v. 6)	Beasts will devour (v. 22)
Sword removed (v. 6)	Sword avenges (v. 25)
Victory over enemies (v. 7)	Defeated by enemies (vv. 17, 25)

---

[127] See also Deuteronomy chapters 27-28.

| God's favour (v. 9) | God's disfavour (v. 17)'.[128] |

In the New Testament, Paul cites verse 12 to exhort the Corinthian believers to loyalty to the Lord, 2 Cor. 6. 16.

A faithful God desires a faithful people – Leviticus chapter 27

Other than the opening and concluding verses – verses 1 and 34 respectively – chapter 27 breaks down as follows:

Vows regarding people, vv. 2-8.
Vows regarding animals, vv. 9-13.
Vows regarding property, vv. 14-25.
Things devoted for the Lord, vv. 26-33.

MACKINTOSH observes that dispensationally Israel failed to keep their vow to the Lord, Exod. 24. 3, and yet He treats them according to grace:

> 'Israel made "a singular vow" at the foot of Mount Horeb; but they were quite unable to meet the claims of law – they were far "poorer than Moses' estimation". But, blessed be God, they will come in under the rich provisions of divine grace. Having learnt their total inability "to dig", they will not be "ashamed to beg"; and hence they shall experience the deep blessedness of being cast upon the sovereign mercy of Jehovah, which stretches, like a golden chain, "from everlasting to everlasting". It is well to be poor, when the knowledge of our poverty serves but to unfold to us the exhaustless riches of divine grace. That grace can never suffer any one to go empty away. It can never tell anyone that he is too poor. It can meet the very deepest human need; and not only so, but it is glorified in meeting it. This holds good in every case. It is true of any individual sinner, and it is true with respect

---

[128] ROOKER, pg. 319.

to Israel, who, having been valued by the lawgiver, have proved "poorer than his estimation". Grace is the grand and only resource for all. It is the basis of our salvation, the basis of a life of practical godliness, and the basis of those imperishable hopes which animate us amid the trials and conflicts of this sin-stricken world. May we cherish a deeper sense of grace, and more ardent desire for the glory'.[129]

Thus, Leviticus ends with the Lord asserting His rights over the people and land of Israel. He is the sovereign master of the history and the future disposition of this world, Ps. 24. 1; Eph. 1. 11. Humans are indebted to Him and yet He offers them matchless grace through His redemptive work.

---

[129] MACKINTOSH, pg. 416.

Bibliography for Leviticus

GEORGE BUSH, *Notes, Critical and Practical, on the Book of Leviticus*, A. McFarren, 1852.

C. A. COATES, *An Outline of the Book of Leviticus*, Stow Hill Bible & Tract Depot, n.d.

JOHN D. CURRID, *A Study Commentary on Leviticus*, EP Study Commentary, Evangelical Press, 2004.

R. LAIRD HARRIS, 'Leviticus', in *The Expositors Bible Commentary*, ed. FRANK GAEBELEIN, Zondervan, 1990. Electronic edition.

R. K. HARRISON, *Leviticus: An Introduction and Commentary*, Vol. 3., Tyndale Old Testament Commentaries, InterVarsity Press, 1980.

H. A. IRONSIDE, *Lectures on the Levitical Offerings*, Loizeaux Brothers, 1929.

S. H. KELLOGG, *Expositor's Bible: Leviticus*, A. C. Armstrong & Son, 1903.

WILLIAM KELLY, *The Priesthood, Its Privileges and Its Duties: An Exposition of Leviticus 8–15*, T. Weston, 1902.

WILLIAM KELLY, *Lectures on the Day of Atonement: Leviticus 16*, W. Walters, 1889.

WILLIAM KELLY, *Israel Holy to Jehovah: Exposition of Leviticus 17–22*, T. Weston, 1903.

JOHN PETER LANGE, PHILIP SCHAFF, and FREDERIC GARDINER, *A Commentary on the Holy Scriptures: Leviticus*, Logos Bible Software, 2008.

ALEXANDER MACLAREN, *Expositions of Holy Scripture: Exodus, Leviticus, and Numbers*, Logos Bible Software, 2009.

C. H. MACKINTOSH, *Genesis to Deuteronomy: Notes on the Pentateuch*, Loizeaux Brothers, 1972.

JAMES G. MURPHY, *A Critical and Exegetical Commentary on the Book of Leviticus*, W. F. Draper, 1872.

B. W. NEWTON, *Thoughts on Parts of Leviticus*, Partridge and Oakey, 1852.

MARK F. ROOKER, *Leviticus*, Vol. 3A, The New American Commentary, Broadman & Holman Publishers, 2000.

WARREN W. WIERSBE, *Be Holy*, 'Be' Commentary Series, Victor Books, 1996.

Numbers

1.   Introduction

The Hebrew name of the book is *bemidhbar*, meaning 'In the wilderness'. This phrase occurs repeatedly in the book, e.g., 1. 1, and accurately describes its setting.[130] In the ancient Greek translation known as the Septuagint the book was known as 'Arithmoi';[131] this, in turn, became 'Numeri' in the – still later – ancient translation known as the Latin Vulgate. Both of these terms refer to the prominent censuses of Numbers chapters 1 and 26.[132] One writer notes that both of the names 'reflect the importance of the census of the Israelite tribes in the book that is the basis for the allocation of territory; the phrase "according to the number of names" is found fifteen times in reference to the distribution of land'.[133]

To contemporary readers, these lists of impossible sounding names might be devoid of interest, but they actually serve an important purpose: they clearly identify God's people. As JOHN NELSON DARBY

---

[130] 'That term [*bemidhbar*] occurs over 40 times throughout the book, and in several places its occurrence is so dense (chapters 14 [8 times], 20 [7 times], and 33 [7 times]) that one cannot help but recognize that it constantly directs the reader's attention to the importance of the wilderness to the context of the narratives in the book'. GREGG WATSON, 'Numbers, Book of', ed. JOHN D. BARRY and LAZARUS WENTZ, *The Lexham Bible Dictionary*, Lexham Press, 2012.

[131] TERTULLIAN, a second-century Latin-speaking Christian, referred to it as 'the book of *Arithmi*,' indicating that the book was called 'Numbers' as early as the first century A.D. [R. DENNIS COLE, *Numbers*, The New American Commentary, Vol. 3B., Broadman & Holman Publishers, 2000, pg. 23].

[132] T. WHITELAW, 'Numbers, Book of,' ed. JAMES ORR et al., *The International Standard Bible Encyclopaedia*, The Howard-Severance Co., 1915, pg. 2163.

[133] BARRY L. BANDSTRA, 'Numbers, Book of', ed. MARK ALLAN POWELL, *The HarperCollins Bible Dictionary (Revised and Updated)*, HarperCollins, 2011, pg. 707.

remarks: 'The first thing to be noticed is, that God numbers His people exactly, and arranges them, once thus recognized, around His tabernacle: sweet thought, to be thus recognized and placed around God Himself!'[134] A modern author adds:

'The census with its careful preserving of the results (there are 46,500 Reubenites; 59,300 Simeonites; 45,650 Gadites...) affirms that everyone belongs to this assembly (Num. 1. 2, 18). There are no second-class citizens in Israel – at least, among the adult men. Everyone counts. Each person is named in these records, as they are named in that book that God has, from which Moses was willing to be excluded if God cancels the membership of the rest of Israel. Counting the people who belong to Israel also implicitly involves noting those who do not belong. This is explicitly true of the numbering recorded after the exile (e.g., Ezra 2). By its nature a census is both inclusionary and exclusionary. You count within the numbers only if you clearly belong to a particular household, community and clan'.[135]

The censuses also demonstrate the Lord's faithfulness to His covenant. The first one is a list of those whom He delivered from Egypt, but who eventually fell under His judgement on account of their unbelief, Num. 14. 29; Heb. 3. 16-19. God promised to curse the unbelieving, Deut. 27. 26, and thus He performed His word. Yet the second census assures the reader that there is a generation that will inherit the blessing by His grace received through faith.[136]

---

[134] J. N. DARBY, *Synopsis of the Books of the Bible: Genesis to 2 Chronicles*, Logos Research Systems, Inc., 2008, pg. 247.

[135] JOHN GOLDINGAY, *Old Testament Theology: Israel's Gospel*, Vol. 1, InterVarsity Press, 2003, pp. 439-440.

[136] ROBERT D. SPENDER, 'Numbers, Theology of', in WALTER A. ELWELL, *Evangelical Dictionary of Biblical Theology*, Baker Reference Library; Logos Library System (Grand Rapids: Baker Book House, 1996), electronic edition, no pagination.

2.   The Purpose of the Book

Numbers is book four of a five-book series: the books of Moses. Although unbelieving academia has fiercely attacked Mosaic authorship since the early nineteenth century, the Son of God affirmed it.[137] As the last verse indicates, the Lord Jesus directly referred back to Numbers, citing the story of the serpent on the poll. The apostles also believed that Moses wrote the Pentateuch, Acts 3. 22; 26. 22; Rom. 10. 5. The more one considers ancient near eastern composition, the more sophisticated these books appear. They clearly teach a unified theme and exceed mere human capability in their grandeur and perfection. As the New Testament affirms: 'All scripture is given by inspiration of God', 2 Tim. 3. 16, and 'For the prophecy came not in old time by the will of man: but holy men of God spake as they were moved by the Holy Ghost', 2 Pet. 1. 21.[138]

These books explain the history of God's central work in the world, which is the creation of a people for Himself who will be a light to the nations. The continuity between Exodus, Leviticus, and Numbers is

---

[137] Matt. 8. 4; 19. 8; Luke 24. 27, 44; John 3. 14.

[138] C. H. MACKINTOSH is worth quoting on this point: 'Each book of the Bible, each section of the inspired canon, has its own distinct place and object: each has its own niche assigned to it by its divine Author. We must not entertain for a moment the thought of instituting any comparison in point of intrinsic value, interest, and importance. All is divine, and therefore perfect. The Christian reader fully and heartily believes this. He reverently sets his seal to the truth of the plenary inspiration of holy Scripture – of all Scripture, and of the Pentateuch amongst the rest; nor is he to be moved one hair's breadth from this by the bold and impious attacks of infidels, ancient, mediaeval, or modern. Infidels and rationalists may traffic in their unhallowed reasonings; they may exhibit their enmity against the book and its Author; but the pious Christian rests, notwithstanding all, in the simple and happy belief that "all is given by inspiration of God"'. *Genesis to Deuteronomy: Notes on the Pentateuch*, Loizeaux Brothers, 1972, pp. 421-422.

explained by J. B. D. PAGE this way: 'Exodus describes the *way out* of Egypt, and the foundational truth of redemption. Leviticus tells of the *way in* to God, detailing the principles of worship. Numbers relates the *way through* the wilderness, with lessons for our conduct in this world. In Leviticus, the *priests* are prominent. In Numbers, the *Levites*, and later the *people*, are foremost'.[139]

Numbers continues the teaching at Sinai begun in Exodus chapter 16 and resumed in Leviticus.[140] It follows Israel as they wander in the wilderness for nearly forty years,[141] learning the folly of disobedience

---

[139] J. B. D. PAGE, 'Introducing Numbers', in *Day by Day through the Old Testament*, ed. C. E. HOCKING AND M. HORLOCK, Day by Day Series, Precious Seed, 1982, pg. 80 [italics original].

[140] JOHN D. CURRID points out the Hebrew verbal clue to Numbers' continuance of the Sinai teaching of the previous two books: 'The book of Numbers begins with the word **"Then"**. In Hebrew this is a *waw*-consecutive with the imperfect of the verb "to be". In older translations it is often rendered as "And it came to pass . . .". This device helps to define the literature as historical narrative, and it demonstrates temporal sequence; in other words, it connects the material with the previous book. Indeed, the tent of meeting had been completed one month earlier, Exod. 40. 17, and during that ensuing month the material of Leviticus had been revealed to the people. And now, at the end of the month, Israel is commanded to take a census of the people'. *A Study Commentary on Numbers*, EP Study Commentary, Evangelical Press, 2009, pg. 26 [boldface original]. The KJV, JND, RV 1881, and ASV render it as 'and'; others have 'now' NKJV, NET; or 'then' NASB. The NIV, RSV, NRSV, and ESV leave it untranslated.

[141] 38 years and 10 months, M. G. EASTON, *Easton's Bible Dictionary*, Harper and Brothers, 1893, no pagination available. JOHN MACARTHUR JR. adds: 'The book of Numbers concentrates on events that take place in the second and fortieth years after the Exodus. All incidents recorded in 1. 1–14. 45 occur in 1444 B.C., the year after the Exodus. Everything referred to after 20. 1 is dated circa 1406/1405 B.C., the 40th year after the Exodus. The laws and events found in 15. 1–19. 22 are undated, but probably all should be dated circa 1443 to 1407 B.C. The lack of material devoted to this 37 year period, in comparison with the other years of the journey from Egypt to Canaan,

and the blessing of obeying the Lord's word. Along the way, the Almighty's faithfulness, mercy, grace, wisdom, and sovereignty. The book also contrasts the blessings that Israel enjoys through Jehovah's covenant fidelity, e.g., Num. 1-10, and their practical failure and recurrent rebellion against His authority, Num. 11-21. As one writer comments: 'Ten chapters of preparation for a straightforward march from Sinai to Canaan are undone by eleven chapters dominated by accounts of let-down, protest, rebellion and chastisement. The macroperspective in Numbers 1–10 envisions Israel in positive theological terms as a people under the blessing, Num. 6. 22–27; cf. Deut. 2. 7. In Numbers 11–21 it looks more like a people under the curse'.[142] The Lord is undaunted by their disobedience, and after severely chastening the nation eventually prepares the next generation for their entry into Canaan, the Promised Land. DARBY points out: 'Now, as Leviticus ended with regulations and warnings respecting the possession of the land, and that with regard to the rights of God, and consequently to the rights of His people, the Book of Numbers brings us through the wilderness to the moment before the entrance of the people into the land at the end of the wilderness journey, and speaks of that grace which justifies the people at the close, notwithstanding all their unfaithfulness'.[143] The twistings[144]

---

communicates how wasted these years were because of Israel's rebellion against the Lord and His consequent judgment'. *The MacArthur Study Bible*, electronic edition, Word Publishing, 1997, pg. 195.

[142] JOHN GOLDINGAY, *Old Testament Theology: Israel's Gospel*, Vol. 1, InterVarsity Press, 2003, pg. 451.

[143] DARBY, pg. 246.

[144] 'The sad aspect of this book is man's penchant for rebellion. In spite of the repeated times God had demonstrated His awe-inspiring power and willingness to act on behalf of His people, they were easily swayed by immediate circumstances. The rebellion of the Israelites reminds each reader of Numbers that human hearts are dark and no one is far from rebellion'. EUGENE H. MERRILL, MARK ROOKER, MICHAEL GRISANTI, et al., *The World and the Word: An Introduction to the Old Testament*, B&H, 2011, electronic edition, no pagination.

and turnings of Israel's history in Numbers do not alter the fact that entrance into the land will occur for those who trust the Lord by faith.[145]

The practical and theological function of the wilderness

While the desert[146] was an austere setting, in God's hand it became the training ground for Israel's future blessing and inheritance. The Psalms often look back to this formative period in Israel's history as a

---

[145] GLEASON ARCHER JR. expresses it well: 'The spiritual lesson enforced throughout the book is that God's people can move forward only so far as they trust His promises and lean upon His strength. The tragedy of Kadesh-barnea was the unavoidable consequence of unbelief; only true believers can enter into God's rest. Without faith they can only die uselessly in the wilderness, cf. Heb. 3. 7–19'. *A Survey of Old Testament Introduction*, 3rd ed., Moody Press, 1994, pg. 265.

[146] On the definition of 'wilderness/desert': 'The Hebrew word for *wilderness (midbār)* means a place for driving flocks. It is not a completely arid desert, but contains a little vegetation and a few trees. The rainfall in such areas is too light, a few inches per year, to support cultivation'. GORDON J. WENHAM, *Numbers: An Introduction and Commentary*, Tyndale Old Testament Commentaries, Vol. 4, InterVarsity Press, 1981, pg. 65. 'Some translate the noun simply as "wilderness," but a modifying word like "barren" needs to be added to portray adequately the arid nature of a *midbār*. It is an area that lacks water, Ezek. 19. 13; Hos. 13. 5, is uninhabited, Job 38. 26, and is uncultivated and usually unfruitful, Jer. 2. 2; 4. 26, though some deserts have enough vegetation for pasturing flocks, 1 Sam. 17. 28. Away from the safety and light of the inhabited areas of the county, the *midbār* is a place of thick darkness and danger, Jer. 2. 31, and is not usually portrayed in a positive light (S. of S. 3. 6 is an exception). Jer. 2. 6 sums up these aspects well when it describes the desert that the Israelites passed through after the exodus: "a land of wilderness plain and gorges . . . a land that is dry and dark . . . a land no one passes through and where no one lives". The only natural inhabitants of the *midbār* are wild animals, such as jackals, Mal. 1. 3, ostriches, Lam. 4. 3, and donkeys, Job 24. 5'. WILLIAM D. MOUNCE, *Mounce's Complete Expository Dictionary of Old & New Testament Words*, Zondervan, 2006, pp. 170-171.

warning against the cost of disobedience and thanksgiving for divine provision, Ps. 106. 14-33. Psalm 78 verse 40 shows the negative side: 'How oft did they provoke him in the wilderness, And grieve him in the desert'. While other psalms dwell on the positive aspect of God's dealings with them: 'The people asked, and he brought quails, And satisfied them with the bread of heaven. He opened the rock, and the waters gushed out; they ran in the dry places like a river. For he remembered his holy promise, And Abraham his servant', Ps. 105. 40-42. Both Stephen and Paul referred to the wilderness experience in their sermons, Acts 7. 37-44; 13. 8. Likewise, Hebrews chapters 3 and 4 use the sin of the first wilderness generation as a solemn warning to mere professors against apostasy. The background to 1 Corinthians chapter 10 verses 1-13 – another serious warning passage – also looks back to Israel's spectacular sins in the wilderness era. Clearly, it left a mark on the consciousness of God's people. Its truth is of trans-dispensational importance, that is, it was valuable for Old Testament Israel and for the New Testament Church, 2 Tim. 3. 16-17; Rom. 15. 4. It keeps believers from extremes concerning sanctification, as one author notes:

'Many a Christian thinks of himself as back in the experience described in the early part of Exodus. He is constantly worrying about his past sins, fretting about whether he really is a child of God or not. He needs to realize that if he has truly looked to Christ for salvation and been born again by simple faith in Him, he has been delivered from Egypt and is now a child of God, headed for the Promised Land. He needs to learn to possess the possessions which God has given him, and to rejoice in them. He must never forget that his sins are under the blood; Jesus has died for him; the transaction is completed; he is now launched on his pilgrim journey. Other Christians tend to make the opposite mistake. They think themselves to be already in the Promised Land. This can lead to an exaggerated idea of the extent of one's sanctification, or to undue discouragement along the way. We need to realize that we are pilgrims, and that this world is still

Satan's territory. We must constantly look to Christ for protection and guidance. The Book of Numbers is the book that typifies our present situation. All through it we find illustrations marvellously planned to show us what we need'.[147]

Believers have derived much spiritual benefit from 'wilderness experiences' through the centuries; its frequency as a motif in Christian hymnody demonstrates this phenomenon. For example, DARBY'S beautiful lyrics speak of the believer's longing for a better home and show that his 'life is hidden with Christ in God', Col. 3. 1-4:

This world is a wilderness wide!
We have nothing to seek or to choose;
We've no thought in the waste to abide;
We have naught to regret, nor to lose.
The Lord is Himself gone before;
He has marked out the path that we tread;
It's as sure as the love we adore,
We have nothing to fear, nor to dread.

MARY BOWLEY PETERS also captures the wilderness sense of the current Christian experience, noting its pilgrim character. This world is not our home, instead we seek a better country with a city that has foundations whose designer and builder is God Himself, Heb. 11. 10, 13-16:

We're pilgrims in the wilderness:
Our dwelling is a camp;
Created things, though pleasant,
Now bear to us death's stamp.
But onward we are speeding,
Though often sorely tried:
The Holy Ghost is leading

---

[147] ALLAN A. MACRAE, 'The Book called "Numbers"', *Bibliotheca Sacra* 111:441 (January 1954), pp. 51–52.

Home to the Lamb, His bride.

With fellow-pilgrims meeting,
Who seek the rest to come,
'Tis sweet to sing together,
'We are not far from home.'
And when we've learned our lesson,
Our work in suffering done,
Our ever-loving Father
Will welcome every one.

Lord, since we sing as pilgrims,
O give us pilgrims' ways,
Low thoughts of self, befitting
Proclaimers of Thy praise;
O make us each more holy,
In spirit pure and meek:
More like to heavenly citizens,
As more of heaven we speak.

A contemporary songwriter, MICHAEL CARD, reminds us of the teaching and testing nature of the wilderness. Trials in the desert of this world serve as the schoolroom for the Lord's instruction of His people and their preparation for eternal dwelling in His kingdom:

In the wilderness, in the wilderness
He calls His sons and daughters to the wilderness
But He gives grace sufficient to survive any test
And that's the painful purpose of the wilderness.

Although the wilderness is not an end point in itself, it is an important pathway that leads toward the destination of enjoying God in His inheritance. It may be temporary, but it is also indispensable for sanctification. Christian character is moulded and formed under the Lord's hand in the desert of this world.[148] As C. H. MACKINTOSH declares: 'It is emphatically a wilderness book, and characterized by journeyings, service, and all the vicissitudes of wilderness life. As such, it is deeply interesting, most instructive, and easily applied to the Christian in this present evil world (compare Numbers 1 and 36. 13 with Deuteronomy 1. 3)'.[149] The celebrated preacher, G. CAMPBELL MORGAN agrees, in these words: 'The patience of God is the supreme revelation of the book. This patience is not incompetent carelessness, but powerful carefulness. Its methods are many. He punished the people for wrongdoing, but always towards the realization of purpose. He placed them in circumstances which developed the facts of their inner life, until they knew them for themselves. That is the meaning of the forty years in the wilderness. They were not years in which God had withdrawn Himself from the people and refused to have anything to do with them. Every year was necessary for the teaching of a lesson, and the revealing of a truth'.[150]

3.   The Plan of the Book

Broadly, the book may be divided generationally. Chapters 1-25 concern the first generation that rebelled and failed to enter the Promised Land. Chapters 26-36 are occupied with matters

---

[148] Epistles such as 1 Peter and James have the imprint of the wilderness very strongly upon them. They are written to a pilgrim people journeying through the wilderness 'to an inheritance incorruptible, undefiled, and that fadeth not away', 1 Pet. 1. 4.

[149] MACKINTOSH, pg. 419.

[150] G. CAMPBELL MORGAN, *Living Messages of the Books of the Bible*, Baker, 1982, pg. 17. A more contemporary scholar, PETER C. CRAIGIE, says something similar: 'if the substance of Numbers is negative and miserable in respect to the light it sheds on human nature, it is entirely positive in respect to its theological perspectives. The picture of Israel's God that emerges in these chapters is of a being who is patient and long-suffering, firm in dealing with human evil, but able to forgive and to restore'. *The Old Testament: Its Background, Growth, & Content*, Abingdon Press, 1986, pg. 112.

concerning the second generation that would eventually enter the land under the leadership of Joshua. Since the book of Numbers prepares Israel for their journey through the wilderness to the edge of Canaan, accordingly the first ten chapters are preparatory for the journey. These instructions reflect the orderly nature of God's dealings with His people, 1 Cor. 14. 40.

The Lord begins by commanding Moses to conduct a census, chapters 1-4, including the preparation of the Levites for service. The censuses of this book are especially concerned with marking out the nation's eligible warriors. Like many modern democracies, the army was composed of 'citizen-soldiers', rather than a professional warrior caste. The camping arrangement around God's sanctuary, the tabernacle, is also laid out, and the camp is purged of defiling and defiled objects or people; this includes the trial of jealousy in chapter 5 verses 11-31. The other side of holiness is detailed in the Nazarite vow, 6. 1-21, which depicts total consecration for the Lord's service. Chapters 7-9 deal with the worship and service of the tabernacle, and detail the sacrifices of the leaders, the arrangement of the lamps in that sanctuary, and the celebration of the Passover. Chapter 10 concludes this preparatory section with instructions concerning the silver trumpets and the movements of the camp as directed by the Lord. This section of the book emphasizes the resources and blessings that Israel enjoys through the goodness of their God.

Chapters 11-21 follow the repeated rebellions of the people and the ensuing discipline from the Lord. There are repeated challenges to His authority – usually focusing on His servant and representative, Moses – followed by divine judgement. Complaints come from sources as varied as the mixed multitude, Moses' siblings Miriam and Aaron, the ten unbelieving spies, Korah and his allies, and even Moses himself. Interspersed within these sad accounts of human disloyalty are reminders of the Lord's gracious and purifying work, chs. 15; 18-19. There are also divinely given victories over various enemies, ch. 21.

While they apparently relate a radically different topic, in actuality chapters 22-25 continue to demonstrate the Lord's faithfulness towards His people, as He protects them from the spiritual machinations and assault of King Balak and his prophet-for-hire Balaam. Despite their best efforts to curse Israel, He turned their malediction into blessing. What is more, He used the false prophet to reveal the tremendous position of Israel in the Almighty's sight, 23. 21. Sadly, chapter 25 shows that the attack came from a different, more alluring direction. The ladies of the Moabite-Midianite coalition invited the Israelite men to a feast, thereby beguiling them and enticing them into both spiritual and physical fornication.[151]

The second census, Num. 26, sweeps the old generation off the scene and turns the reader's attention to the new generation that will inherit the land. Preparations for entering the land are made as teaching concerning inheritance laws, chs. 27 and 36; daily and seasonal sacrifices, chs. 28-29; laws regarding vows, ch. 30; victory over their enemies the Midianites, ch. 31; and instructions concerning the Transjordanian settlement of Reuben, Gad, and the half-tribe of Manasseh, ch. 32; the establishment of Levitical cities and cities of refuge, ch. 35, are all set forth. Chapter 33 verses 1-49 looks back on where the Israelites have travelled during their wilderness wanderings, and verses 50-56 give teaching concerning the future conquest of Canaan. The boundaries of the land are delineated, 34. 1-15, and administrators are chosen to divide the inheritance, vv. 16-29. Perhaps most importantly, there is a change of leadership, as Moses inaugurates Joshua as his successor to lead God's people into the land of their inheritance, 27. 18-22.

---

[151] Num. 31. 15; Ps. 106. 28; Rev. 2. 14.

A simple breakdown of the book is:

- Preparation for travels, chs. 1-10
- Journeying from the desert to the edge of the Promised Land, chs. 11-25
- Preparation for entering the Promised Land, chs. 26-36

Some writers divide the book based on geographical setting:

1. 'The people of God prepare to enter the Promised Land (1. 1-10. 10)
2. From Sinai to Kadesh (10. 11 – 12. 16)
3. Forty years near Kadesh (13. 1 – 19. 22)
4. From Kadesh to the plains of Moab (20. 1 – 22. 1)
5. Israel in the plains of Moab (22. 2 – 36. 13)'[152]

Other scholars note the repetitive cycles of grace and rebellion in the book:

'(1) Sinai Cycle A: The Community in Faithfulness and Purity (1. 1 – 6. 27)

(2) Sinai Cycle B: The tabernacle and the Community of Faith (7. 1 – 10. 10)

(3) Rebellion Cycle A: People and Leaders (10. 11 – 15. 41)

(4) Rebellion Cycle B: Priests and Levites (16. 1 – 19. 22)

(5) Rebellion Cycle C: From Moses to Balaam and Back to the People (20. 1 – 25. 18)

(6) Advent Cycle A: The Birth of the New Generation Who Will Inherit the Land (26. 1 – 30. 16)

(7) Advent Cycle B: Preparation for War and Entry into the Promised Land (31. 1 – 36. 13)'[153]

---

[152] WENHAM, pp. 61-62.
[153] COLE, pp. 44-52.

A detailed content outline of Numbers:

'I. Israel Prepares to Enter the Land, 1. 1 – 10. 10
  A. The first census, 1. 1-46
  B. The responsibilities of the Levites, 1. 47-54
  C. Israel in camp and on the march, 2. 1-34
  D. Two censuses of the Levites, 3. 1 – 4. 49
      1. Census of all male Levites, 3. 1-51
          a. The sons of Aaron, 3. 1-4
          b. The duties of the Levites, 3. 5-10
          c. Reason for the Levitical census, 3. 11-13
          d. The clans' numbers, positions, and
          responsibilities, 3. 14-39
          e. Redemption of the firstborn, 3. 40-51
      2. Census of mature Levites, 4. 1-49
          a. The tasks of the Kohathites, 4. 1-20
          b. The tasks of the Gershonites, 4. 21-28
          c. The tasks of the Merarites, 4. 29-33
          d. The results of the second census, 4. 34-49
  E. Cleansing the camp, 5. 1 – 6. 27
      1. Exclusion of the unclean from the camp, 5. 1-4
      2. Atonement for perjury, 5. 5-10
      3. Test of suspected adultery, 5. 11-31
      4. Rules for Nazarites, 6. 1-21
          a. Definition of a Nazarite, 6. 1-6
          b. Nazarites and uncleanness, 6. 7-12
          c. Completion of a Nazarite vow, 6. 13-20
          d. Summary of the law, 6. 21
      5. The priestly blessing, 6. 22-27
  F. Offerings for the tabernacle, 7. 1-89
  G. The lampstand, 8. 1-4
  H. The dedication of the Levites, 8. 5-22
  I. The retirement of the Levites, 8. 23-26
  J. The second Passover, 9. 1-5
  K. The delayed Passover, 9. 6-14

5. The distributors of the land, 34. 16-29
6. Cities for the Levites, 35. 1-8
I. The cities of refuge, 35. 9-34
   1. The selection and purpose of these cities, 35. 9-15
   2. Homicide that warrants the death penalty, 35. 16-21
   3. Homicide that does not deserve death, 35. 22-29
   4. Final points, 35. 30-34
   5. Zelophehad's daughters marry, 36. 1-13'[154]

4.   The Author and Date of the Book

Contrary to liberal and non-believing scholarly consensus, like the rest of the Pentateuch Numbers was written by Moses, circa 1405/1406 B.C. Its material focuses on events between the second and fortieth years after the exodus.[155]

5.   Important Themes in the Book

A) God as a God of order.
B) Unity of the people of God.
C) Spiritual warfare.
D) Holiness and its practical development.
E) God's view of His people and their position of favour in His sight.
F) The danger of murmuring.
G) The human propensity to sin.
H) Grace after human failure.
I) God's sovereignty in carrying out His will.

---

[154] CROSSWAY BIBLES, *The ESV Study Bible,* Crossway Bibles, 2008, pp. 261-264.

[155] Many conservative commentators hold to this date, seeing the Exodus around 1445 B.C. See MACARTHUR JR., ed., *The MacArthur Study Bible,* pg. 195 and WILLIAM MACDONALD, *Believer's Bible Commentary: Old and New Testaments,* ed. ARTHUR FARSTAD, Thomas Nelson, 1995, pg. 169.

J) God's faithfulness to His people and His promises, e.g., the ongoing fulfilment of the Abrahamic Covenant.

Preparation				
1-4	**5.1 – 6.21**	**6.22-27**	**7-8**	**9-10**
Numbering for the TRIBES	Keeping the Camp clean	The Aaronic blessing	Dedications	Regulations for the Journey
A. THE TRIBES 1. For war 2. For camping and marching	A 1. Physical uncleanness 2. Business trespass 3. TRIAL OF JEALOUSY	The Lord • BLESS THEE • Keep thee • Make his face to shine upon thee and be gracious to thee • Lift His countenance upon thee • Give thee peace • My name upon them • I will BLESS THEM	A Offerings of the Princes at the DEDICATION OF THE ALTAR	A. 1. Passover 2. Guidance by CLOUD Guidance by TRUMPETS
B. THE LEVITES 3. Levites for firstborn 4. Duties to transport Tabernacle	B. NAZARITE'S VOW & rules about defilement		B. The LAMPSTANDS & the OFFERING of the LEVITES as a living sacrifice	B. 1. Order of march 2. Hobab as eyes 3. Movements of ARK

Journey

11-15	16-19	20-24	25-31	32-36
A. REBELLION 1. Murmuring 2. Lusting 3. Criticism of Moses 4. REFUSAL to enter the LAND	A. REBELLION OF KORAH, Levites, and others	A. REBELLION OF MOSES AND AARON 1. Moses smites rock 2. Opposition of the Kings 3. Serpent on pole 4. Wars of Lord 5. The Well	A. REBELLION Israel joins himself to BAAL-PEOR	A. REBELLION? Refusal to journey further
	Censers of rebels nailed to the altar		GOS IS JEALOUS	Settlement of the inheritance for the TRIBES
B. SACRIFICES ... when you have entered the land ...	B. SACRIFICES The rights of Aaron and sons as priests LEVITES	B. SACRIFICES By Balaam 'GOD HAS BLESSED'	B. SACRIFICES For each day of FEASTS OF THE LORD	B. NO RANSOM For murdered or homicides
	The Red Heifer		VOWS	Settlement of LEVITES & CITIES OF REFUGE

1	2	3	4	5	6	7	8	9	10
1.1 – 4.49	5.1 – 6.21	6.22 – 6.27	7.1 – 8.26	9.1 – 10.36	11.1 – 15.41	16.1 – 19.22	20.1 – 24.25	25.1 – 31.54	32.1 – 36.13
Numbering 1. Ordering for the wilderness A. Tribes 1. Men armed for war 2. Order of the camp and marching B. Levites 1. Numbering 2. Substitution for firstborn 3. Numbering and procedures for carrying Tabernacle	**Sanctification of camp** A. Discharges 1. Leprosy 2. Trespass 3. Ordeal of Jealousy B. Nazarite Vow 1. from wine 2. cutting hair 3. contact with dead	**True blessing of Israel by the priests** The Lord bless A. Security B. Grace C. Peace 'So shall ye put my name on them'	**Ordering of worship and service** A. Offerings of Princes at dedication of altar [Sacrifices] B. Lamp-stand and the living sacrifices of priests	**Regulation for journeying** A. 1. Passover 2. Cloud (controlled) 3. Trumpets B. Journey commences 1. Princes of host 2. Hobab? Eyes? 3. Ark – eyes	**Rebellion** Murmuring – refusal to enter promised land or inheritance God's judgement, 14.13 Intercession Cloud Ark – when you start and where you finish	**Rebellion** Korah, Dathan, and Abihu. Moses and Aaron Sign 1 – Altar and Censors, ch. 17 Sign 2 – Aaron's rod that budded Levites, wave offering, tithes, red heifer, ch. 18	**Rebellion** People strive with Moses, 20. 24 Moses and Aaron rebel against God, 27. 14 Rock smitten Serpent on pole Balaam's attempt to curse Cannot reverse God's blessing	**Rebellion** Israel joins himself to Baal-Peor God is jealous, 1 Cor. 8 & 10 [Promise?] of everlasting priesthood Joshua stands before M.P. 1. Festival sacrifices 2. Vows 3. Spoils devoted to God	**Rebellion** Suspicion of rebellion – Moses thought refusal to pass over armed for war Settling tribes in their inheritance Settling Levites in cities of refuge Ransom expiation
					Sacrifices ch. 15	Sacrifices ch. 18-19	Sacrifices chs. 22-24	Sacrifices ch. 28	

Numbers Outline

Chronology of Events in Exodus, Leviticus, and Numbers		
Date	Scripture	Event
1.14.1	Exod. 14. 6, 30-31	Exodus from Egypt
3.14.1	Exod. 19. 1	Israelites arrive at Sinai
1.1.2	Exod. 40. 2, 17	Tabernacle erected with Tent of Meeting
	Lev. 8. 1-36	Priestly sanctification begins
	Lev. 1. 1 – 7. 38	Altar offerings commence
	Num. 7. 1, 3	Tribal offerings begin
	Num. 9. 15	Cloud covers tabernacle
1.8.2	Lev. 9. 1	Priestly sanctification concluded
1.12.2	Num. 7. 78–83	Tribal offerings completed
1.14.2	Num. 9. 1	Second Passover
2.1.2	Num. 1. 1–2	First census commences
2.14.2	Num. 9. 11	Second Passover for the Unclean
2.20.2	Num. 10. 11	Cloud moves – Israel departs Sinai[157]

---

[156] The preceding charts are by brother DAVID GOODING and were part of a packet of outlines shared at the Florida Men's Bible Study, January 2015, held at Camp Horizon, Leesburg, FL. USA.
[157] COLE, pg. 135.

CALENDAR OF EVENTS FROM THE EXODUS TO THE PLAINS OF MOAB				
Year	Month	Day	Event	Biblical Reference
1	1	14	Exodus: Departure from Egypt	Exod. 12. 1-50
1	3	14	Arrival in Sinai Desert	Exod. 19. 1
2	1	1	Tabernacle Erected	Exod. 40. 17
2	1	1–12	Israelite Tribe Dedication Offerings	Num. 7. 1-89
2	1	14–22	Passover & Unleavened Bread Celebration	Num. 9. 1-14
2	2	1	First Tribal Military Census	Num. 1. 1-46
2	2	14	Passover Alternative for Unclean and Distant	Num. 9. 6-13
2	2	20	Departure from Sinai Desert	Num. 10. 11
2	2	23	Kibroth Hattaavah (Quail)	Num. 10. 33; 11. 34
2			Spies Sent from Kadesh in Paran Desert	Num. 13. 3, 26
40	1		Miriam Dies in Kadesh in Zin Desert	Num. 20. 1
40	5	1	Aaron Dies	Num. 20. 22-29; 33. 37-39
40	11	1	Moses Speaks to the People	Deut. 1. 3[158]

---

[158] COLE, pg. 172.

6.   The Contents of the Book

Beginning census of the first Israelite generation

Chapter 1 outline:

- instructions for the census and selection of tribal representatives, vv. 1-16;
- numbering the tribes (excluding Levi), vv. 17-46;
- instructions for Levi, vv. 47-54.

Managing 2-3 million people in the wilderness required organization. Beyond this practical reality, God is a being who delights in order. He gave specific directions for the building of the tabernacle and told Moses to construct everything according to the divinely revealed pattern, Exod. 25. 9. Later the temple would also be constructed in keeping with God's instructions, 1 Chr. 22. 11. The New Testament Church likewise is designed by the Lord.[159] In every age, believers' lives must be regulated by His teaching so that they may please Him and grow spiritually in their own walk.

These censuses serve as more than mere organizational principles for the multitudes. Numbers chapter 1 verse 3 demonstrates that these men are being selected for warfare: 'all that are able to go forth to war in Israel'. This was a roll call for fighting men. Entrance into the inheritance requires combat; it is serious business. God's blessings demand a choice: for them, it was Egypt or Canaan. For present-day saints it is this world or the age to come, Gal. 1. 4; 2 Tim. 4. 10. Like the Israelites, modern believers are engaged in warfare for the Lord. The key difference is that their battles were physical and geographical; whereas in this dispensation, the struggle is against spiritual powers in the heavenlies, Eph. 6. 10-19; 2 Cor. 10. 3-6. ISAAC

---

[159] See 1 Tim. 3. 15; Acts 2. 42; 1 Cor. 11. 2.

WATTS captures the spirit in his classic hymn, 'Am I a soldier of the cross?'

Sure I must fight if I would reign;
Increase my courage, Lord.
I'll bear the toil, endure the pain,
Supported by Thy word.

Thy saints in all this glorious war
Shall conquer, though they die;
They see the triumph from afar,
By faith's discerning eye.

When that illustrious day shall rise,
And all Thy armies shine
In robes of victory through the skies,
The glory shall be Thine.

Certain leaders from each tribe were appointed to oversee the census among the various 'families', v. 2. 'The house of their fathers' is a smaller group than 'families', which approximates to the modern term 'clans'.[160] The tribal leaders' names are interesting and may warrant devotional meditation:

'Of Reuben, Elizur the son of Shedeur ("whose rock is God" – son of the stream of fire).
Of Simeon, Shelumiel the son of Zurishaddai (God's peace [Godfried], – Rock of the Almighty).

---

[160] 'The noun *mišpāḥâ* designates a subgroup of a larger division, and is, therefore, variously translated as "clan, family, people" as well as "kind, kingdoms, nation"'. MOUNCE, pg. 465; '*Family* (Hebrew *mišpāḥâ*) would be more appropriately translated "clan". It is the main social unit, intermediate in size between a tribe and the *father's house* (Josh. 7:14). The *father's house* might be better rendered "family", though it was a somewhat larger unit than our nuclear families, cf. Judg. 6. 15. But in some cases the terms are used more flexibly (Num. 4. 18; 17. 2)'. WENHAM, pg. 66 [italics original].

Of Judah. Nahshon the son of Amminadab (sorcerer? serpent standard? – Atheling).

For Issachar, Nethaneel, the son of Zuar (gift of God – littleness, or the little one).

For Zebulun, Eliab the son of Helon (whose father is God – man of sorrows? Dream?).

For Ephraim, Elishama the son of Ammihud (whom God hears – "From the people of Judah?" impossible! it signifies rather: my people are the objects of praise).

For Manasseh, Gamaliel the son of Pedahzur, (Gamliel: God's recompense, God's rule – his rock is his deliverer).

For Benjamin, Abidan the son of Gideoni (the father of the judge or the father-judge – the woodman as a powerful warrior).

For Dan, Ahiezer the son of Ammishaddai (brother of help? Brotherly help – from the people of the Almighty).

For Asher, Pagiel the son of Ocran (God's destiny – the afflicted one = Benoni?).

For Gad, Eliasaph the son of Reuel (whom God has added, God's Joseph – Invocation of God).

For Naphtali, Ahira the son of Enan (brother of uproar? Brother of festivity – abounding in springs)'.[161]

Their tabulations of the warriors runs as follows (the second column has the numbers from chapter 26):

Numbers 1	Numbers 26
Reuben: 46,500	Reuben: 43,730
Simeon: 22,200	Simeon: 59,300
Gad: 40,500	Gad: 45,650
Judah: 76,500	Judah: 74,600

---

[161] JOHN PETER LANGE ET AL., *A Commentary on the Holy Scriptures: Numbers*, Logos Bible Software, 2008, pg. 10. I changed LANGE'S order and the numbering of the leaders' names to match the order in Numbers chapter 1 verses 5-15. The same men also appear in: 2. 3-31; 7. 12-83; 10. 14-27.

Issachar: 64,300   Issachar: 54,400
Zebulun: 60,500   Zebulun: 57,400
Manasseh: 52,700   Manasseh: 32,200
Ephraim: 32,500   Ephraim: 40,500
Benjamin: 45,600   Benjamin: 35,400
Dan: 64,400   Dan: 62,700
Asher: 53,400   Asher: 41,500
Naphtali: 45,400   Naphtali: 53,400
Total: 601,730 - v. 46   Total: 603,550 - v. 51

The order of names is slightly different in Numbers chapter 1 and chapter 26 – Ephraim precedes Manasseh in the first list and the order is reversed in the second. Otherwise the population numbers are extremely similar between the two lists. This indicates that the population of the second generation was virtually the same as the first generation. Though the Almighty's dealings with Israel were complicated by the first generation's rebellion at Kadesh Barnea, chs. 13-14, His plans for His people were not thwarted. The statistics manifest God's faithfulness to His covenant people, Gen. 12. If the first generation failed because of unbelief, God will graciously bring in their children by faith, Heb. 3. 16-18; Num. 14. 26-35.

Of course, the Levites are a notable omission from the census rolls (since Joseph is divided into Ephraim and Manasseh, Gen. 48. 14-21, the number in the list still comes to twelve despite their absence). That is because they were selected to be the Lord's tribe for priestly and sacred service. Their genealogy is listed separately in chapters 3 and 4, where their numbers are detailed. They formed the inner layer encamped around the holy dwelling place of the Lord, the tabernacle. This book will discuss their duties when we examine chapters 4 and 5, but chapter 1 focuses on one vital task that they performed in the encampment: they guarded[162] the Almighty's tent from unauthorized

---

162 'This word can also mean "guard." For example, in Num. 3. 7, the Levites are commanded to keep guard (*mišmeret*) over the tabernacle. One way they

encroachment, Num. 1. 51-53. 'The stranger' of Numbers chapter 1 verse 51 apparently indicates a non-Levite, rather than a mere foreigner; *The New King James Version* and *English Standard Version* render it 'outsider'.[163] If such a person came too close to the tabernacle, they incurred the death penalty, 3. 10. Clearly, approaching the presence of the holy God demanded special authority. Unlike believers on our side of the cross, there was no coming boldly before the throne of grace by the non-levitical Israelite, Heb. 4. 14-16. The modern believer's authorization comes from our link to the Melchizedekian high priest who offered the perfect propitiatory sacrifice for the sins of the world.[164]

---

kept guard over the tabernacle was to prevent foreigners from approaching it, Num 3. 38'. RON CLARK and DOUGALD MCLAURIN III, 'Duty', ed. DOUGLAS MANGUM ET AL., *Lexham Theological Wordbook*, Lexham Bible Reference Series, Lexham Press, 2014. 'The object used with this is the cognate noun מִשְׁמֶרֶת (*mishmeret*): "The Levites must care for the care of the tabernacle." The cognate intensifies the construction to stress that they are responsible for this care'. NETmg.

[163] *zār* '(one who is) **unauthorized**: non-Aaronite Lev. 22. 10, non-Levite Num. 1. 51, one who does not share in the cult, i.e. layman Exod. 30. 33'. WILLIAM LEE HOLLADAY and LUDWIG KÖHLER, *A Concise Hebrew and Aramaic Lexicon of the Old Testament*, Brill, 2000, pp. 91-92 [boldface original]; NASB has 'layman'; NET has 'unauthorized person' with this marginal note: 'The word used here is זָר (*zar*), normally translated "stranger" or "outsider." It is most often used for a foreigner, an outsider, who does not belong in Israel, or who, although allowed in the land, may be viewed with suspicion. But here it seems to include even Israelites other than the tribe of Levi'. It is the same Hebrew word used for 'strange' in the well-known expression 'strange fire' in Leviticus chapter 10 verse 1; it is also used in Numbers chapter 3 verse 4 referring to the same incident.

[164] See 1 John 2. 1-2; Heb. 7. 23-28; 8. 1-2; 9. 11-15; 10. 14, 19-22.

Tribal encampment surrounding the tabernacle

Encampment of the twelve tribes

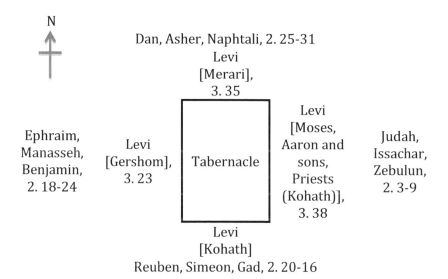

Break Camp
1) Judah, 2. 9;
2) Reuben, 2. 16;
3) Ephraim, 2. 24;
4) Dan, 2. 31.

Marching order of the twelve tribes

Dan 2. 31	Ephraim 2. 24	Levi 2. 17	Tabernacle	Levi 2. 17	Reuben 2. 16	Judah 2. 9

Rear ⟶ Front

Chapter 2 outline:

Camping directions for the tribes, vv. 1-34

Verse 2 instructs the Israelites to camp by their 'standard with the ensign of their father's house'. The erudite nineteenth-century Hebrew scholar, C. F. KEIL described these markers well:

'[A] standard, banner, or flag, denotes primarily the larger *field sign*, possessed by every division composed of three tribes, which was also the banner of the tribe at the head of each division; and secondarily, in a derivative signification, it denotes the *army* united under one standard . . . the *signs* (ensigns), were the smaller flags or banners which were carried at the head of the different tribes and subdivisions of the tribes (the fathers' houses). Neither the Mosaic law, nor the Old Testament generally, gives us any intimation as to the form or character of the standard (*degel*)'.[165]

The *New English Translation* margin further adds:

'The standard was the symbol fastened to the end of a pole and carried to battle. It served to rally the tribe to the battle. The Bible nowhere describes these, although the serpent emblem of Numbers 21. 8–9 may give a clue. But they probably did not have shapes of animals in view of the prohibition in the Decalogue. The standards may have been smaller for the families than the ones for the tribes'.[166]

---

[165] CARL FRIEDRICH KEIL and FRANZ DELITZSCH, *Commentary on the Old Testament*, Vol. 1, Hendrickson, 1996, pp. 659–660 [italics original].

[166] NETmg.; compare this statement: 'During the wilderness journey each Israelite tribe had its own banner or standard, Num. 2. 2; cf. 1. 52. A single standard represented each division of three tribes as the twelve tribes encamped around the tabernacle, 2. 3, 10, 18, 25, 34, and as they marched,

122

The encampment was orderly and well-defined – every family was in their proper place in keeping with their clan affiliation. Their identities were marked out by banners and ensigns that publicly declared their connection to the household of Israel. Likewise, every believer today should identify himself with the Lord's people. The saints ought to declare their lineage as redeemed members of the body of Christ, 1 Cor. 12. 12-13; Eph. 4. 4-6.[167] They are members of a spiritual family that identifies itself with the One who called them into this blessed position.[168] Ultimately, the Lord is the believer's banner, Exod. 17. 15 KJVmg., NKJV. Christian identity and hope is only found in God's faithfulness.

The passage concludes with a beautiful statement of Israel's obedience to the Lord's instructions: 'And the children of Israel did according to all that the LORD commanded Moses: so they pitched by their standards, and so they set forward, every one after their families, according to the house of their fathers', Num. 2. 34.

---

10. 14, 18, 22, 25'. ALLEN C. MYERS, 'Banner', in *The Eerdmans Bible Dictionary*, Eerdmans, 1987, pg. 123.

[167] As MACKINTOSH declares: 'What is the standard of God's militant host? Let us hear and remember. It is Christ. This is the only standard of God, and the only standard of that warrior-band which musters in this wilderness-world to wage war with the hosts of evil and fight the battles of the Lord. Christ is the standard for everything. To have any other would only unfit us for that spiritual conflict to which we are called. What have we, *as Christians*, to do with contending for any system of theology or church organization? Of what account, in our estimation, are ordinances, ceremonies, or ritualistic observances? Are we going to fight under such banners as these? God forbid! Our theology is the Bible; our church-organization is the one Body, formed by the presence of the Holy Ghost, and united to the living and exalted Head in the heavens. To contend for anything less than these is entirely below the mark of a true spiritual warrior'. MACKINTOSH, pg. 431 [italics original].

[168] See John 1. 9-12; Eph. 3. 15; 1 John 3. 1-2.

Duties of the Levites

Chapters 3-4 highlight the role of the Levites in the camp and on the march. These chapters are structured using an ancient parallel structure called chiasmus. One commentator explains it like this:

'Structurally the cycle development and Levitical elements merge to heighten the emphasis on the priestly tribe. In content chaps. 3-4 parallel chaps. 1-2, which set forth the census of the other twelve tribes and the structural organization of the larger community. The section divides into seven parts in the following structural pattern:

A Genealogical Listing: Aaronic Line, 3. 1-4
B Responsibilities of the Levites, 3. 5-10
C Dedication of the Levites for the Firstborn, 3. 11-13
A′ Genealogical Listing: Levitical Clans, 3. 14-20
B′ Responsibilities and Census of the Levite Clans, 3. 21-39
C′ Dedication of the Levites for the Firstborn, 3. 40-51
B″ Responsibilities and Census of the Levite Clans: Age 30-50, 4. 1-49'.[169]

A content outline of chapters 3-4:

- genealogy of Aaron and Moses, 3. 1-4;
- selection of the Levites in place of the firstborn and their subsequent bestowal to the high priest, vv. 5-13;
- genealogy of the Levites (including a breakdown by families: Merari, Gershon, and Kohath), vv. 14-39;
- selection of the Levites, their livestock, and the redemption money, vv. 40-51;
- Kohathite duties, supervised by Eleazar the priest, 4. 1-20;

---

[169] COLE, pp. 89-90.

- Gershonite duties, supervised by Ithamar the priest, vv. 21-28;
- Merarite duties, supervised by Ithamar the priest, vv. 29-33;
- Census of 30-50-year-olds Kohath, Gershon, and Merari, vv. 34-49.

The genealogy of Aaron and Moses begins with a familiar biblical expression, 3. 1: 'These are the generations of',[170] which functions as a literary marker dividing the sections of the book of Genesis.[171] Whereas in that book it usually introduces a narrative section of stories about 'the heavens and the earth' or 'Isaac' or the like, here it begins a section of genealogical material, with directions for camping, marching, and transporting the tabernacle.

The Levites were selected by the Lord to take the place of all of the firstborn sons of Israel's tribes, vv. 11-13. The logic is that the Almighty purchased them on the Passover night when death was striking the firstborn in Egypt. Sheltered by the blood of an unblemished lamb, the household's firstborn would experience redemption from judgement, resulting in deliverance from the divine wrath. Because of this sacrificial victim's death – whose shed blood testified to the execution of the death penalty – the Lord Himself would 'pass over' their dwellings, forbidding the avenging angel to slay any firstborn sons within, Exod. 12. 12-13. So they were redeemed to be the Lord's possession – His own special people, 13. 1. He wanted them to be 'a kingdom of priests', 19. 6, but their disobedience made this impossible. That tragic idolatrous episode was noteworthy for the way it brought out devotion in the tribe of

---

[170] Alternative renderings include: 'the records of' NKJV, NET; '*the records of the generations of*' NASB [italics original]; and 'the family records' HCSB. Other translations retain the KJV phraseology including JND, ASV, ESV, and RSV.

[171] See Gen. 2. 4; 5. 1; 6. 9; 10. 1; 11. 10, 27; 25. 12, 19; 36. 1, 9; 37. 2; cf. Matt. 1. 1.

Levi, 32. 26-29, which may be the very reason that they were selected to serve in connection with the tabernacle and its furniture. Of course, it is only by grace that God should enable anyone to approach His holy presence in service. Like them, believers today in this dispensation are bought with a price, 1 Cor. 6. 19-20, to be living sacrifices, Rom. 12. 1, and serve the Lord, Acts 27. 23; 1 Thess. 1. 9.

The firstborn sons of the other tribes exceeded the Levites by 273 persons; therefore, God demanded a redemption price of five shekels per person for a total of 1,365 shekels, Num. 3. 44-51. This shows God's interest in every one of His redeemed. He has purchased them by blood – Exodus chapter 12 for Israel and Acts chapter 20 verse 28 for the church. He intends to use every one of them. They each belong to Him, and He will not lose one of them. They all have value to Him. As one commentator writes:

'May we not regard this as exhibiting His high estimate of men? We are so precious in His sight that He will not lose one of us if He can prevent it. His heart yearns in unutterable love towards every prodigal wanderer from His service, His home, and His heart . . . God is so exact in His claims upon us, because His love toward us is so great . . . There is no exaggeration in His claims, nor anything unreasonable. He means what He says. He really requires what He demands. He claims from us the unreserved consecration of ourselves and our possessions – that all shall be used in accordance with His will, etc. Have we duly considered His claims? Are we complying with them?'[172]

C. A. COATES adds another side to the picture:

'The fact that there were more firstborn males in Israel than there were numbered Levites would perhaps suggest that in a practical

---

172   WILLIAM JONES, *Numbers*, The Preacher's Complete Homiletic Commentary, Funk & Wagnalls Co., 1892, pp. 60-61.

sense more persons are hallowed to God through redemption than are found in the definite place of being numbered for levitical service. The disparity in the numbers would probably be very great at the present time, but God requires that the obligation shall be owned, the ransom given. If you are a redeemed "firstborn" you are hallowed to God. If you have no counterpart as a Levite – that is, if you have never recognised your obligation to serve in relation to holy things – you have to consider the question of ransom. However young you are, however immature or unintelligent, God would impress upon you that you have definite value for His holy service. Now what is your value for levitical service? "Five shekels . . . according to the shekel of the sanctuary". Think of the value God puts upon you as one hallowed for His service! You have fivefold sanctuary value, and each of the five shekels is, as it were, drawn out in the full detail of its worth as comprising "twenty gerahs". It seems designed to impress the youngest believer with his value in God's estimation in view of the service that is due from him, even though he may be, as yet, too young to take it up in any practical way. In a babe only "a month old" there is a potentiality that is worth a hundred gerahs in the sanctuary. If such is God's estimate of your value for His holy service, when you are as yet only "one month old", when He may have to wait a long time before you are mature for that service, does it not encourage you to cherish the thought that you are already valued by Him as hallowed for His service? God would give every young believer, even though he may never have thought seriously of taking up any service in relation to the tabernacle of testimony, a distinct impression that he has sanctuary value. Perhaps, there are old believers, too, who need to learn the lesson of the "five shekels"! If we really wake up to the value which God puts upon us in relation to levitical service it would move us to desire to be of the tribe of Levi! And we are not debarred from this; it is but another aspect of our place and calling through grace. If I am a hallowed firstborn, it is through infinite grace, and the same grace entitles me to be of the assembly of the firstborn ones, which answers to the tribe of Levi: But if I am of that tribe I must recognise the character of the service in which I am called to have part. I must seek to learn, under priestly instruction, what to do, and how to do it'.[173]

The coverage of the number of the firstborn and the necessity of the redemption money demonstrates that the immense payment made by the Lord at the cross, 1 Pet. 1. 18-19, was much more than the value of what He received in the redeemed. They are purchased to serve, but their value must be supplemented by the five shekel gift. Likewise, today the Lord has redeemed believers – who are described in the New Testament as 'firstborn', Heb. 12. 23 – yet not all of them appreciate the necessity of service in the things of God. Many are content to enjoy salvation's benefits without taking on the responsibilities of spiritual service in the Lord's house, 1 Tim. 3. 16.

Although He selected them for Himself, the Almighty gave the Levites to the High Priest to serve in matters pertaining to the tabernacle, Num. 3. 5-10. Because they were substitutes for the entire nation's firstborns, the genealogy in chapter 3 calculates their number from one month old and upward, v. 15. In contrast, chapter 4 focuses on their duties and therefore counts them from 30-50 years old, which was their age span during their term of service, 4. 3.[174] Their duties breakdown as follows:

---

[173] C. A. COATES, *An Outline of Numbers*, electronic edition, no pagination.
[174] The minimum age of service for the Levites is recorded differently in different passages of scripture. Some verses say it is 25 years old, Num. 8. 24; others say 20 years old, 1 Chron. 23. 24-25. This diversity has been explained in various ways: 1. Some see 25-30 as a time of apprenticeship, while young Levites grow into the full strength of manhood required to carry the tabernacle vessels and equipment. They could serve around the tabernacle, but only carry it at age 30 and beyond. 2. Others see the age as being increased from 25 to 30 because there was a surplus of Levites and this would diminish the carrying work force by about 20%. 3. Still others think the age was raised from 25 to 30 after Nadab and Abihu were

I. Kohath: They carried the tabernacle's furniture, and moved it in this order:

1. The priest covered the ark with the veil, then a layer of badger skins, followed by a blue covering and then the poles would be inserted for carrying, vv. 4-6.
2. The priests covered the table of shewbread with a blue cloth, then put the shewbread and utensils on it, then covered it with a scarlet cloth followed by a badger skin, and then inserted the polls, vv. 7-8.
3. The priests covered the lampstand and its utensils with a blue cloth, followed by badger skins; it was then carried on a beam, vv. 9-10.
4. The priests covered the golden altar with a blue cloth and then badger skins; the utensils were then carried in a blue cloth, covered with badger skins; they were carried on a beam; the ashes were also carried along with the utensils, covered by a purple cloth, and badger skins, vv. 11-14. Eleazar the priest supervised their activity, v. 16.

II. Gershon: They carried the curtains and coverings of the tabernacle, the screens for the tabernacle and the court, the hangings of the court, and the cords, vv. 24-26. Ithamar the priest supervised their activity, v. 28.

---

executed by God; this is supposition and seems to have no clear basis in the text. 4. Others think that the age was lowered once the tabernacle was stationary in the land and reflected the changing needs of the Levitical service. I incline towards this last view, but would not be dogmatic on the point. It is obvious that there are several plausible suggestions to account for the difference. As always, God's word is perfect and man's understanding is incomplete. The Septuagint harmonized Numbers chapter 4 verse 3 and chapter 8 verse 24 by having both read '25'. For an excellent summary of the various views and the arguments supporting them, see COLE, pg. 154.

III.   Merari: They carried the boards, bars, pillars – including their sockets, pegs, and cords, vv. 29-33. Ithamar the priest also supervised their activity, v. 33.

Levitical service was of such a sombre nature that twice the passage declares that failure to respect the sanctity of the holy things results in death, vv. 15, 20. Accordingly, they laboured under the priestly authority of Aaron and his sons and were supervised by them, vv. 16, 27, 33. Clearly, approaching the Lord and ministering in sacred service is not a responsibility to take lightly. Eleazar also took care of the oil for the lamps, the sweet incense, the daily grain offering, and the anointing oil, v. 16. According to the priests' count, the Levites who were available for duty were 8,580, v. 48. Even though modern believers are under grace rather than law, they must remember that handling divine things – the word of God, service in the Church, worship – is serious business. Even in the Church age, the Head of the Church has severely disciplined His members for profaning His Church.[175]

Purification and discipline

Chapters 5 and 6 concern the necessity for purity in the camp. If the holy God is dwelling in their midst, the Israelites must purge themselves of any defiling or offending element. A content outline of the chapters demonstrates this:

- Putting offending people outside the camp, 5. 1-4.
- Confession of sin and presenting the requisite offerings, vv. 5-10.
- The test of bitter water exonerating a wife from infidelity or proving her guilt, vv. 11-31.
- The Nazirite vow and its demand for personal holiness, 6. 1-21.

---

[175] See 1 Cor. 3. 16-17; 11. 20-22, 27-32.

- The Priestly blessing pronounced over the people, vv. 22-27.

These passages deal with one of the major themes of Numbers: the subject of the Lord's holiness.[176] Concerning those who needed to be excluded from the camp, it is marvellous to see that the Lord Jesus healed these types of people during His earthly ministry: lepers, Mark 1. 40-45, people with defiling flows from their bodies, 5. 25-34, and corpses which defiled those around them, 5. 35-43. Christ is able to cleanse from defilement and reconcile sinners to God, 1 John 1. 7.

The Lord's presence in the camp also casts human sin in a different light. Sin is viewed here as something that does damage – a specific act that harms someone else. The KJV renders *ma'al* as 'trespass', Num. 5. 6; while other versions translate it 'in unfaithfulness against the Lord', NKJV,[177] or 'by breaking faith with the Lord', ESV, RSV.[178]

---

[176] As SPENDER affirms: 'Holiness, directly associated with the presence of God, 5. 3; 35. 34, necessitated that unclean persons, 5. 1; 19. 11-20, events, 5. 6-7, or objects, 31. 22-23, be cleansed or be removed from the camp. In addition, priests and Levites, the divine caretakers and mediators of God's holiness, had to be purified before they could serve, 8. 21, and they alone were charged with the oversight of the holy things, 4. 4, which they could not touch, 4. 15, or even look at, 4. 20! Violation of the holiness of God or his commands brought plague, 8. 19, exile, 5. 3; 12. 14, or death, 9. 13; 15. 35. The grace of God, also evident in Numbers, should be understood in relationship to his holiness. His willingness to forgive Israel was seen as a manifestation of his grace but not in opposition to his holiness, 14. 18-19. The people were held responsible for their actions, 14. 22-23, 40-41, and Moses' challenge – "be sure that your sin will find you out", 32. 23 – was a reminder of their continued responsibility as they anticipated entering the land'. ROBERT D. SPENDER, *Numbers, Theology of,* electronic edition, no pagination.

[177] Other renderings include: 'acting unfaithfully against the Lord' NASB; 'acts unfaithfully toward the Lord' HCSB.

[178] One dictionary defines it thus: 'a violation of a standard and so incurring guilt, with a focus on not being steadfast and faithful to a person in a committed relationship'. JAMES SWANSON, *Dictionary of Biblical Languages*

The related Hebrew verb is used to describe marital infidelity in Numbers chapter 5 verses 12 and 27, among other verses. The trespass offering both acknowledges the person's guilt and the harmful consequences of their actions against the Lord and others.

Since the Lord is encamped among them, Israel must be holy. As KEIL and DELITZSCH explain: 'No crime against the property of a neighbour was to remain without expiation in the congregation of Israel, which was encamped or dwelt around the sanctuary of Jehovah; and the wrong committed was not to remain without restitution, because such crimes involved unfaithfulness . . . towards Jehovah'.[179] This terminology shows a dimension to sin that is often forgotten: it is disloyalty towards the holy God. Trespasses violate divine law. THOMAS BROOKS, a seventeenth-century Puritan preacher, spoke of this dimension of iniquity:

'Certainly the commands of sin are of all commands the vilest commands; they are all illegal; sin hath no ground, no reason to command our souls. Sin is but a usurper, a traitor, and therefore has no authority over us. All sin's commands are purely sinful; they are plain and notorious rebellions against the laws of Christ, the life of Christ, and against the crown, honour, and dignity of Jesus. All sin's commands are grievous, burdensome, and painful commands; of all yokes, none so heavy as that which sin lays upon the sinner'.[180]

---

with *Semantic Domains: Hebrew (Old Testament)*, Logos Research Systems, Inc., 1997. VINE'S DICTIONARY adds: 'Most of the usages support the idea of "faithlessness, treachery". It is an act committed by a person who knows better but who, for selfish motives, acts in bad faith' W. E. VINE, MERRILL F. UNGER, and WILLIAM WHITE JR., *Vine's Complete Expository Dictionary of Old and New Testament Words,* Nelson, 1996, pg. 268.

[179] KEIL AND DELITZSCH, pg. 668.

[180] THOMAS BROOKS, 'A Cabinet of Jewels', in *The Complete Works of THOMAS BROOKS,* ed. ALEXANDER BALLOCH GROSART, Vol. 3. G. Herbert, 1866, pg. 322.

SPURGEON eloquently agreed:

> 'Every sin has in it the very venom of rebellion, and is full of the essential marrow of traitorous rejection of God. But there be some sins which have in them a greater development of the essential mischief of rebellion, and which wear upon their faces more of the brazen pride which defies the Most High . . . The fact is, that while all transgression is a greatly grievous sinful thing, yet there are some transgressions which have a deeper shade of blackness, and a more double scarlet dyed hue of criminality than others'.[181]

On a practical level one can see how sins that harmed a neighbour or their property required restitution; otherwise, animosity and bitterness would sour the fraternal spirit among the tribes. True repentance leads to restitution. If the offended person was deceased and there was no family representative – the well-known *goel* or 'kinsman-redeemer' of the book of Ruth fame – to receive compensation, then it passed to the Lord Himself who gave it to His priests. Furthermore, the sacrificial atonement ram and heave offerings all belonged to the Almighty and were passed on to His servants, the sons of Aaron, for their use, vv. 9-10. The principle of a believer making restitution for the negative effects of their sins is seen in Zachaeus' life, Luke 19. 8-10.

The test of jealousy

Among trespasses that show disloyalty towards the Lord, adultery is a serious breach of the peace. Even the suspicion of this sin could cause immense turmoil in the home – even where the wife was completely innocent of the charge. Therefore, God gave a test to

---

[181] C. H. SPURGEON, 'Presumptuous Sins', in *The New Park Street Pulpit Sermons*, Vol. 3. Originally preached on 7 June 1857, Passmore & Alabaster, 1857, pg. 225.

manifest her guilt or innocence in the matter. Modern feminist theology views such a trial as some sort of chicanery meant to oppress women. Actually, it was intended to protect a woman's virtue and reputation, as well as to safeguard the purity of the marital bed. Modern believing scholarship recognizes the righteousness of the procedure, explaining: 'This procedure in Numbers 5 is not an example of magic; it is a procedure through which God punishes the guilty'.[182]

The elements of the test:

1. A meal offering of 1/10 of an ephah of barley without oil or frankincense, v. 15. Being bloodless, the meal offering speaks of life rather than death, see Lev. 2. If her life is clean, it will be manifested through the test.

2. Holy water with dust from the tabernacle floor is put into an earthen vessel. The woman stands bareheaded before the Lord, holding her meal offering, vv. 17-18. On the ground of the Lord's presence in the midst of His people, holiness is required of His people and demonstrated in this ceremony; compare Church discipline in the New Testament, Matt. 18. 18-20; 1 Cor. 5. 1-13.

3. Under oath she drinks the 'bitter water' – water where the dust and the written curses are scrapped within. A portion of the memorial offering is burned on the altar. If she is innocent, no harm ensues; if, however, she is guilty, then her womb suffers drastic judgement: a stomach that indicates pregnancy and reproductive organs that shrivel,[183] but in

---

[182] MERRILL, ROOKER, GRISANTI, ET AL., *The World and the Word*, electronic edition, no pagination.

[183] The KJV's 'thigh', v. 22, probably indicates the reproductive organs; the NRSV has 'the LORD makes your uterus drop, your womb discharge'. The Jewish sages believed it to be a case of the punishment fitting the crime: 'If her thigh went first to sin, and afterwards her stomach – behold the thigh is struck first, and afterwards the stomach. And the rest of her body does not

reality is barren. Permanent infertility occurs and her name is accursed in Israel, vv. 19-28.

Undoubtedly such a procedure would make one think twice about going astray from one's marital vows! Believers in this dispensation are held to the same divine standard of absolute purity in sexual conduct before, during, and after marriage. Hebrews chapter 13 verse 4 declares: 'Marriage is honourable in all, and the bed undefiled: but whoremongers and adulterers God will judge', showing that even today the Almighty requires holiness in conjugal life. In the Old Testament, He speaks of His relationship with Israel in marital terms,[184] and in the New Testament uses the same thing to depict His connection to the Church, Eph. 5. 22-33. Since marriage is a fundamental institution in society, He guards its sanctity in the face of a world that seeks to pervert it.

Devotion to the Lord pictured in Nazariteship

After a ritual that potentially reveals unfaithfulness, chapter 6 presents an ordinance for demonstrating faithfulness to the Lord. The Nazarite[185] vow provided an opportunity for men or women to dedicate themselves to their God for holy service. It manifests practical holiness manifested through consecration. The institution's two-sided nature shows both the positive and negative aspects of holiness. As ERDMAN remarks: 'In holiness and consecration the essential idea is that of separation, more definitely of separation from sin and separation for service'.[186] In Numbers chapter 6 it is

---

escape'. MISHNAH, 'Seder Nashim', 'Tractate Sotah' 1:7; electronic edition accessed here:
https://en.wikisource.org/wiki/Translation:Mishnah/Seder_Nashim/Tracta te_Sotah/Chapter_1/7. See also WENHAM, pg. 95.
[184] See Isa. 50. 1; Hos. 2. 2-3; Jer. 2. 1-2; 3. 1.
[185] The term comes from a word meaning to withhold something from oneself and therefore connotes 'separation'. See COLE, fnn. 121, 119.
[186] CHARLES R. ERDMAN, *The Book of Numbers,* Baker, 1952, pg. 25.

described as voluntary and temporary,[187] 6. 1-5, 13, but other passages show instances of perpetual Nazariteship, as in the cases of Samson, Judg. 13. 3-5, Samuel, 1 Sam. 1. 11, and John the Baptist, Luke 1. 15. Some also suggest that Paul's vow in Acts chapter 18 verse 18 was a Nazarite vow of the temporary variety.[188]

The components of the Nazarite vow:

1. Abstaining from the fruit of the vine in the form of all grape products, Num. 6. 3-4. The Lord's service sometimes requires putting aside natural pleasures for the greater purpose of doing His will. In a society obsessed with personal rights, it is a refreshing reminder that God's interests come first. Wine is frequently a type of 'joy' in the scriptures, Psa. 104. 15; S. of S. 2. 4;[189] John 2. 1-10. In other words, some legitimate joys are laid aside for a time in order to please the Lord.

2. He will let his hair grow freely and not cut it, v. 5. Possibly this indicates that a man is willing to bear shame for the Lord, 1 Cor. 11. 14, but since the Nazarite vow was open to both genders, this is not certain. Rabbinic tradition suggests that

---

[187] 'In contrast to Judg. 13, *nāzîr* status here is not lifelong but continues only for a specific period of abstention, a period determined by the *nāzîr*'s vow'. J. KÜHLEWEIN, 'נָזִיר *nāzîr* **consecrated person**', in ERNST JENNI AND CLAUS WESTERMANN, *Theological Lexicon of the Old Testament*, Hendrickson Publishers, 1997, pg. 728. 'According to the Mishna, the normal time for keeping a Nazarite vow was thirty days; but sometimes a double vow was taken, lasting sixty days. In fact, a vow was sometimes undertaken for a hundred days'. VINE, UNGER, and WHITE JR., pg. 223.

[188] I. HOWARD MARSHALL, 'Acts' in *Commentary on the New Testament Use of the Old Testament*, ed. D. A. CARSON AND G. K. BEALE, Baker, 2007, pg. 596. He also believes that Acts chapter 21 verse 24 concerns a Nazirite vow. VINE also suggests this possibility for Acts chapter 18 verse 18. VINE, UNGER, and WHITE JR., pg. 223.

[189] The KJVmg., NKJVmg., NASBmg., ESVmg., and JND all give the literal Hebrew rendering of 'house of wine' for the KJV's 'banqueting house'.

136

the women would keep their hair unkempt as their statement of not carrying for their own glory. Others have noted that the Hebrew expressing Nazariteship is related to the word for 'diadem' - 'the gold plate' on the mitre, Lev. 8. 9, that the high priest wore.[190] Thus, it was comparing the Nazarite to the priests in their consecration. In any case, it was the most visible reminder to others of the Nazarite's separation for God's service.

3. He will separate himself from anything dead – even the corpse of a deceased relative, v. 6. Repeatedly, the scriptures connect death with sin, Rom. 3. 23; Jas. 1. 15. Corrupting, sinful influences must be rejected by the believer in favour of an undefiled life. Suddenly contacting a dead body was enough to forfeit the past time of consecration for the Nazarite, Num. 6. 12.[191] In the event of sudden defilement, he

---

[190] COLE, fn. 121, pg. 119.

[191] 'Let us, then, beware how we trifle with sin. Let us remember that ere one stain of the guilt of sin – even the very smallest – could be removed, the blessed Lord Jesus Christ had to pass through all the unutterable horrors of Calvary. That intensely bitter cry, "My God, My God, why hast Thou forsaken Me?" is the only thing that can give us any proper idea of what sin is; and into the profound depths of that cry no mortal or angel can ever enter. But though we can never fathom the mysterious depths of the sufferings of Christ, we should at least seek to meditate more habitually upon His cross and passion, and, in this way, reach a much deeper view of the awfulness of sin in the sight of God. If, indeed, sin was so dreadful, so abhorrent to a holy God, that He was constrained to turn away the light of His countenance from that blessed One who had dwelt in His bosom from all eternity; if He had to forsake Him because He was bearing sin in His own body on the tree, then what must sin be?

Oh, let us seriously consider these things. May they ever have a place deep down in these hearts of ours, that are so easily betrayed into sin. How lightly, at times, do we think of that which cost the Lord Jesus everything – not only life, but that which is better and dearer than life, even the light of God's countenance! May we have a far deeper sense of the hatefulness of sin. May we most sedulously watch against the bare movement of the eye in a

would shave his hair and bring two turtledoves to the priest to be sacrificed as a burnt and a sin offering respectively, v. 11, and then present a lamb of the first year as a trespass offering, v. 12. All of these offerings point to Christ's multifaceted sacrifice that provides cleansing from defilement and deliverance from the wrath that sin warrants, 1 Cor. 15. 1-11.

Upon completing the days of his consecration the Nazarite offered the following:

1. A burnt offering: an unblemished male lamb of the first year, v. 14.
2. A sin offering: an unblemished ewe lamb of the first year, v. 14.
3. A peace offering: an unblemished ram, v. 14. (The order of the offerings by the priest is sin, burnt, and peace, vv. 16-17.)
4. A basket of unleavened bread, cakes of fine flour mixed with oil, unleavened wafers anointed with oil and a grain offering with its drink offering, v. 15.
5. A meal offering and a drink offering, v. 17.

Then, he shaved his head and burned the hair on the fire of the peace offering. Afterwards, he offered:

6. A wave offering: boiled shoulder of a ram with one unleavened cake from the basket and one unleavened wafer, v. 19.

---

wrong direction; for we may rest assured that the heart will follow the eye, and the feet will follow the heart, and thus we get away from the Lord, lose the sense of His presence and His love, and become miserable, or, if not miserable, what is far worse, dead, cold, and callous – "hardened through the deceitfulness of sin."

May God, in His infinite mercy, keep us from falling'. MACKINTOSH, pp. 466-467.

7. The breast of the wave offering and the thigh of the heave offering, v. 20. These wave offerings were given to the priests by the Lord after they were presented to Him.

The priestly blessing

God's grace is seen in the benediction[192] that ends chapter 6. Verses 24-27 not only pronounce the Lord's blessing upon His people, they also put His name upon them, v. 27. The Lord's name connotes both authority and identity. They are blessed by His mandate and belong to Him by virtue of His name invoked upon them, v. 27 NKJVmg. The Hebrew grammar underlying these verses shows that it is not wishful thinking, but an actual oracle.[193] In other words, the Lord put His

---

[192] The beauty of the Hebrew poetry is well-described in this comment: 'The first line consists of three words in Hebrew with a total of twelve syllables, the second five words and fourteen syllables, and the third seven words with sixteen syllables. Even the number of Hebrew consonants builds up steadily, fifteen, twenty, twenty-five. If one subtracts the thrice-repeated name of the Lord, there are twelve words left, no doubt symbolizing the twelve tribes of Israel. Grammatically there is no need to repeat God's name, but the repetition emphasizes that the Lord is the source of all Israel's benefits, as does the last clause *I will bless them* (27): "I" is emphatic in the Hebrew.

As the lines of the blessing lengthen, their content becomes richer, producing a crescendo that culminates in the word *peace* (26). Each line has the Lord as its subject and is followed by two verbs, the second of which expands on the first: *bless, keep; shine, be gracious; lift up, give peace'.* WENHAM, pp. 101–102 [italics original].

[193] 'The formal subject of the verb is the LORD, and the speaker pronouncing the blessing is the priest, notably after emerging from the holy of holies where atonement has been made. The LORD says in this passage that when the priest says this, then the LORD will bless them . . . It is a declaration of what the LORD imparts. It is as binding and sure as a patriarchal blessing which once said officially could not be taken back. The priest here is then pronouncing the word of the LORD, declaring to the congregation the outcome of the atonement'. NETmg.

name upon His people and promised to bless them. The verb 'keep' in verse 24 often signifies 'to guard'[194] and occurs six times in Psalm 121 concerning God's protection over Israel; it expresses His power to keep them secure. The parallel images of the divine face and countenance in the middle of the blessing express the Lord's favour towards His people as well as His ability to comfort them.[195] Verses 25-26 also bring up grace and peace to common blessings enjoyed by His people in all ages. The threefold repetition of the Lord's name reminds us that God is triune, as a later benediction expresses: 'The grace of the Lord Jesus Christ, and the love of God, and the communion of the Holy Ghost, be with you all. Amen', 2 Cor. 13. 14.

It is also interesting to note that the oldest portions of scripture ever discovered have this blessing from Numbers chapter 6. The celebrated Ketef Hinnom silver scrolls, which were found in a Jerusalem tomb excavation in 1979, contain this benediction. These small amulets date from the late seventh to the early sixth centuries B.C. By comparison, the oldest of the famous Dead Sea Scrolls dates to the third century B.C. – i.e., about three centuries newer than the silver scrolls. These objects are important confirmation of the antiquity of the Pentateuch – including Numbers – and the overall accuracy of the Bibles that we use.[196]

---

[194] MOUNCE, pg. 313.
[195] CURRID, pg. 110.
[196] GORDON FRANZ, who is a personal friend of this author and an esteemed brother in the Lord, was one of the archaeologists working on this dig under the leadership of PROF. GABRIEL BARKAY. For a riveting account of the discovery of the scrolls and their subsequent publication, see GORDON FRANZ, 'Remember, Archaeology is NOT a Treasure Hunt', accessed here: http://www.lifeandland.org/2009/02/remember-archaeology-is-not-a-treasure-hunt/. For the dating of the scrolls and their implications for the Pentateuch, see ERIK WAALER, 'A Revised Date For Pentateuchal Texts: Evidence from Ketef Hinnom', in *Tyndale Bulletin* 53:1, 2002, pp. 53-54; and STEPHEN CAESAR, 'The Blessing of the Silver Scrolls', in *Bible & Spade,* Spring, 2006; Accessed here:

The centrality of the Lord's presence and His guiding function among His people

Chapters 7-10 concern matters of the tabernacle and following the Lord's guidance.

Content outline

- Anointing the tabernacle and receiving offerings from the twelve tribes for the dedication of the altar, Num. 7. 1-88.
- The Lord's instructions for Moses regarding the lamps' arrangement and the dedication of the Levites for service, 7. 89 – 8. 26.
- Celebrating the Passover and contingency for missing the proper day, 9. 1-14.
- The Lord's presence and guidance by the pillar of fire and cloud, 9. 15-23.
- The Lord's guidance by silver trumpets, 10. 1-10.
- Departing from Sinai, following the Lord, 10. 11-36.

Numbers chapter 7 describes the identical offerings that were presented by representatives of each of the twelve tribes. Their order of presentation matches the order of encampment listed in chapter 2.

Six carts – one for two of the leaders – and twelve oxen hauled the gifts for the altar, v. 3. The carts and oxen were given to the Merarite and Gershonite clans of Levi. But the Kohathites were pointedly not given such a conveyance, v. 9, because they carried the holy furniture on their shoulders. Sadly, this truth was forgotten in the time of King David with tragic repercussions, 2 Sam. 6. 1-11. Each leader presented, vv. 10-88:

---

http://www.biblearchaeology.org/post/2010/01/06/The-Blessing-of-the-Silver-Scrolls.aspx.

1. One silver charger ('platter', NKJV) weighing 130 shekels.
2. One silver bowl weighing seventy shekels.

(Both of these were filled with fine flour mixed with oil as a grain offering.)

3. One gold spoon ('pan', NKJV) weighing ten shekels, full of incense.
4. One bull, one ram, and one male lamb of the first year = burnt offering.
5. One kid of the goats = sin offering.
6. Two oxen, five rams, five male goats, and five male lambs in their first year = peace offering.

Verses 84-88 give the aggregate of these items – it obviously was an expensive offering. What is more, the fact that each tribe gave identically demonstrates their equal standing before the Lord and their unity as His people. Just as there is only one foundation for Christian churches, 1 Cor. 3. 11-12, so there was only one offering for the Israelites participation in the dedication of the altar. In this section of Numbers the people are viewed collectively and positionally – that is, the way the Lord sees them, after His electing purposes for them shall be fulfilled. They stand on the ground of the same sacrifice and have equal access to His presence (of course, they were represented practically by the Levitical priesthood of the sons of Aaron in actual service within the tabernacle night and day).

Arranging the lamps

The Lord is spoken of as 'dwelling between the cherubim' several times in scripture.[197] The *English Standard Version* translates the

---

[197] See 1 Sam. 4. 4; 2 Sam. 6. 2; 2 Kgs. 19. 15; 1 Chr. 13. 6; Pss. 80. 1; 99. 1; Isa. 37. 16.

phrase as 'enthroned above the cherubim'; thus picturing the mercy seat as Jehovah's throne. It is from this holy and exalted location that He speaks with Moses in Numbers chapter 7 verse 89. As the other references show, this phrase is usually associated with divine sovereignty in the face of extreme human need. In the present context, it indicates the seriousness of arranging things within the tabernacle. A more modern rendering of Numbers chapter 8 verse 2 depicts the activity more clearly: 'Speak to Aaron and say to him, When you set up the lamps, the seven lamps shall give light in front of the lampstand', ESV. Aaron is to 'raise up', NASBmg., the lamps upon each branch of the lampstand in such a way that they shine frontwards upon the table of shewbread. The symbol of the Lord's provision for His people – twelve loaves, enough for each tribe – is illuminated by this simulated tree of life.[198] It typifies the Lord Jesus Christ of whom it was written: 'in him was life and the life was the light of men', John 1. 4.

These instructions are followed by the presentation of the Levites as a wave offering – a type of living sacrifice for the auxiliary service of the tabernacle. As this volume's discussion of the Levitical passages in chapters 3 and 4 indicates, they were presented as helpers to the Aaronic priesthood, vv. 13-19. At the stage in the narrative, the Holy Spirit is indicating that Jehovah's presence among them requires consecrated vessels, chapter 7, a dedicated priesthood, chapter 8, and the remembrance of the basis of their life with God – the Passover, chapter 9.

Chapter 9 verses 15-23 recount the guidance that comes from the Lord's presence in the form of the pillar of cloud by day and pillar of

---

[198] Its description in Exodus chapter 25 verses 31-39 mimics a living tree. Since light is metaphorically connected with truth, knowledge, and eternal life in the Bible it is not a far leap to see overtones of the ancient trees of the garden that will reappear in the new heavens and new earth, Pss. 36. 9; 119. 30; John 8. 12; 17. 3; 1 John 1. 7; Rev. 2. 7; 22. 2. For further discussion see COLE, pg. 146.

fire by night. What is more, under the Almighty's instruction further directions were given to the tribes by their human leaders through the blowing of the silver trumpets, Num. 10. 1-10, 13. The pillar demonstrated it was time to move; the trumpets directed the specific movement of Israel's clans. Silver, the material of redemption, 18. 16, reappears as the material for the trumpets. They were used to direct camp movement, vv. 5-8, sound alarm as in the case of being attacked, v. 9, and signal rejoicing at festival time, v. 10. One of the Feasts of Jehovah was called the Feast of Trumpets, Lev. 23. 23-25, which prophetically refers to the Lord's future regathering of Israel, Isa. 41. 8-20. A trumpet will also figure prominently in the Lord's catching up of His church, 1 Cor. 15. 52; 1 Thess. 4. 16. Whether eschatologically, or in the regular rhythms of everyday life, the Lord desires to guide His people.

From Sinai to Kadesh Barnea

Israel's first journey is one of 'three days' journey', Num. 10. 33, which usually indicates a new beginning in the scriptures – as in Christ's resurrection, 1 Cor. 15. 4; Jehovah's covenant at Sinai, Exod. 19. 11; and the divided monarchy, 1 Kgs. 12. 12. Before departing, Moses invites his 'father-in-law' – or some would translate it 'brother-in-law', NLT, NAB[199] – to join them on their journey to the

---

[199] 'There is a problem with the identity of Hobab. The MT says that he is the son of Reuel, making him the brother-in-law of Moses. But Judg. 4:11 says he is the father-in-law. In Judg. 1. 16; 4. 11 Hobab is traced to the Kenites, but in Exod. 3. 1 and 18. 1 Jethro (Reuel) is priest of Midian. Jethro is identified with Reuel on the basis of Exod. 2:18 and 3:1, and so Hobab becomes Moses' חֹתֵן (*khoten*), a relative by marriage and perhaps brother-in-law. There is not enough information to decide on the identity and relationships involved here. Some suggest that there is one person with the three names (G. B. Gray, *Numbers* [ICC], 93); others suggest Hobab is a family name (R. F. Johnson, *IDB* 2:615), and some suggest that the expression "the son of Reuel the Midianite" had dropped out of the genealogy of Judges, leading to the conflict (J. Crichton, *ISBE* 2:1055). If Hobab is the same as Jethro, then Exod.

Promised Land, Num. 10. 29-32. He offers him to share in the blessings that come to the Lord's covenant people, a reminder of the blessings of the Abrahamic covenant, Gen. 12. 2-3. It is also a harbinger of good things to come: God is going to bless Israel and do great things for them. This is a fitting reminder as the book transitions from the Almighty's plans for Israel and the real-time reactions of the Israelites under His government in their journey.

The camp's movement is also preceded by Moses' wonderful benediction: 'Rise up, Lord, and let thine enemies be scattered; And let them that hate thee flee before thee. And when it rested, he said, Return, O Lord, unto the many thousands of Israel'. Everything was contingent upon God's work among them – He protected and preserved them in the wilderness. ROY HILL notes the application for believers today:

'This was a prayer for His presence to be felt individually and corporately. Even as the company moved forward, individual time with the Lord was very important. Such experiences are precious and as we enjoy seasons of rest we feel closer to Him. Not just involved in the activity and excitement of a forward movement, but also resting when He rests, and having time for worship as well as service. Let us pray, as did Moses, for the things that will help us through – a sense of His presence and an appreciation of His return. So armed, the people of God as individuals, as churches, and in general, can have the confidence to move forward. He delights to demonstrate His power to us and we delight in the promise of His presence here and now, as well as in

---

18:27 does not make much sense, for Jethro did go home. On this basis many conclude Hobab is a brother-in-law. This would mean that after Jethro returned home, Moses conversed with Hobab, his brother-in-law. For more discussion, see the articles and the commentaries'. NETmg.; an alternative rendering: 'Moses said to Hobab, son of Moses' father-in-law Reuel the Midianite', HCSB.

His promise, "I will come again". We happily respond, "Even so, come Lord Jesus'".[200]

Murmuring resulting in quail

Numbers chapter 11 marks a change in tone, as the people begin to complain against the Lord. It is a sad pattern that recurs during the first generation, whose history is discussed throughout the middle section of the book, Num. 11-25. As GOLDINGAY comments: 'The opening of Numbers 11 . . . summarizes the dominant features of the story from Sinai to Moab: trouble, protest, chastisement, plea, remission'. Others observe the repeating pattern in these murmuring incidents:

1. Complaining.
2. Divine Response.
3. Wrath.
4. Intercession by Moses.
5. Cessation of wrath.
6. Incident commemorated by naming the place.[201]

Two of these complaint passages are grouped together at the beginning of the eleventh chapter. While the first concerns generic murmuring against the Lord, vv. 1-3, the second occurrence deals with the mixed multitudes' lust for food, vv. 4-6. The first results in a burning plague – 'Taberah' as the place became known – and the second brings another plague, vv. 31-35, as the moniker 'Kibroth

---

200 ROY HILL, 'January 30th: Rise Up, Lord . . . Return, O Lord, Numbers 10. 35-36', in *Day by Day in Prayer*, ed. IVAN STEEDS, Day by Day Series, Precious Seed, 1997, pg. 46.
201 The other complaint passages are Num. 11. 1-3; 4-35; 12. 1-16; 13. 1 – 14. 45; 16. 1-50; 20. 2-13; 21. 4-9; and 25. 1-19. GREGG WATSON, 'Numbers, Book of', in *The Lexham Bible Dictionary*, electronic edition, no pagination.

Hattaavah' ('graves of craving' NKJVmg.) commemorates.[202] This second incident demonstrates their discontent with the Lord's provision of manna as food, vv. 4-6, and a revisionist history of their experience in Egypt. They were slaves in that land, and could hardly have been barbecuing down by the Nile! The mixed multitude's influence[203] did not help, but the Israelites rebelled of their own volition, v. 4. Upon encountering difficulty, they demonstrate the woeful human propensity to question God's goodness and vainly imagine that life is better without Him.

These stressful incidents of rebellion drove Moses to plead with the Lord to relieve him of the burden of leading the nation, vv. 11-15 – even by execution if necessary. His desperation resulted from an overly introspective mindset – note the personal pronouns 'I' and 'me' in his complaint. In mercy, God provided help by putting His Spirit upon seventy elders in order to mark them out as magistrates in the nation, vv. 16-17, 24-29. He also alleviated Moses' anxiety over meat by miraculously giving quail to the people, vv. 18-23, 31-34.

---

[202] This is probably the incident that the New Testament refers to when it says: 'Now these things were our examples, to the intent we should not lust after evil things, as they also lusted', 1 Cor. 10. 6. Probably, Psalm 106 verses 14-15 also looks back on this notable sin.

[203] One scholar explains the identity of 'the mixed multitude' in this way: 'The narratives of Exodus 12. 38 and Numbers 11. 4 make it clear that many of these slaves took advantage of the Israelite departure from Egypt to make good their own escape. These non-Israelite elements formed a considerable proportion of the liberated slaves and serfs whom Moses led out into the desert regions beyond the borders of Egypt. This movement was the beginning of a journey that lasted for a whole generation, during which time an unruly mob was forged into a worshiping community in preparation for the occupation of the Promised Land of Canaan'. R. K. HARRISON, *Old Testament Times,* Hendrickson Publishers, 2001, pg. 136.

Attacks on the Lord's authority as vested in Moses

Wounded by friends

Great leaders are often criticized and misunderstood; although superlatively humble,[204] Moses was no exception to this phenomenon. Numbers chapters 12 to 17 show some notable attacks on his authority, as well as that of his brother Aaron. Surprisingly, the first attack came from his own family. Apparently out of a mixture of personal pride – they disapproved of his Ethiopian wife[205] – and professional jealousy, his siblings Aaron and Miriam asserted their own importance against Moses' authority.

The Lord personally defended His spokesman's honour by differentiating His close relationship with Moses from His manner of communication with other prophets. For him, revelation does not come indirectly through visions or dreams; instead, He manifests His 'form'[206] to this favoured leader. It was a theophany, because no man can see God in His fully unveiled glory, John 1. 18; 1 Tim. 6. 16. Nevertheless, Moses saw more of the divine glory than anyone else of

---

[204] NKJV, NASB, and NET translate this word as 'humble'. The NETmg. comments: 'The word ‏ענו‎ (*'anav*) means "humble". The word may reflect a trustful attitude, as in Pss. 25. 9, 37. 11, but perhaps here the idea of "more tolerant" or "long-suffering". The point is that Moses is not self-assertive. God singled out Moses and used him in such a way as to show that he was a unique leader'. Two esteemed Hebrew experts add: 'No doubt it was only such a man as Moses who could speak of himself in such a way – a man who had so entirely sacrificed his own personality to the office assigned him by the Lord, that he was ready at any moment to stake his life for the cause and glory of the Lord'. KEIL AND DELITZSCH, pg. 703 [italics original].

[205] She was probably his second wife, since he acquired Zipporah in Midian, Exod. 2. 21.

[206] 'The word "form" (Hebrew *tĕmûnâ*) is used of visual representations, pictures or images, of earthly and heavenly beings, Exod. 20. 4'. WENHAM, pg. 127.

that era, Exod. 33. 18-23. The Almighty's defence is written poetically and follows the literary parallelism known as chiasmus so common to the ancient world.[207] To sum it up in a phrase, Moses was 'faithful in all mine house', Num. 12. 7, and thus is a type of Christ in His faithful stewardship of divine things, Heb. 3. 1. DAVID GOODING remarks:

'I wonder how he ever managed to keep his temper. He had given his life for this nation. He might have been at that very moment reclining on soft cushions in the palace in Egypt. Yet there he was amongst this race of ill-mannered and uncouth ex-slaves, doing his very best for them, and getting in return constant naggings and grumblings on every side. What was it that kept the man so faithful to Israel? It was his faithfulness to God who had appointed him to his house'.[208]

---

[207] It is called this in academia, because it follows the shape of the Greek letter 'chi'. COLE describes the structure here:
'A Introduction: Hear my words (6)
  B If your prophet is of Yahweh,[84]
    C In a vision to him I make myself known
      D In a dream I speak to him.
        E Not so my servant Moses (7)
        E′ In all my household he is trustworthy
      D′ Face to face I speak with him (8)
    C′ And in[85] a presence[86] that is not in riddles
  B′ And the form of Yahweh he beholds
A′ Rhetorical Conclusion: How then were you not afraid, To speak against my servant Moses?

At the focal point (E-E′) of the literary structure one can seen the emphasis in the passage is on the uniqueness of Moses . . . a man who stands above the others among the Israelites, such as the recently endowed seventy elders, as well as above Miriam and Aaron'. COLE, pp. 202-203.
[208] DAVID W. GOODING, *An Unshakeable Kingdom: The Letter to the Hebrews for Today,* Myrtlefield Trust, 2014, pp. 96-97.

Due to her apparent instigation of this attack, Miriam is disciplined by the Lord with the scourge of leprosy. As Leviticus chapters 13 and 14 show, this disease is pervasive and corrupting; therefore, it is a fitting picture of the ravaging nature of sin – something like a spiritual cancer. It may be that this was a case of the punishment fitting the crime: she opposed a dark skinned woman, so God's chastisement came forth in the skin. The devastating nature of the discipline leads Aaron to plead for mercy and confess their sin. Moses' heart for intercession is demonstrated by his willingness to immediately pray for her healing, Num. 12. 13. But there are no short cuts in God's school, and she is separated for seven days before being restored. The Almighty's desire for reconciliation is evidenced by the fact that the congregation of Israel remained where they were until she could be restored to the blessings of fellowship, vv. 15-16.

Spy games at Kadesh Barnea

Numbers chapters 13 and 14 detail the tragic national sin that barred most of a generation from Canaan and consigned the remnant of the people to sojourn in the wilderness for almost forty years. The content may be outlined as follows:

- Sending and instructing the spies, Num. 13. 1-20.
- The spies' mission and subsequent report, vv. 21-33.
- The congregations' unbelieving response and Moses and Aaron's grief, 14. 1-5.
- Caleb and Joshua's grief and dissent from the ten spies' bad report, vv. 6-10.
- The Lord's response pronouncing judgement against the unbelieving generation, vv. 11-38 (including Moses' intercession for the people, vv. 13-19).
- The unbelievers' ill-fated invasion attempt, vv. 39-45.

The spies were not lowly foot-soldiers, but respected members of the community's elite – 'every one a ruler among them', Num. 13. 2.[209] Leaders must be faithful to the Lord, or their social position and worldly attainments are worthless. The true elite are those who believe God's word – in this case, Caleb and Joshua.[210] God promised a land flowing with milk and honey. The spies confirmed the prosperity of the land – even bringing back a massive cluster of grapes as proof of the reality of His inheritance, vv. 23-24. They verified that the land was exactly how the Almighty described it, v. 27. If only they had stopped there!

Regrettably they disbelieved the Lord's word, looking instead at the size of the enemies rather than the size of the mighty God. As G. CAMPBELL MORGAN laid out the choice: 'Everything depends upon whether we see the walled cities and the giants, or God. Nothing less than a triumphant faith, born of a clear vision of God Himself, will enable us to go forward. It is only faith which can cooperate towards infinite issues. Sight can do small things. Faith alone is equal to infinite things'.[211] But they refused to obey the gospel, Heb. 4. 2, which is the same as saying that they did not believe. To put it in New Testament language: 'And to whom sware he that they should not enter into his rest, but to them that believed[212] not?' Heb. 3. 18.

---

[209] 'But the men chosen here by Moses were not . . . "military scouts"; they were influential men whose report could sway the community'. J.A. BECK, 'Geography and the Narrative Shape of Numbers 13', in *Bibliotheca Sacra* 157:627, July, 2000, pg. 272.

[210] Formerly known as 'Hoshea' – 'Deliverence/salvation' but elongated to 'Joshua' – 'Jehovah is salvation'/'Jehovah saves', Num. 13. 16. Names are significant in the Bible – especially when they are changed, cf. 'Abram' to 'Abraham' and 'Sarai' to 'Sarah' in Genesis 17; Simon being given the name 'Cephas' in Aramaic – 'Peter' in Greek, John 1. 42.

[211] MORGAN, pp. 18-19.

[212] This word, *apeitheo*, means 'disobey' VINE, pg. 173; and SWANSON, electronic edition, no pagination. The NKJV renders the phrase: 'those who did not obey'; 'them that were disobedient' ASV; NASB, ESV, RSV, NRSV,

Throughout Hebrews chapters 3 and 4 the Holy Spirit interchanges these ideas of unbelief and disobedience, putting them both squarely on the shoulders of the unfaithful exodus generation. Despite seeing God do signs and wonders against the mightiest superpower of their time, they disbelieved that He could vanquish weaker enemies in Canaan. As one brother described them: 'They were believers who did not believe'.[213] This highlights the danger of mere profession versus possession of the truth.

In contrast, Caleb and Joshua went against the enormous peer pressure of their colleagues, asserting that the Lord would give them victory over their enemies as well as the land just as He promised, Num. 14. 6-9. They vainly tried to remind the people of the seriousness of rebelling against God, the richness of the 'exceeding good land . . . which floweth with milk and honey', and the divine power that would render their enemies weak and defenceless, vv. 7-9. For their trouble, they were threatened with stoning! Nonetheless, God rewarded their true faith by promising them entrance into Canaan; albeit after the disobedient generation died off. The unbelievers maintained that their children would be killed. But God, who knows better how to care for children than any human being, affirmed that they would be the inheritors of His land, v. 31.

The Lord's glory was at stake. If He failed to bring Israel into the land, then Egypt would be vindicated in their unbelief. Moreover, His promises would be utterly discredited. But the gospel proclaimed in their days of bondage asserted that He would bring the Israelites out of slavery and into the freedom of a new relationship with Him in

---

NET, and other translations are similar. D. W. Gooding points out that this word and its cognates – twenty-nine New Testament appearances in all – are never used to describe true believers, Gooding, pp. 104-106; his entire chapter on Hebrews chapters 3 to 4 is worth studying in detail.

213 Randal P. Amos, oral ministry, Rochester, NY, USA, circa 2000. We see this phenomenon in other passages of the Bible as well, e.g. John 2. 23-25; 6. 66; 8. 31-59.

their inheritance. Despite the unbelieving spies' insinuation, God does not do things by half. As the hymn says:

> *'The work which His goodness began*
> *the arm of His strength will complete'.*[214]

He will demonstrate His glory by bringing the second generation into the land, vv. 13-24.

The people then tried to enter the land under their own power and were soundly defeated. They were obviously unconcerned with God and attempted to gain the blessings without bothering with Him. The Almighty would wait until that generation passed off the scene to bring in their offspring by faith, vv. 35-45. Caleb and Joshua would get in, but they would have to bide their time in the desert until the children were of age to possess Canaan.

Chapter 15 offers hope after the Israelites' tragic failure in the previous two chapters. It opens with the beautiful statement: 'Speak to the children of Israel, and say to them: "*When you have come into the land* you are to inhabit, which I am giving to you"', v. 2 NKJV, [my italics for emphasis]. The Lord will invariably bring them into Canaan. He then describes sacrifices, which form the basis of their interaction with their God. Only through Christ's death on the cross are people able to have forgiveness and a relationship with their Creator. They will gain the inheritance by grace and not through personal merit. Therefore, the possession of the land is not in doubt – the Almighty will give it to them by His working. The passage ends with the reaffirmation of His connection to Israel: 'I am the Lord your God, who brought you out of the land of Egypt, to be your God: I am the Lord your God', v. 41.

---

[214] AUGUSTUS M. TOPLADY, 'A debtor to mercy alone'.

Content outline of chapter 15

- Faith expressed through burnt, drink, and grain offerings, vv. 1-29.
- Unbelief expressed through presumptuous sin – such as Sabbath violation, vv. 30-36.
- Faith expressed through the blue tassel – reminding them of holiness and the requirements of God's law, vv. 37-41.

The reaffirming of Moses' and Aaron's authority and the re-established credentials of the Levitical service

Chapters 16 and 17 concern the challenges of Moses and Aaron's God-given authority and their subsequent vindication. Of course, an assault on these divinely called servants is rebellion against the Lord's authority. The first salvo comes from a surprising source: their own family – cousins this time – attacks their position in Israel, Exod. 6. 18, 20-24; Num. 16. 1. In the Hebrew Bible these chapters are the literary midpoint of the book, which highlights the importance of maintaining God's authority in the centre of His people.[215]

Content Outline

- The challenge against God's representatives, Moses and Aaron, Num. 16. 1-14.
- Divine wrath against the rebels, vv. 15-35.
- Renewed safeguards against someone challenging God's holy representatives and the sacred tabernacle, vv. 36-40.
- The people's challenge against Moses and Aaron for the deaths of Korah and his allies, vv. 41-50.
- The Lord sets up a test to show His legitimate priest, Num. 17. 1-7.

---

[215] CURRID, pg. 229.

- Aaron is vindicated by the budding rod and the people fear the Lord, vv. 8-12.

The rebels came from the ranks of the elite: Korah was of the Kohathite clan of the Levites who were privileged to carry the tabernacle's holy furniture; his 250 allies were 'princes', v. 2, 'leaders', NKJV, among the tribes of Israel. Their privileges did not stop them from accusing Moses and Aaron of taking an unduly prominent position in the nation, asserting that all of the Israelites were holy. Thus, they undermined God's selected representatives. Korah and company erroneously thought that they could usurp the priesthood, but Moses' countered that they were taking too much on themselves, vv. 8-11. This brash revolt was so serious that God employed an uncommon method of capital punishment: they were suddenly swallowed alive with all that pertained to them, vv. 28-31; cf. Exod. 15. 12. He mercifully spared some of Korah's sons who apparently separated themselves from their wicked father, Num 26. 11.[216] Jude verse 11 remembers him as the forerunner of spiritual rebels who appear all too frequently throughout church history and still plague the modern church. Like Korah, many of them have enjoyed spiritual light, but they turn aside from this truth in the desire for position, power, and earthly pleasures.[217]

The censer test demonstrated the Lord's choice of Moses and Aaron and His rejection of the unholy mob. The incorrigibly rebellious attitude of these upstarts is manifested in their resolute refusal to present themselves before the proper authorities, which was emphatically bookended by the phrase 'We will not come up', vv. 12-14. But the group whose incense offering in their censer was

---

[216] The sons of Korah later became celebrated singers and gatekeepers, as well as doing other service in the Solomonic temple, 1 Chr. 9. 28-33; 26. 19. Eleven psalms are dedicated to them: Pss. 42, 44, 45, 46, 47, 48, 49, 84, 85, 87, and 88.

[217] See Acts 1. 16-20; Isa. 14. 12-21; Ezek. 28. 12-19.

accepted by the Almighty would be decisively vindicated in their intercession. So it was: Aaron was accepted and the 250 imposters were executed by fire from the Lord's presence. Like Nadab and Abihu before them, they were killed for their temerity in offering unauthorized worship. God must be sanctified by those who approach Him. They must come by invitation, with the divinely ordained sacrifice. In the New Testament, all believers are priests, but their priesthood is based on Christ's perfect sacrifice. They worship and serve by His invitation and appointment, 1 Pet. 2. 5, 9.

In the aftermath of the judgement, Aaron's son Eleazar is instructed to reaffirm the holiness and necessary exclusivity of the holy things. No 'stranger',[218] v. 40 – in this case a non-Aaronite – is to approach the Lord's altar. Unauthorized incense offering always ends badly – for example, the ill-advised action of King Uzziah, 2 Chr. 26. 16-21. Since the upstarts' censers were presented before the Almighty they were now considered holy. Accordingly, they were made into plates to cover the altar, as a visible memorial of God's holiness, Num. 16. 39-40. Soon Aaron's legitimate censer was called upon to save the murmuring multitude from the wrathful plague, vv. 46-50. His action prefigures the saving work of Christ, who also stands 'between the living and the dead', v. 48, by making propitiation for sin and delivering believers from God's just vengeance, John 5. 24.

Lasting vindication for the Aaronic priesthood

Chapter 17 also has a test, involving rods for each tribe's representative as lasting testimony of the Lord's choice. He marked out Aaron as His man by making his rod produce buds, blossoms, and

---

[218] As CURRID points out: 'Interestingly, this word "stranger" is a cognate of the term "strange" that was used with regard to the sinful offering of Nadab and Abihu, Lev. 10. 1-2. If anyone does offer such a thing, he will become like Korah and his congregation; this means that he will simply share the same fate and ending'. CURRID, pg. 243.

fruit – almonds in this case, v. 8. This pictorial sign is reminiscent of the tabernacle lampstand's composition, Exod. 25. 31-36. As Numbers chapter 17 verse 10 declares: 'And the Lord said to Moses, "Bring Aaron's rod back before the Testimony, to be kept as a sign against the rebels, that you may put their complaints away from Me, lest they die"', NKJV. Like the preceding chapter, there is a lasting sign to guard the way of approach to God. Formerly, it was a covering for the altar; latterly it was this beautiful and fruitful rod.

Carrying on with the theme of the priestly service and guarding God's sanctuary, chapter 18 reiterates the Aaronic duty to protect the tabernacle from iniquitous incursions like the earlier challenges from Korah and his friends, Num. 16. Aaron and sons are to 'bear the iniquity' of the sanctuary and of their priesthood, 18. 1. This means that they are responsible to keep 'strangers' away from the holy furniture and the holy place and holy of holies. LANGE defines this 'iniquity'[219] – some render it 'guilt' NKJVmg. – of the tabernacle as:

> '[N]ot merely offences against laws for the priests and against the sacred utensils (*Knobel*), nor even the uncleannesses and defects that attached to those that stood in the sanctuary and even to their gifts (for that there was the great Day of Atonement), but all assaults on the central Sanctuary, corruptions of worship, such as the murmuring congregation had given example of; while the high-priestly atonement of Aaron gave an example of bearing

---

[219] *'āwōn* is usually translated "sin, guilt, wickedness, iniquity" and is one of the three primary words for sin in the OT, an offense against God that ranges from willful rebellion to unintentional sins. *'āwōn* usually has an ethical function, but it sometimes is a catch-all word to designate any sin against God'. MOUNCE, pg. 655; 'The word signifies an offense, intentional or not, against God's law. This meaning is also most basic to the word *chattaʼt*, "sin", in the Old Testament, and for this reason the words *chattaʼt* and *'āwōn* are virtually synonymous'. VINE, UNGER, AND WHITE, JR., pp. 121-122.

(atoning for) the guilt . . . what is done sinfully within this institution Aaron and his sons are to take upon their hearts'.[220]

WENHAM agrees, adding this: 'Indeed, if mistakes are made and unauthorized persons usurp the privileges of the priests or Levites, blame will fall on them for failing in their guard duty . . . The priests and Levites thus act as spiritual lightning conductors,[44] taking upon themselves God's anger when individuals sin so that the people as a whole is spared'.[221] The bearing of iniquity for the nation reminds one of the Lord Jesus who became the ultimate sin bearer and purifies His people so that they may approach the true sanctuary, Heb. 9. 11-15.[222]

As daunting as the ministry is, the Lord gave the priests much help. They had the Levites as their assistants in the peripheral work that surrounded the movement, setting up, and ongoing support of the tabernacle, Num. 18. 2-6. The actual service inside the tent was given as 'a service of gift' to the priests, v. 7 literal Hebrew rendering as

---

[220] LANGE et al., pp. 96–97.
[221] WENHAM, pg. 160. Footnote 44 within his quotation is as follows 'Cf. J. MILGROM, *Studies in Levitical Terminology*, p. 31'.
[222] 'Here there is One who is competent to carry His people through. Now, therefore, we see the "iniquity of the sanctuary" made to rest upon Him, "that there be no wrath upon the children of Israel". In the work of intercession, Aaron's house may share with Aaron, – the under-priests with the high-priest, only remembering well that it is the high-priest's rod that budded, and that ultimately all rests upon him. Thus He who died for us carries us on to full, final salvation, "in the power of an endless life". "He ever liveth to make intercession for us". With the value of a work done which is of infinite efficacy, we have also a hand of power which sustains us, – all put into His hand who is "Son over the house of God",* every way divinely competent, at once "Jesus Christ the righteous, and the propitiation for our sins", 1 John 2. 1, 2'. [*Heb. 3. 6; in the Greek, 'His,' – *i.e.*, God's 'house'; not 'his own'.] F. W. GRANT, *The Numerical Bible: The Pentateuch*, Loizeaux Brothers, 1890, pg. 451.

reflected in DARBY'S *New Translation* and the *New American Standard Bible's* margin, demonstrating that worship and intercession flow from the Most High's grace. A further boon to their ministry was that their material support was provided by the Lord. Although they did not inherit allocations of land like the other tribes, they were given the privilege of directly relying on God for their maintenance, 1 Cor. 9. 13; Num. 18. 20. Their food was taken from portions of the meal, sin, trespass, and heave offerings as well as the firstborn cows, sheep, and goats, vv. 8-19. To put it succinctly, He fed them from His portion. The Levites in turn were supported by the Israelite tithes, from which they then offered a heave offering to the Lord, vv. 21-32. God provides for His servants and they certainly cannot exceed Him in what little they give back.

Purification by the red heifer

Chapter 19 continues the sanctuary's defence by concentrating on cleansing from defilement through the red heifer's ashes[223] mixed with water, cedar wood, hyssop, and scarlet yarn, v. 6. The sacrificed

---

[223] On the ashes, two gifted brethren of the past comment: 'The body burnt outside the camp denoted the *holiness* of God, who must banish sin from His presence, even when borne by Christ. What then was the severity of His judgment, since this judgment consumed the holy victim who bore the sin! The victim, it is said, was a thing most holy. But the ashes of the burnt heifer loudly proclaimed at the same time that sin was *not imputed* to the sinner, and that this great question had been definitely settled between Christ and God'. H. L. ROSSIER, 'The Red Heifer', in *The Christian Friend*, Vol. 15, 1888; electronic edition accessed here:
http://www.stempublishing.com/authors/rossier/RedHeif.html   'The Spirit of God brings me the ashes, that is, He tells me the fire of God's judgement *has been* there. It is not that it *is* there; if it were there it would be fire and not ashes . . . It is not the question of an atonement, and it is not a fresh application of the blood, but it is that you judge yourself about the thing that God has set aside on the cross.' J. B. STONEY, 'Liberty', in *Steps In Light* in *Collected Writings*, Vol. 1, 1887, pg. 15; electronic edition.

animal's blood was sprinkled seven times in front of the tabernacle and the carcass was burned entirely, vv. 4-5. It prefigures Christ's propitiatory work, which is the basis of the repentant sinner's forgiveness and purification. He gave His life by pouring out His blood, and was completely offered to God as a payment for sin, 2 Cor. 5. 21; 1 John 1. 7.

Numbers chapters 11 to 16 give the moral flavour of Israel in the wilderness. There was no shortage of defiling things – especially with the first generation dying under God's judgement for their unbelief and disobedience, Heb. 3. 16-19; Ps. 90. 3, 5-10. T. ERNEST WILSON sets the scene: 'Masses of dead bodies, dying from disease, war or natural causes must have been a common sight to the Israelites in their aimless desert wanderings. This is the sad and sobering background to the fact of ceremonial defilement by contact with the dead and how it must be dealt with. It is described in Numbers 19'.[224] People were made unclean by contacting dead things in the tent or the field. The former shows the need to guard private and home-life from things that defile; the latter, demonstrates the chance for contacting impurity in public. Bones and graves also defile, and ROSSIER unpacks the implications of this evocative metaphor: 'A grave might be unwittingly walked over, Luke 11. 44. The Lord makes use of the figure of a sepulchre to portray the hypocrisy of a heart which presents a pleasant appearance, whilst within it is full of dead men's bones and all uncleanness, Matt. 23. 27, 28. The grave is a heart that voluntarily hides its internal corruption beneath a fair exterior'.[225] Some bones are the defiling aftermath of battle – the product of this world's violence; others are merely the outcome of death by natural

---

[224] T. ERNEST WILSON, 'The Ordinance of the Red Heifer', in *Precious Seed*, 39:3, 1988, electronic edition accessed here:
http://www.preciousseed.org/article_detail.cfm?articleID=1294&keyword=red+heifer.
[225] H. L. ROSSIER, 'The Red Heifer', in *The Christian Friend*, Vol. 15, 1888; electronic edition accessed here:
http://www.stempublishing.com/authors/rossier/RedHeif.html.

causes, manifesting that this sinful scene is filled with impurity that contaminates those who unwittingly contact it, Num. 19. 14. Thankfully the ceremony of the red heifer demonstrates that God has established a means of complete cleansing. The Israelite could be sprinkled on the third and seventh days. The number three presents a new beginning – e.g., Christ's resurrection day; seven presents perfection. So cleansing is readily available and perfectly purifies those who go to the Lord for it, 1 John 1. 9.

Moses' sin and its drastic repercussions

Content outline of chapters 20 and 21

- Miriam's death, Num. 20. 1.
- The Israelites' complaint and Moses' sin at Meribah-Kadesh, vv. 2-13.
- Moses' unsuccessful diplomatic correspondence with Edom, vv. 14-21.
- Aaron's death and the passing of the mantle to Eleazar, vv. 22-29.
- Israel's victory over Arad and establishment of Hormah, 21. 1-3.
- Fiery serpents and the bronze serpent remedy, vv. 4-9.
- Travelling to Moab; a divinely provided well, vv. 10-20.
- Israel's victory over Sihon and Og in preparation for the conquest of Canaan, vv. 21-35.

Numbers chapters 20 to 21 begin the narrative of the closing of the Exodus generation. Personal tragedies alternate with challenges from the nations that border Canaan, demonstrating both man's failure and God's faithfulness. Chapter 20 begins with Miriam's death and ends with the passing of the priestly mantle from father to son, followed by the passing of the first Levitical high priest. In between the departure of these two luminaries, Moses fails to sanctify the Lord before Israel and is told that he will not lead Israel into the land.

Instead of carefully following God's instructions to speak to the rock and receive water, Moses became angry and misrepresented the Almighty's character to His people. He claimed that Aaron and he were the ones who must provide the water. He also used Aaron's rod – the symbol of priesthood and mediation on Israel's behalf – and violently struck the rock, vv. 7-11. This implied that the Lord was uncaring towards His people's needs. As DAVID GOODING comments:

'When the Lord's people are suffering, it is a very serious thing to bring down the rod of judgment on them and accuse them of being rebellious, when what they need is to be shown the mercy and sympathy of God through their High Priest. It was not the people who on that occasion were rebelling against God. God's verdict was that it was Moses and Aaron that were rebelling against Him, and misrepresenting His character to the people'.[226]

On balance, Moses was a faithful leader in his divinely appointed mission, Heb. 3. 2; on this occasion he failed spectacularly. To be led into the fullness of God's inheritance one must be faithful and not disobey His instructions. Thankfully, our heavenly inheritance – not to mention Israel's future inheritance in the land, Gal. 3. 16 – is secured by a perfect prophet, priest, and king: the Lord Jesus Christ. As GOODING further explains:

'That act of impatience cost Moses his entry into the Promised Land. It seems hard on Moses, doesn't it? But God had appointed Moses to look after Israel, and if Moses could not do it without losing his temper and so misrepresenting God to the people, then Moses must be set aside. And God has appointed us a captain of our salvation, and made him responsible for seeing us through this world home to glory. Thank God we can count on his faithfulness and know that he will never fail, never once lose his patience or his temper with any of us, but will fulfill his God-

---

[225] DAVID W. GOODING, personal e-mail to this author, 12 August 2008.

appointed task to the very end. He will save to the uttermost all who come to God by him'.[227]

Through his disobedience, Num. 20. 12, Moses was forbidden to lead the nation into the land. He would be graciously permitted to view it from afar on Mount Nebo, Deut. 34. 1. Eventually he would get into the land, but under glorified conditions, Matt. 17. 3. Moses and Aaron's failure is commemorated by the name 'Meribah', meaning 'Contention' NKJVmg., Num. 20. 13. Although the place is different from the one in Exodus chapter 17, it is given the same name; only this time the strife comes from the leaders who ought to know better, rather than the people, as in the first case. Aaron's judgement comes at the end of the chapter, v. 24.

Meeting the Gentile neighbours and pervasive old habits

These chapters also relate Israel's dealings with Edom, Arad, and the Amorites. These points of contact met with rejection in the first case and combat in the latter two cases. Such experiences prepared them for larger conflicts in the future conquest of Canaan. On the pathway to God's inheritance there are tribulations and afflictions, Acts 14. 22.

In the midst of these variegated hardships, they also encountered the enemy within. Once again, they murmured against the Lord, resulting in wrath in the form of 'fiery serpents',[228] Num. 21. 4-6. Their deadly bite took the lives of many Israelites, but God provided a means of salvation that took the image of the thing that was killing them: a 'brass'[229] serpent, 2 Cor. 5. 21. The Lord Jesus referred back to this

---

[227] GOODING, *An Unshakeable Kingdom*, pg. 97.

[228] In five of the seven occurrences of this term in the Hebrew Bible the term refers to 'fiery serpents', Deut. 8. 15; Isa. 14. 29; 30. 6. Two other times it refers to heavenly beings and is transliterated as 'seraphim', Isa. 6. 2, 6.

[229] Many scholars translate this metal as 'copper' due to the proximity of this event to Timna, ancient site of copper mines; see ANSON F. RAINEY and R.

happening as a picture of His death on the cross as a sacrifice for sin, John 3. 14-16. 'Look and live' is still the principle undergirding the gospel, Num. 21. 8.

An attack from on high

Numbers chapters 22 to 24 deal with an attempted occult assault on Israel. In spite of the many failings of the Israelites, God is graciously committed to protecting and blessing Israel. He will eventually bring them to their inheritance according to His faithfulness. In this part of Numbers, He looks at them positionally and will deal with them according to His purposes.[230] Of course, the other side of the coin is that this blessed people will only receive the divine allotment and lasting salvation through the Messiah, Rom. 11. 26-27.

Fearing the advance of the Israelites, a Midianite-Moabite coalition led by King Balak[231] hired a celebrated soothsayer named Balaam[232]

STEVEN NOTLEY, *Carta's New Century Handbook and Atlas of the Bible*, Carta, 2007, pg. 41. Whether 'brass', KJV, 'bronze', NKJV, or copper, the underlying Hebrew word is related to the word for 'serpent', see COLE, pp. 347-348.

[230] It is well-stated in these words: 'When God looks at His people, He beholds in them His own workmanship; and it is to the glory of His holy name, and to the praise of His salvation, that not a blemish should be seen on those who are His – those whom He, in sovereign grace, has made His own. His character, His name, His glory, and the perfection of His work are all involved in the standing of those with whom He has linked Himself. Hence, therefore, the moment any enemy or accuser enters the scene, Jehovah places Himself in front to receive and answer the accusation; and His answer is always founded, not upon what His people are in themselves, but upon what He had made them through the perfection of His own work. His glory is linked with them, and in vindicating them, He maintains His own glory'. MACKINTOSH, pp. 566-567 [italics original].

[231] Spiritual forces act upon people in high places: 'Kings and statesmen, however talented and well intentioned they may be, are helpless pawns in the hands of diabolical spirits, if they have not learned the need of absolute dependence upon God'. W.W. FEREDAY, *Jonah The Preacher & Balaam The*

to curse the newcomers. Chapter 22 recounts the complicated negotiations between the clients and their prophet-for-hire. Out of greed, he begs Jehovah to let him go on this mission, but He first forbids this and then permits him to go with the strict charge to only speak what the Almighty tells him, vv. 1-20. A notable encounter with the Angel of the Lord – famously involving a talking donkey – reinforces this mandate to become God's spokesman, vv. 21-35. The donkey shows more awareness of divine activity than the so-called 'seer'. The threefold movement of this animal foreshadows the three moving encounters with the Moabite king that occur in chapter 23.[233]

Some suggest that Balaam was a genuine prophet, who prostituted his gifts for financial gain; however, the scriptures seem to indicate otherwise. He is more likely a false prophet; consider:

1. Although he uses the name of Israel's God 'Jehovah', Num. 22. 18, Balaam has no apparent love for His people. His prophecies might be adduced as proof, 23. 8-10, but it needs

---

False Prophet, John Ritchie Publishers, 1992, pp. 54-55. Elsewhere he adds: 'Men who know not God, and to whom the Bible is a sealed book, have no resource in their anxieties but alliances and treaties. God's saints, instructed by the Holy Spirit, have no confidence in these devices, and they wait for Christ. This is the proper moral effect of the reverent study of prophecy. 'Horns' and 'beasts' may be very interesting, and may furnish much material for discussion; the aim of the Spirit of God in disclosing to us the future is to separate us from man's hopelessly evil order of things, and fix our minds upon Christ'. FEREDAY, pp. 99-100.

[232] In 1967 archaeologists uncovered an inscription talking about Balaam's prowess in sorcery at a place called Tell Deir Alla near the Jabbok River in Jordan. Although it dates from about 600 years after the book of Numbers, scholars feel that it represents a much older tradition. Of course, the Bible is accurate in every detail and this is just one of the many examples of its historicity. See BRYANT G. WOOD, 'Balaam Son of Beor', *Bible and Spade,* Vol. 8, Autumn, 1995, pp. 114-116.

[233] CURRID, pp. 319, 321-322.

to be remembered that he is speaking under the Holy Spirit's guidance in those instances. He is like many who say 'Lord, Lord', Matt. 7. 22-23, 'having a form of godliness but denying the power thereof', 2 Tim. 3. 5.

2. The term 'diviner's fee', Num. 22. 7, and its related words are always associated with false prophets.[234]

3. The New Testament classes Balaam's methodology and teaching as paradigmatic of the exploitation of spiritual things for financial gain, 2 Pet. 2. 15; Jude 11, and licentiousness, Rev. 2. 14.

Rather than a misguided prophet of Jehovah, Balaam was a charlatan who probably was accustomed to trafficking with demons, 1 Cor. 10. 20, while he syncretistically incorporated true names and concepts to enhance his credentials as a sorcerer, cf. the witch at Endor, 1 Sam. 28. 7-25; Simon the sorcerer, Acts 8. 9-24; the Jewish exorcists, Acts 19. 13-17.[235]

---

[234] WILHELM GESENIUS AND SAMUEL PRIDEAUX TREGELLES, 'Qesem', in *Gesenius' Hebrew and Chaldee Lexicon to the Old Testament Scriptures*, Logos Bible Software, 2003, pg. 736.

[235] Two teachers of the past capture his personality: 'A man may be full of the knowledge of God and yet utterly destitute of the grace of God, may receive the truth in the light of it and yet be a stranger to the love of it . . . *he saw the vision of the Almighty*, but not so as to be *changed into the same image*. He calls God the *Most High*, and the *Almighty*; no man could speak more honourably of him, nor seem to put a greater value upon his acquaintance with him, and yet he had no true fear of him, love to him, or faith in him, so far may a man go towards heaven, and yet come short'. MATTHEW HENRY, *Matthew Henry's Commentary on the Whole Bible*, Hendrickson, 1994, pg. 225 [italics original]. 'Balaam had some knowledge of the true God, and could use Jehovah's name, but there was with him an unholy mixture of the divine and the satanic, for he used enchantments also. He was a corrupt and money-loving man, the prototype of the false teachers and ungodly persons who appear in times of departure and apostasy, and in whom is concentrated intense opposition to all that is spiritual, see 2 Peter 2. 15, 16; Jude 11'. COATES, pg. 289.

Balaam's prophecies

The mercenary-seer is brought to three different locations to observe Israel from the heights and curse them. There is no indication in the text that Israel knew anything about this until much later. Much to Balak's consternation, Balaam blesses God's people instead of cursing them. The theme of the first prophecy, Num. 23. 7-10, is Israel's unique status as the ones who are unassailably blessed among the nations. The second prophecy, vv. 18-24, concerns God's presence among them and refusal to retract His promises. The third prophecy, 24. 3-9, takes up the future prosperity and blessing of Israel. There is a fourth prophecy[236] thrown in at the end of the passage as a summary of Israel's future. It concerns the Messiah's triumph and reign over the nations that surround the land when He returns. He is described in regal terms: 'a star', Isa. 14. 12; Matt. 2. 2, and a 'sceptre', Gen. 49. 9-10; Num. 24. 17. Balaam describes His defeat of each of these enemies of Israel: Edom, Amalek, the Kenites,[237] and Assyria ('Asshur'), vv. 18-24. After all of the varied sacrifices and changing vantage points, as guided by the Almighty, the greedy prophet blesses God's people as was prophesied centuries earlier, Gen. 12. 3. SHEARMAN remarks: 'Let the heathen touch God's people, and He would show where His love and blessing lie. They were the apple of His eye. His delight was to bless them. God's grace provided the basis, for Christ was 'made a curse for us . . . that the blessing of Abraham might come'''.[238]

---

[236] Since verses 15, 20, 21, and 23 all use the term 'parable', KJV – or 'oracle' as others translate it, NKJV – some Bible students say these are four distinct messages. But since they are united in theme and proximity I am treating them as one.

[237] Nomadic metal-working 'smiths' who attached themselves to various nations at different times. See COLE, pg. 430.

[238] A. T. SHEARMAN, 'April 1st: Ebal and Gerizim (Deuteronomy 27. 1-13; 28. 1-19)', in *Day by Day through the Old Testament*, ed. C. E. HOCKING AND M. HORLOCK, Day by Day Series, Precious Seed, 1982, pg. 107.

The first generation culminates with idolatrous failure at Baal Peor

Having failed in their attempt to weaken Israel by occultic cursing under Balaam's tutelage, Num. 31. 16; Rev. 2. 15, the Midianite-Moabite coalition used a physical means of assault: they lured the Israelite men into idolatry and fornication by the feminine charms of their women, and thereby brought God's wrath upon the congregation, Num. 25. 1-3. Carnal adultery led to spiritual adultery as they joined in the sacrificial meals to the false fertility god Baal of Peor, Ps. 106. 28. MATTHEW HENRY wisely explains this insidious tactic's subtlety:

'If Balak had drawn out his armed men against them to fight them, Israel had bravely resisted, and no doubt had been more than conquerors; but now that he sends his beautiful women among them, and invites them to his idolatrous feasts, the Israelites basely yield, and are shamefully overcome: those are smitten with these harlots that could not be smitten with his sword. Note, we are more endangered by the charms of a smiling world than by the terrors of a frowning world'.[239]

COATES also notices this danger:

'The friendliness and invitations of the world are more to be feared than its curses. And it must not be supposed that it is only young believers who are exposed to this snare. For it comes in at the end of the wilderness, as acting upon those who have, typically, made a good deal of spiritual progress, and who have known something of the good of the indwelling Spirit, both for inward satisfaction and as power to get the victory over enemies. The fact that persons have come distinctly into view as subjects of divine working makes it a definite object with Satan to seduce and corrupt them. And sometimes it becomes sorrowfully

---

[239] HENRY, pg. 226.

manifest that those who have successfully resisted persecution fall before what appeals to fleshly gratification. How often the friendliness of the world, and even an appeal to the lowest lusts of the flesh, have succeeded in casting the people of God down from their excellency! It is not to little children, but to young men – who are strong, and who have the word of God abiding in them, and who have overcome the wicked one – that the warning is addressed, "Love not the world, nor the things in the world", 1 John 2. 15'.[240]

Desperate times require desperate measures. Israel's sin reached its climax as a leader of the Simeonites, Zimri the son of Salu, Num. 25. 6, 14-15, brazenly led a Midianite princess named Cozbi into the middle of the congregation to commit immorality in his tent. In a bold action reminiscent of his grandfather's intercession for the people in time of judgement, 16. 46-50, Phinehas boldly put a stop to this wanton flouting of God's law by impaling them both with his javelin, 25. 7-8.[241] His defining characteristic was zeal, vv. 10, 13, and he was an ardent example to the other Israelites that the Lord's holiness must

---

[240] COATES, pg. 313.

[241] In an apparent case of the punishment fitting the crime, the text notes that Phinehas struck these fornicators through their bodies with his javelin, striking the woman in her 'belly' KJV. This Hebrew word also refers to an inner room used as a shrine, NETmg.; if she would misuse her body to abet idolatry, then wrath fell on her body – many commentators feel that her reproductive organs are meant here, see COLE, pp. 441-442 and WENHAM, pg. 210. There is also a covenantal aspect to this action, as noted by GOLDINGAY: 'The form of execution, by sword or spear, suggests a link with the ritual of covenant-making. If it should break the covenant, Israel has asked that it should be cut up as the animal in a covenant-making was cut up (Gen. 15. 17-21; cf. Jer. 34. 18). That happens'. GOLDINGAY, pg. 419. Clearly, Zimri suffered the penalty of covenant breaking: capital punishment.

be guarded[242] – even by swift and painful judgement. BERNARD OSBORNE unpacks his character this way:

'He could not fold his arms and see God's law insulted, His rule defied. The servant's heart moved in one blaze of godly indignation. He must be up to vindicate God; he "stood up". This is a picture of one zealous man rising up from the midst of the inactive multitude who sit still and make no effort . . . Phinehas stood up from the rest, and presented himself before the people, assuming the office and discharging the duty from which the regular, official leaders seemed to shrink. His bold resolve feared nothing in a righteous cause'.[243]

---

[242] The scriptures later describe Phinehas as the head of the gate-keepers of the tabernacle, 1 Chr. 9. 20. On this aspect of his work, C. A. COATES remarks: 'As ruler over the door-keepers we are told of Phinehas that "Jehovah was with him". No doubt he was as jealous for God in regard of those whom he admitted to the tent of meeting as he was jealous in killing Zimri: We have to deplore that there has been great lack of this holy watchfulness in the Christian profession; the door has been left unguarded, and much that is worldly and carnal has got in . . . Something of the spirit of Phinehas is needed'. COATES, pp. 317-320.

[243] BERNARD OSBORNE, 'Righteousness, Justice, Judgment', in *Day by Day in the Psalms*, ed. ARTHUR T. SHEARMAN AND JOHN HEADING, Day by Day Series, Precious Seed, 1986, p. 105. MACKINTOSH offers a similar assessment: 'God's glory and Israel's good were the objects that ruled the conduct of the faithful Phinehas on this occasion. It was a critical moment. He felt there was a demand for the most stern action. It was not time for false tenderness. There are moments in the history of God's people in which tenderness to man becomes unfaithfulness to God; and it is of the utmost importance to be able to discern such moments. The prompt acting of Phinehas saved the whole congregation, glorified Jehovah in the midst of His people, and completely frustrated the enemy's design. Balaam fell among the judged Midianites, but Phinehas became the possessor of an everlasting priesthood'. MACKINTOSH, pp. 571-572.

Phinehas' faithfulness flowed from his faith in God and resulted in a 'covenant of peace' and 'an everlasting priesthood' from the Lord, Num. 25. 12-13; Ps. 106. 30-31. His priesthood flows through the line of Zadok, 1 Chr. 6. 8, all the way into Christ's future millennial reign, Ezek. 40. 46. As a warrior-priest he covered Israel's sin by judging it. Although the Lord Jesus died as a substitute for sinners on the cross, those who reject Him will meet Him one day as their judge, John 5. 22-23; Acts 17. 31.

The infidelity of the men who sinned at Baal Peor brought on a plague that slew 24,000 people, v. 9. Paul cites this incident as a warning to believers in our age to abstain from sexual sin, 1 Cor. 10. 8.[244] To modern people this divine wrath might seem overly harsh, but it actually gives a fitting sense of the gravity of idolatry and sexual sin. JAMES PHILIP describes the Almighty's ire against sin thus: 'God is, apparently, not in the least afraid of being thought censorious – or of His servants and champions being thought censorious, either. Rather, it is a question of calling some ugly things by their proper names and dealing with them accordingly. In this permissive and morally decadent age, we could certainly do with some of this spirit'.[245] Believers must be zealous in putting their sinful inclinations to death. The New Testament equivalent to Phinehas' decisive ministry is the mortification of the flesh, Col. 3. 5-7.

---

[244] Paul cites the number killed by the plague as 23,000, while the Numbers passage says 24,000. Various suggestions have been put forth, but VINE seems to capture the right idea: 'We do not agree with those who suppose that Paul was quoting from memory. Nor is there any question of a difference of readings in the original. The passage in Numbers does not say 24,000 fell in one day. Accordingly, the apostle may be giving the immediate result here, while the record given by Moses mentioned the full result'. W. E. VINE, 1 Corinthians, in *Collected Writings of W.E. Vine,* Thomas Nelson, 1996.
[245] JAMES PHILIP, *Numbers,* The Preacher's Commentary Series, Vol. 4, ed. LLOYD J. OGILVIE, Thomas Nelson, 1987, pg. 250.

The second census – a picture of God's faithfulness after His people's failure

Numbers chapter 26 offers the book's second census of the Israelite tribes. As noted in the introductory section of this book, the nation's population remained fairly stable after almost forty years of wandering in the desert. The second generation was roughly the same in number as their parents' generation – the group that came out of Egypt in the exodus. God disciplined the unbelieving ones and is now poised to take their children into the Promised Land, Num. 14. 31-34. With all of Israel's ups and downs, He remains faithful to His promises. As a contemporary author notes:

'So we see that Israel's sin does not negate God's purposes in grace. The Lord punishes Israel severely for their sins, but He remains in their midst. Over and over He disciplines and restores them because of His promises to the fathers. The new generation whose census is taken in chapter 26 is then prepared anew for the entrance into the Promised Land (chs. 27-36). Hope is still alive because of the Lord's faithfulness'.[246]

Guarantee of the inheritance as seen in the case of the daughters of Zelophehad

Five different Old Testament passages mention Zelophehad and his daughters. This family's plight became case law in Israel regarding the inheritance of the land by daughters, where there were no sons in the family. At stake was the prospect of an Israelite man's name perishing from the roles of the people of God. The Most High God would not permit this; instead He determined that the daughters were permitted to inherit in their father's name, 27. 1-11. Later, their tribe, Manasseh, worried that they would marry members of another tribe, thereby losing a portion of their inheritance. Therefore, the

---

[246] GEORGE BRISTOW, *The Promise of God,* Gospel Folio Press, 1997, pp. 87-88.

Lord determined that they must marry within their own tribe so as to continue the tribe's possession, Num. 36. This manifested His care for individuals, families, and tribes, as well as demonstrating His fidelity to His promises. Their story serves an important literary function in the book of Numbers. As one teacher explains:

'Emphasizing deep-rooted faith, Num. 27. 1-11 provides a fitting introduction to the second half of the book. The material that follows, 27. 12-35, 34, contains warnings and promises that pertain to the land . . . The second half of Numbers, then, deals with the second generation's preparation both to enter the land and to retain the privilege of staying in it. Failure to obey God would result in expulsion, 33. 55-56'.[247]

Moses' successor

The old adage says that 'the Lord buries His workers, but carries on His work'. We see this principle at this point in the book of Numbers, as Moses is instructed to prepare his successor for his duties as the leader for the era of Israel's invasion of Canaan. The Lord's people need spiritual oversight, and having them scattered like shepherdless sheep is an undesirable situation, Matt. 9. 36-38. Once more one observes Moses' humility, for he bows to God's will by uncomplainingly anointing his replacement. Joshua is consistently represented positively in the book of Numbers.[248] With Caleb he is one of two faithful spies, Num. 14. 30, and is described as 'Moses' assistant, one of his choice men', 11. 28, NKJV.[249] He consistently

---

[247] DEAN R. ULRICH, 'The Framing Function of the Narratives about Zelophehad's Daughters', *Journal of the Evangelical Theological Society* 41:4, December 1998, pp. 535-536.
[248] Eleven times we read his name in this book: Num. 11. 28; 13. 16; 14. 6, 30, 38; 26. 65; 27. 18, 22; 32. 12, 28; 34. 17.
[249] Some render it alternatively: 'the attendant of Moses from his youth' NASB, or 'the assistant of Moses from his youth' ESV.

fought the Lord's battles, demonstrated loyalty to Moses, and devoted himself to the Lord's things. With the added benefit of some of Moses' authority, 27. 20, he is an excellent choice to lead the nation. He will be guided by the Lord through Eleazar, the high priest, who will use the Urim to ascertain the Almighty's will, 27. 22.

This changing of the guard was an emotional moment, as PARMENTER notes: 'Moses a mature man of God, still in prime physical condition, would have dearly loved to be there when his people finally crossed the Jordan into the land of Canaan. There must have been a tinge of disappointment in his heart, yet Moses unflinchingly obeyed Jehovah to the very end'.[250]

The sacrificial basis of Israel's life

The second generation's entrance into the inheritance would be conditioned by grace and not by any merit of their own. The rhythms of their lives revolved around sacrifice. Daily, weekly, monthly, and throughout their harvest calendar, different types of offerings reminded them of the Lord's grace and that their standing depended on His redemptive work. Their lives were filled with pictures that pointed to substitutionary atonement, holiness, and divine mercy. The perfect accomplishment and continual efficacy of Christ's sacrificial death is collectively stressed by the various offerings in these chapters. As MACKINTOSH maintains:

'[T]he special theme here is, God's delight in Christ. Morning and evening, day by day, week after week, from one new moon to another, from the opening to the close of the year, it is Christ in His fragrance and preciousness to Godward. True it is – thanks be to God, and to Jesus Christ His Son – our sin is atoned for, judged,

---

[250] ERIC PARMENTER, 'February 8th: Set a Man Over (Numbers 27:15–17)', in *Day by Day in Prayer*, ed. Ivan Steeds, Day by Day Series, Precious Seed, 1997, pg. 55.

and put away forever – our trespasses forgiven and guilt cancelled; but above and beyond this, the heart of God is fed, refreshed, and delighted by Christ'.[251]

Vows and oaths are included in this section because they are a form of sacrifice, cf. Num. 29. 39 and chapter 30, binding oneself to do or give to God or abstain from something as He requires. Such sacrifices were safeguarded, and family authority must be affirmed in the theocracy that the Lord was establishing in the Promised Land.

The content outline of these passages is:

- Daily morning and evening offerings, Num. 28. 1-8.
- Sabbath offerings, vv. 9-10.
- Monthly offerings, vv. 11-15.
- Passover and Unleavened Bread offerings, vv. 16-25.
- Feast of Weeks offerings, vv. 26-31.
- Feast of Trumpets, 29. 1-6.
- Day of Atonement offerings, vv. 7-11.
- Feast of Tabernacles offerings, vv. 12-40.
- The sanctity of vows and oaths (another form of sacrifice), 30. 1-2.
- The procedure for an unmarried woman's vows, vv. 3-5.
- The procedure for a married woman's vows, vv. 6-8.
- The procedure for a widow or divorced woman's vows, vv. 9-15.

---

[251] MACKINTOSH, pg. 578; brother GRANT adds: 'Thus then, beyond all desert experiences, in the first part of this last division of Numbers God is seen enthroned, sin powerless to blur for a moment the brightness of His glory, which through sacrifice has only the more wondrously displayed itself. True, after all, man's heart is found unable worthily to take it in: he cannot, as he might be expected, answer to it; all the more is it proved that grace is what he absolutely needs, and that to grace he must be debtor. Grace, then, will be his song for eternity'. GRANT, pg. 501.

- Summation concerning vows and oaths, v. 16.

Judgement day for the Midianites

Chapter 31 forms the sequel to chapter 25, when the Midianites enticed the men of Israel to sexual immorality and idolatry at Baal Peor. The Lord now instructs His people to 'avenge the Lord of Midian', Num. 31. 3, for this crime. This transcends mere revenge, and is the execution of righteous judgement against His enemies. Modern readers sometimes think this is a disquieting example of jihad. On the contrary, the Creator of the universe gives life and also has the right to rescind that gift according to His perfect will, Deut. 32. 39; Heb. 9. 27. He extends His light and mercy to everyone, John 1. 9, but there are limits to His grace. If there is persistent rejection of His overtures, then He does 'His strange work', Isa. 28. 21, of pouring out His righteous anger. As in chapter 25, Phinehas is once more the Lord's deliverer. The eradication of these wicked people is a holy endeavour, led by a priest who was zealous for righteousness. As the grapes of wrath are trampled out, Balaam – the architect of Midian's seduction of the Israelite men – is executed for his iniquity, Num. 31. 8.

God's judgement is also discriminating: 'The LORD is longsuffering, and of great mercy, forgiving iniquity and transgression, and by no means clearing the guilty, visiting the iniquity of the fathers upon the children unto the third and fourth generation', Num. 14. 18. One sees this righteous discernment in His treatment of the Midianite women, 31. 15-20. Only the guilty were executed; the innocent were incorporated into the nation who had a covenant with God. All of the battle spoils are purified by the holy water, vv. 19-24; Num. 19; the whole campaign is conducted in a holy fashion.

Spiritual opportunists or turncoats? Reuben, Gad, and the half tribe of Manasseh

The two-and-a-half tribes that are prominent in chapter 32 have often been maligned by commentators as 'world borderers'. Yet one should be careful in rushing to judgement against these people – especially since they were the victims of misunderstanding and character assassination elsewhere in the Bible, Josh. 22. 10-34. Moses obviously feared a repetition of the apostasy at Kadesh Barnea forty years earlier, Num. 32. 6-15. They were willing to fight Israel's Canaanite enemies, however, and they only settled in their Transjordanian allotments after their brethren had inherited their portions on the river's western side, Josh. 22. 1-9. They desired territory that was divinely given to Israel by their conquest over the Gentile foes Sihon and Og, Num. 21. 21-35. Moreover, the aftermath of their behaviour in Joshua chapter 22 makes it plain that they were not defecting from the Lord. They consistently maintained their loyalty to their God. Their territorial claims were later described by God as their 'inheritance', 34. 14-15.

The review of Israel's wilderness wanderings and the prospect of an inheritance

Chapters 33 and 34 look back as well as forwards in regard to the movements of God's pilgrim people. The geographic history of their journey is recounted and instructions are given for the conquest of Canaan and the boundaries of the land and distribution of the inheritance to the tribes. As a whole, they depict the nature of following the Lord by faith to the Promised Land. This world is not our home; we seek a better city in a better country, Heb. 11. 10, 13-16. As SPURGEON eloquently reminds us:

'And so the whole chapter is a succession of removings and encampings, till at last they ceased to dwell in tents, and came to live in their own walled cities in the land of Canaan. Just such has been the history of the Church – it has always been removing its place, and such has been the condition of each individual. Here we have no abiding city. "We seek a city which hath foundations, whose builder and maker is God." Here we have but an earthly house of our tabernacle which is soon to be dissolved, and we are continually men of the weary foot, who rest not, but journey onward to the place of rest'.[252]

MACKINTOSH writes in a similar vein:

'Such is the Church of God in the world – a separated, dependent, defenceless thing, wholly cast upon the living God. It is calculated to give great vividness, force, and clearness to our thoughts about the Church to view it as the antitype of the camp in the desert; and that it is in no wise fanciful or far-fetched to view it thus, 1 Corinthians 10. 11, does most clearly show. We are fully warranted in saying that what the camp of Israel was literally, that the Church is morally and spiritually. And further, that what the wilderness was literally to Israel, that the world is morally and spiritually to the Church of God. The wilderness was the sphere of Israel's toil and danger, not of their supplies or their enjoyment; and the world is the sphere of the Church's toil and danger, not of its supplies or its enjoyment'.[253]

Content outline of chapters 33 and 34

- Israel's geographical journeys, Num. 33. 1-49.
- Instructions for the conquest, vv. 50-56.
- The delineation of Canaan's borders, 34. 1-13.
- Reuben, Gad, and the half tribe of Manasseh's inheritance, vv. 14-15.

---

[252] C. H. SPURGEON, 'The March', in *The Metropolitan Tabernacle Pulpit Sermons*, Vol. 7, Passmore & Alabaster, 1861, pg. 162.
[253] MACKINTOSH, pp. 433-434.

- The appointment of the dividers of the inheritance, vv. 16-29.

The cities of refuge as a picture of the gospel

Since the Lord Himself was the Levites' possession – in lieu of actual territorial allotments like the other tribes – Israel was instructed to give them forty-two cities, plus six cities that were to be used as asylums for those who were guilty of manslaughter, Num. 35. 1-8. To avoid unrestrained bloodshed that would pollute the land, vv. 33-34, the duty of the executioner was subjugated to the authority of the congregation who maintained 'cities of refuge', v. 11. They adjudicated the cases that determined whether a slayer was a murderer or merely guilty of the unpremeditated crime of manslaughter. Of course, to benefit from this tribunal they must flee to one of these protected cities. There they were spared instant execution at the hands of the 'avenger of blood'[254] – known in other contexts as the 'kinsman-redeemer' (such as Boaz in the book of Ruth) – and were only delivered into his hands if a verdict of murder was handed down based on a proper judicial inquiry with two or three witnesses attesting the slayer's guilt, v. 30; Deut. 19. 15.

The gospel overtones of these cities of refuge are clear. Transgressors are mercifully spared from death, and are kept safe in the city. When the high priest died, they were then permitted to return home. Modern believers are kept safe, having a high priest who ever lives to make intercession for His people, Heb. 7. 25. As WENHAM notes: 'Thus the high priest of ancient Israel anticipated the ministry of our Lord, not only in his life of offering sacrifice and prayer on behalf of the people, but also in his death, cf. Heb. 4–9'.[255] Another author comments:

---

[254] WILHELM GESENIUS AND SAMUEL PRIDEAUX TREGELLES, *Gesenius' Hebrew and Chaldee Lexicon to the Old Testament Scriptures,* Logos Bible Software, 2003, pg. 151; See also KEIL AND DELITZSCH, pp. 835–836, and CURRID, pg. 439.
[255] WENHAM, pg. 266.

'The blood of Christ has, in mercy, magnified the claims of divine justice, and the gates of salvation are flung wide open to receive the transgressor. God declares His name of love, and by His servants, His Levites, who expound His word, invites sinners to enter in and partake of His grace. Love now cries aloud from the throne of the majesty on high – the Lord Jesus in heaven is proclaimed as assuring the life of those who are of the guilty race that slew Him. And not only is security theirs who have fled to Christ for refuge, but being saved in hope – in hope of coming glory – a glorious inheritance is theirs in anticipation'.[256]

Some commentators also see the cities of refuge as a picture of God's dispensational dealings with Israel. WITHERBY'S remarks are helpful on this point:

'Eighteen hundred years ago the manslayer lifted up his hand, innocent blood was shed, and from that day the land of Canaan has been defiled by the blood of Jesus. The manslayer has lost his inheritance, he has fled from his own city; the Jews are banished from their land. Strangers dwell in the lots which Jehovah apportioned to the tribes; the possession is forfeited, and, to appearance, lost. But within the veil, in the heavenly sanctuary, the High Priest dwells. The Lord has passed through the heavens, and though unknown to the nation, who with wicked hands slew Him, He lives above. So long as He abides thus, Israel will remain without their inheritance. But He will come forth, the heavenly High Priest, and then Israel shall receive full forgiveness, and shall once more inherit every man his dwelling place. On that day, in millennial glory, shall the Name of the Lord and His presence be

---

[256] H. FORBES WITHERBY, 'Cities of refuge', in *The Book of Joshua*, electronic edition accessed here:
http://www.stempublishing.com/authors/HF_Witherby/HFW_Joshua31.ht ml.

the centre, the true Shiloh, the Peace of the promised possession on earth'.[257]

FEREDAY similarly writes: 'He graciously regards Israel as a "slayer", rather than a "murderer", to be restored in due time to the good land, the land of their possession'.[258] Since He deals with them on the grounds of ignorance, He is able to extend mercy towards them. One day He will restore them to their inheritance and they will enjoy it like never before under the rule of the Messiah, Zech. 12-14.

Zelophehad's daughters revisited

The Book of Numbers ends with the seemingly anticlimactic discussion of a point of real estate case law; yet, it is extremely important to the theme of the book as a whole. Numbers reveals God to be a powerful, holy, and merciful Being who is able to overcome His people's failure and preserve them for His inheritance. Just as individual inheritance rights were to be safeguarded – e.g., the first Zelophehad story in chapter 27 – so the collective rights of the tribe to their portion in the land is also to be affirmed and maintained. To put it bluntly, the Lord's people will not lose their inheritance! For the church today we have the same security, Rom. 8. 31-39; 1 Pet. 1. 3-5.

---

[257] *Ibid.*

[258] W. W. FEREDAY, 'The Man Slayer', electronic edition accessed here: http://www.stempublishing.com/authors/fereday/Trsry/Man_Slayer.html.

Bibliography for Numbers

ALBERT BARNES, *Notes on the Old Testament: Exodus to Ruth*, ed. F. C. Cook and J. M. Fuller, John Murray, 1879.

GEORGE BUSH, *Notes, Critical and Practical, on the Book of Numbers*, Ivison & Phinney, 1858.

C. A. COATES, *An Outline of the Book of Numbers*, Stow Hill Bible & Tract Depot, n.d.

D. A. CARSON, R. T. FRANCE, J. A. MOTYER, and G. J. WENHAM, eds., *New Bible Commentary: 21st Century Edition*, 4th ed, Inter-Varsity Press, 1994.

R. DENNIS COLE, *Numbers*, Vol. 3B, The New American Commentary, Broadman & Holman Publishers, 2000.

CROSSWAY BIBLES, *The ESV Study Bible*, Crossway Bibles, 2008.

JOHN D. CURRID, *A Study Commentary on Numbers*, EP Study Commentary, Evangelical Press, 2009.

J. N. DARBY, *Synopsis of the Books of the Bible: Genesis to 2 Chronicles*, Logos Research Systems, Inc., 2008.

CHARLES R. ERDMAN, *The Book of Numbers*, Baker, 1952.

F. W. GRANT, *The Numerical Bible; Being a Revised Translation of the Holy Scriptures with Expository Notes: Arranged, Divided, and Briefly Characterized according to the Principles of Their Numerical Structure: The Pentateuch (Study Text)*, Loizeaux Brothers, 1890.

MATTHEW HENRY, *Matthew Henry's Commentary on the Whole Bible*, Hendrickson, 1994.

CARL FRIEDRICH KEIL and FRANZ DELITZSCH, *Commentary on the Old Testament*, Vol. 1, Hendrickson, 1996.

JOHN PETER LANGE, PHILIP SCHAFF, SAMUEL T. LOWRIE, and A. GOSMAN, *A Commentary on the Holy Scriptures: Numbers*, Logos Bible Software, 2008.

JOHN MACARTHUR, JR., ed., *The MacArthur Study Bible*, electronic edition, Word Publishing, 1997.

WILLIAM MACDONALD, *Believer's Bible Commentary: Old and New Testaments*, ed. Arthur Farstad, Thomas Nelson, 1995.

C. H. MACKINTOSH, *Genesis to Deuteronomy: Notes on the Pentateuch*, Loizeaux Brothers, 1972.

GORDON J. WENHAM, *Numbers: An Introduction and Commentary*, Vol. 4, Tyndale Old Testament Commentaries, InterVarsity Press, 1981.

Deuteronomy

1.   The Name of the Book

Like the other parts of the Pentateuch, the title 'Deuteronomy' originates from the ancient Greek translation known as the Septuagint. As one writer explains with greater technical precision:

'The name Deuteronomy derives from the Greek rendering of a phrase in 17. 18 where the king who is to rule over Israel is commanded to prepare *a copy of this law*. The LXX rendered this phrase mistakenly as *to deuteronomion touto*, lit. "this second (or, repeated) law". Subsequently the Vulgate rendered the Greek noun *deuteronomium*. The contents of the book were thus regarded as a second law. The first had been given on Mount Horeb (Sinai). The second was a repetition of the first on the plains of Moab. Despite a mistaken translation of the Hebrew *mišnêh hattôrâ hazzō't* the name of the LXX translators is not entirely inappropriate since Deuteronomy is, in some measure at least, a re-presentation of the law of Sinai, albeit in the form of an exposition of the Mosaic law'.[259]

In Jewish tradition the book bears various names, including 'These are the words', 'Book of admonitions', 'This Law', 'The words of the covenant', and 'This commandment'.[260] Modern Jews refer to it simply as 'Debarim' – that is, 'Words'. All of these titles emphasize that this book is a direct communication from the Lord to His people

[259] J. A. THOMPSON, *Deuteronomy: An Introduction and Commentary*, Tyndale Old Testament Commentaries, Vol. 5, InterVarsity Press, 1974, pg. 16.
[260] GEORGE ADAM SMITH, *The Book of Deuteronomy in the Revised Version With Introduction and Notes*, The Cambridge Bible for Schools and Colleges, Cambridge University Press, 1918, pp. ix-x; and THOMPSON, pg. 16.

Israel. He is giving His law – the Hebrew word 'Torah' also means 'Instruction'[261] – to them in carefully chosen words.

2. The Purpose of the Book

As the fifth and final book of the Pentateuch – also known as the Torah or Books of Moses – this book is an important transition from Israel's early history looking forward to their conquest of the land under Joshua. The book is a recapitulation of God's law with particular application to their impending occupation of Canaan. It emphasizes the oneness of the true and living God in contrast to the false deities of the nations that they were going to fight. It also holds forth the exalted ethics of the legal system that the Almighty designed to govern their individual and national lives.

Deuteronomy takes place over the course of one month and is Moses' farewell message to his people.[262] He recounts the Lord's faithfulness in the past, charges them to obey Him in the present, and both warns and encourages them regarding the future. SHEARMAN offers this explanation of the book:

'Deuteronomy is a proclamation of Israel's laws. Moses spelt out the statutes and ordinances, and amplified them, that as the

---

[261] FRANCIS BROWN, SAMUEL ROLLES DRIVER, and CHARLES AUGUSTUS BRIGGS, *Enhanced Brown-Driver-Briggs Hebrew and English Lexicon,* Logos Research Systems, 2000, pg. 435.

[262] 'In fact, Moses' death is not recorded until chapter 34, so that the whole book of Deuteronomy is framed between the announcement of Moses' impending death and the announcement of his actual death. The book is thus, in a sense, the spiritual testament of Moses, Israel's great Lawgiver', THOMPSON, pg. 117. HALL asserts Moses' Spirit-led eloquence in these words: 'Its language is the lively exhortation of a master preacher and teacher whose admonitions transcend time and culture'. GARY HARLAN HALL, *Deuteronomy,* The College Press NIV Commentary, College Press Publishing Co., 2000, pg. 13.

nation entered the new sphere of the Promised Land, they would have no doubts as to the Lord's requirements. Some of the details now may seem trivial and irrelevant, yet they speak one message, "Holy laws for a holy people!" Well-being for them and satisfaction for a holy God would be the result of their obedience'.[263]

Another author describes it this way:

'There is much of retrospect in it, but its main outlook is forward. The rabbins speak of it as "the Book of Reproofs". It is the text of all prophecy; a manual of evangelical oratory; possessing "all the warmth of a St. Bernard, the flaming zeal of a Savonarola, and the tender, gracious sympathy of a St. Francis of Assisi". The author's interest is entirely moral. His one supreme purpose is to arouse Israel's loyalty to Jehovah and to His revealed law. Taken as a whole the book is an exposition of the great commandment, "Thou shalt love Jehovah thy God with all thy heart, and with all thy soul, and with all thy might". It was from Deuteronomy Jesus summarized the whole of the Old Covenant in a single sentence, Matt. 22. 37; cf. Deut. 6. 5, and from it He drew His weapons with which to vanquish the tempter, Matt. 4. 4, 7, 10; cf. Deut. 8. 3; 6. 16, 13'.[264]

---

[263] A. T. SHEARMAN, 'Mar. 31st: Laws for a Holy People, Deut. 22. 1-8; 24. 10-22; 25. 1-3; 26. 16-19', in *Day by Day through the Old Testament*, ed. C. E. HOCKING AND M. HORLOCK, Day by Day Series, Precious Seed, 1982, pg. 106. Another writer elucidates the theme further: 'The real understanding of Deuteronomy lies in the fact that God is to be feared, followed, loved, served, and obeyed, Deut. 10. 12-13. So the personal God's will is law in the revealing of himself in love. The mere adherence to a constitutional law or the acceptance of a creed is not sufficient to fulfill even the first command of God. The first command is to establish a real covenant'. JOHN JOSEPH OWENS, 'Law and Love in Deuteronomy', *Review & Expositor* 61:3 (Summer 1964), pg. 278.

[264] GEORGE L. ROBINSON, 'Deuteronomy', ed. JAMES ORR ET AL., *The International*

The Lord Jesus quotes it more often than any other Old Testament book, and Paul regularly cites it to support his arguments for salvation and Christian living.[265] KALLAND adds this: 'The theological value of Deuteronomy can hardly be exaggerated. It stands as the wellspring of biblical historical revelation. It is a prime source for both OT and NT theology. Whether the covenant, the holiness of God, or the concept of the people of God is the unifying factor of OT theology, each finds emphasis and remarkable definition in Deuteronomy'.[266] The frequent citations of the book in the New Testament attest to its lasting value for God's people in all ages.[267] Others compare it to the Gospel of John as a digest of the preceding forty years of history. Whereas Deuteronomy summarizes the Pentateuch's key doctrines, John brings together the key truths of the Gospels. Theologically, its systematic presentation of doctrine makes it the Old Testament equivalent of Romans. As a commentator remarks: '[L]ike the gospel of John, the book of Deuteronomy functions as a theological manifesto, calling on Israel to respond to God's grace with unreserved loyalty and love'.[268]

Standard Bible Encyclopaedia, The Howard-Severance Co., 1915, pg. 835.

[265] See Rom. 10. 6-8, 19; 11. 8; 12. 19; 1 Cor. 5. 13; 8. 6; 9. 9; Gal. 3. 13; Eph. 6. 2-3. Also DANIEL I. BLOCK, *The NIV Application Commentary: Deuteronomy*, ed. TERRY MUCK, Zondervan, 2012, pg. 26.

[266] EARL S. KALLAND, *Expositor's Bible Commentary: Deuteronomy*, ed. FRANK GAEBELEIN, Zondervan, 1999, electronic edition, no pagination.

[267] 'Deuteronomy is one of the greatest books of the Old Testament. Its influence on the domestic and personal religion of all ages has not been surpassed by any other book in the Bible. It is quoted over eighty times in the New Testament[1] and thus it belongs to a small group of four Old Testament books[2] to which the early Christians made frequent reference'. [Fn. 1: 'References occur in all but six books of the New Testament, namely John, Colossians, 1 Thessalonians, 2 Timothy, and 1 and 2 Peter'. Fn. 2: 'Genesis, Deuteronomy, Psalms and Isaiah'.] THOMPSON, pg. 16.

[268] BLOCK, pg. 25.

3.   The Plan of the Book

Many Bible students notice that Deuteronomy uses the literary structure of an ancient suzerainty treaty – a covenant where a suppliant nation enters into an agreement with a more powerful nation. KLINE's outline demonstrates this understanding of the book:

'1. Preamble: The covenant mediator, 1. 1-5.
2. The historical prologue; covenant history, 1. 6 – 4. 49.
3. The covenant stipulations: covenant life.
   (a) The great commandment, 5. 1 – 11. 32.
   (b) Ancillary commandments, 12. 1 – 26. 19.
4. The covenant sanctions: covenant ratification, blessings and curses, covenant oath, 27. 1 – 30. 20.
5. Dynastic disposition: covenant continuity, 31. 1 – 34. 12'.[269]

Of course, the lesser party is Israel, who are given instructions from the greater, who is the Lord.

Deuteronomy may also be divided according to Moses' exhortations to the nation:

Moses' first sermon, Deut. 1 – 4;
Moses' second sermon, Deut. 5 – 28;
Moses' third sermon, Deut. 29 – 30;
The Conclusion of Moses' Life, Deut. 31 – 34.

FARSTAD and MACDONALD give a more detailed outline along similar lines:

'I.   MOSES' FIRST DISCOURSE – APPROACHING THE LAND, Chs. 1 – 4

---

[269] MEREDITH G. KLINE, *Treaty of the Great King* (1963); quoted in THOMPSON, pg. 23.

A. Introduction, 1. 1-5
B. From Horeb to Kadesh, 1. 6-46
C. From Kadesh to Heshbon, Ch. 2
D. Trans-Jordan Secured, Ch. 3
E. Exhortation to Obedience, Ch. 4

II. MOSES' SECOND DISCOURSE – PURITY IN THE LAND, Chs. 5 – 28

A. Review of the Sinai Covenant, Ch. 5
B. Warnings Against Disobedience, Ch. 6
C. Instructions on Dealing with Idolatrous Nations, Ch. 7
D. Lessons from the Past, 8. 1 – 11. 7
E. Rewards for Obedience, 11. 8-32
F. Statutes for Worship, Ch. 12
G. Punishment of False Prophets and Idolaters, Ch. 13
H. Clean and Unclean Foods, 14. 1-21
I. Tithing, 14. 22-29
J. Treatment of Debtors and Slaves, Ch. 15
K. Three Appointed Feasts, Ch. 16
L. Judges and Kings, Ch. 17
M. Priests, Levites, and Prophets, Ch. 18
N. Criminal Laws, Ch. 19
O. Laws Concerning Warfare, Ch. 20
P. Various Laws, Ch. 21-25
Q. Rituals and Ratifications, Ch. 26
R. Curses and Blessings, Ch. 27, 28

III. MOSES' THIRD DISCOURSE – COVENANT FOR THE LAND, Chs. 29, 30

A. The Covenant Made in Moab, 29. 1-21
B. Punishment for Breaking the Covenant, 29. 22-29
C. Restoration for Returning to the Covenant, Ch. 30

IV. MOSES' LAST DAYS – DEATH OUTSIDE THE LAND, Chs. 31 – 34

A. Moses' Replacement, Ch. 31
B. Moses' Song, Ch. 32
C. Moses' Blessing, Ch. 33
D. Moses' Death, Ch. 34'.[270]

WIERSBE's outlines are always useful; here are two:

'I. Historical Concerns: Moses Looks Back, Chs. 1 – 4

A. The tragedy of unbelief, Ch. 1
B. Journeys and Victories, Chs. 2-3
C. Closing appeal that they obey, Ch. 4

II. Practical Concerns: Moses Looks Within, Chs. 5 – 26

A. The testimonies, Chs. 5 – 11
1. The law proclaimed, Ch. 5
2. The law practiced, Ch. 6
3. The law preserved, Chs. 7-10
a. Dangers from without, Ch. 7
b. Dangers from within, Chs. 8 – 10
4. The closing appeal, Ch. 11
B. The statutes, Chs. 12 – 18
C. The judgments, Chs. 19 – 26

III. Prophetical Concerns: Moses Looks Ahead, Chs. 27 – 30

A. Blessings and curses, Chs. 27 – 28
B. Repentance and return, Chs. 29 – 30

---

[270] WILLIAM MACDONALD, *Believer's Bible Commentary: Old and New Testaments*, ed. ARTHUR FARSTAD, Thomas Nelson, 1995, pp. 202-203.

IV. Personal Concerns: Moses Looks Up, Chs. 31 – 34

A. A new leader, Ch. 31
B. A new song, Ch. 32
C. A new blessing, Ch. 33
D. A new home, Ch. 34'.[271]

'I. Remembering God's blessings, Chs. 1. 1 – 5. 33

1. God led them, Chs. 1. 1 – 3. 29
2. God came to them, Ch. 4. 1-43
3. God taught them, Ch. 4. 44 – 5. 33

II. Responding to God's goodness, Chs. 6 – 11

1. Loving God, Ch. 6
2. Obeying God, Ch. 7
3. Showing gratitude to God, Chs. 8. 1 – 10. 11
4. Fearing God, Ch. 10. 12 – 11. 32

III. Reviewing God's Word, Chs. 12. 1 – 26. 19

1. Worship and obedience, Chs. 12. 1 – 16. 17; 18. 9-22
2. Civil officials, Chs. 16. 18 – 17. 20
3. Offerings, Chs. 18. 1-8; 26. 1-19
4. Cities of refuge, Chs. 19; 21. 1-9
5. Waging war, Ch. 20
6. Miscellaneous laws, Chs. 21. 10 – 25. 19

IV. Renewing God's covenant, Chs. 27. 1 – 30. 20

---

[271] WARREN W. WIERSBE, *Expository Outlines of the Old Testament: Deuteronomy*, Zondervan, electronic edition, no pagination.

1. Obedience and disobedience, Chs. 27 – 28
2. The terms of the covenant, Chs. 29 – 30

V. Replacing God's servant, Chs. 31 – 34

1. Moses encourages his successor, Ch. 31. 1-13
2. Moses warns the nation, Ch. 31. 14 – 32. 52
3. Moses blesses the tribes, Ch. 33
4. Moses leaves the people, Ch. 34'.[272]

Others observe the parallelism of its chiastic structure:

'A. The Outer Frame: A Look Backward, Deut. 1–3
B. The Inner Frame: The Great Peroration, Deut. 4–11
C. The Central Core: Covenant Stipulations, Deut. 12–26
B[1]. The Inner Frame: The Covenant Ceremony, Deut. 27–30
A[1]. The Outer Frame: A Look Forward, Deut. 31–34'.[273]

Detailed content outline

Date and setting, Deut. 1. 1-5

First speech

- Historic Review = Call to enter the land and appointing of elders, 1. 6-21.
- Sending the Spies; the evil report; divine judgement due to their rebellion, vv. 22-46.

---

[272] WARREN W. WIERSBE, *Be Equipped*, 'Be' Commentary Series, Chariot Victor Publishing, 1999, pg. 9.
[273] DUANE L. CHRISTENSEN, *Word Biblical Commentary: Deuteronomy 1-21. 9*, Word Biblical Commentary, Vol. 6A, Word Inc., 2002, pg. xli; quoted in HALL, pg. 23.

- Passing through wilderness: through the land of Edom and Moab, 2. 1-12.
- End of first generation and passing by Ammonite territory, vv. 13-23.
- Rise of second generation with defeat of Sihon and Og, 2. 24 – 3. 22.
- God's refusal to permit Moses to enter the land, vv. 23-29.
- Charge to obey God's commands; reiteration of their position established at Horeb, 4. 1-14.
- Prohibition of idolatry stemming from greatness of God's character, vv. 15-40.
- Three cities of refuge on east side of Jordan River, vv. 41-43.
- Conclusion of first speech, vv. 44-49.

Second speech

- Recounting the giving of the Ten Commandments at Sinai, 5. 1-22.
- The people's fearful response to God's holy presence and the appointment of Moses as mediator, vv. 23-31.
- Charge to obey the Law, vv. 32-33.
- Charge to obey the Law based on the uniqueness of God's person at the true and living God, 6. 1-9.
- When they possess and prosper in the land, they are not to forget the Lord who saved them from Egypt and delivered them into Canaan, vv. 10-25.
- No agreement with Canaanites; fight them and be loyal to God, 7. 1-11.
- Physical blessings of fruitfulness based on loyalty to God, vv. 12-15.
- An assurance of their triumph over the Canaanites through their loyalty to the Lord, vv. 16-26.
- Remembrance of God's past provision in the wilderness, 8. 1-6.

- Looking forward to God's provision in the future, vv. 7-10.
- Warning not to forget God when they enter the land and prosper, vv. 11-20.
- God will destroy the giants and Canaanite nations for them, 9. 1-3.
- They should not arrogantly assume that it is because of their moral worth, vv. 4-6.
- Recounting their history of disobedience in the wilderness and Moses' intercession to save them from utter destruction, vv. 7-29.
- Ten Commandments re-given on new tablets, 10. 1-5.
- Appointing the Levites for divine service, vv. 6-9.
- Moses, Sinai, and the command to begin the long journey to the land, vv. 10-11.
- Call to obedience based on God's person and work for them, vv. 12-22.
- Charge to obey based on the remembrance of God's past judgements on Egypt and in the wilderness, 11. 1-9.
- The nature of Canaan = dependent on God's providence [rain], vv. 10-17.
- Charge to teach the law to the children, vv. 18-21.
- Promise of obedience leading to the conquest of the land, vv. 22-25.
- Obedience leads to blessing and disobedience leads to cursing, vv. 26-32.
- Destroy idolatrous shrines in the land and the prohibition against syncretism, 12. 1-4.
- Sacrifices are to be offered where God puts His name, vv. 5-14.
- Where to kill and eat meat in the land and with reference to where He puts His name, vv. 15-28.
- Charge against adopting the idolatry of the vanquished Canaanites, vv. 29-32.
- How to deal with false prophets, 13. 1-5.

- How to deal with family who suggest idolatry, vv. 6-11.
- How to deal with cities that suggest idolatry, vv. 12-18.
- Personal holiness prohibiting sharing or cutting, 14. 1-2.
- Personal holiness: clean and unclean foods, vv. 3-21.
- Personal holiness: tithing, vv. 22-29.
- Sabbatical year, God's blessings, and generosity towards the poor, 15. 1-11.
- Proper treatment of Hebrew slaves and their emancipation, vv. 12-18.
- Killing and eating first born of herd and flock, vv. 19-23.
- Feast of Passover and Unleavened Bread, 16. 1-8.
- Feast of weeks, vv. 9-12.
- Feast of Tabernacles, vv. 13-15.
- Three mandatory feasts: 1) Unleavened Bread 2) Weeks 3) Tabernacles, vv. 16-17.
- Appointing judges and officers and maintaining justice, vv. 18-20.
- Prohibition against idolatrous trees or pillars near the Lord's altar, vv. 21-22.
- Pure offerings and the punishment of idolatry = death penalty, 17. 1-7.
- Appellate judgement from priests and Levites, vv. 8-13.
- The establishment of a king who follows the Law, vv. 14-20.
- Provision for the priests and Levites, 18. 1-8.
- Rejection of idolatrous practices – including child sacrifice – of Canaanite nations, vv. 9-14.
- Promise of the Messiah-prophet and assurance of prophet's truthfulness, vv. 15-22.
- Establishment of cities of refuge in the land, 19. 1-13.
- Establishment of landmarks, v. 14.
- Law concerning witnesses – two or three required for conviction, vv. 15-21.
- Rules governing warfare, 20. 1-20.
- Law of unsolved murder, 21. 1-9.

- Law of female captives, vv. 10-14.
- Law of firstborn son's inheritance, vv. 15-17.
- Law of rebellious son, vv. 18-21.
- Curse associated with hanging on a tree, vv. 22-23.
- Law of lost property, 22. 1-4.
- Women shall not wear a man's garment, v. 5.
- Instruction regarding birds, their nests, and young, vv. 6-7.
- Parapet around house roof to prevent manslaughter, v. 8.
- Agriculture laws regarding mixed seed and missed animals, vv. 9-10.
- Laws regarding garments: 1) No woollen and linen 2) Tassel on four corners of garment, vv. 11-12.
- Laws regarding sexual morality: especially concerning virginity and engagement and against incest, vv. 13-30.
- Laws regarding who may enter the Lord's assembly, 23. 1-8.
- Laws regarding hygiene in the camp, vv. 9-14.
- Laws regarding social relationships, vv. 15-25.
- Laws concerning wives, 24. 1-5.
- Miscellaneous laws concerning pledges, kidnapping, leprosy, hired servants, proper treatment of strangers, children, and orphans, reaping harvest, etc., vv. 6-22.
- Judgement must be just, 25. 1-3.
- Don't muzzle ox when treading the corn, v. 4.
- Levirate marriage = brother raising seed for his brother, vv. 5-10.
- Judgement against woman who seizes man's genitals, vv. 11-12.
- Establishment of trustworthy weights and measures, vv. 13-16.
- Command to destroy Amalekites, vv. 17-19.
- Offering firstfruits and tithes after entering the land of their inheritance, 26. 1-15.
- Reaffirmation to keep commandments based on their status as God's people, vv. 16-19.

- Set up white stones with the Law on them and charge to obey, 27. 1-10.
- Curses pronounced on Ebal for disobedience, vv. 11-26.
- Blessings pronounced for obedience, 28. 1-14.
- Cursings and negative consequences of disobedience (God's judgement), vv. 15-68.

Third speech

- Renewed covenant between the Lord and Israel, 29. 1-29.
- Covenant stipulations calling them to obedience (receiving blessing and cursing), 30. 1-20.

Closing section

- Moses' successor Joshua, 31. 1-8.
- The Law is to be read every seven years, vv. 9-13.
- Inauguration of Joshua and prediction of Israel's rebellion, vv. 14-23.
- Book of the Law put in the Ark for preservation, vv. 24-29.
- The Song of Moses and its presentation to Israel, vv. 30-47.
- Moses is called to Nebo to preview the land, vv. 48-52.
- Moses' final blessing of Israel, 33. 1-29.
- The death and burial of Moses on Mount Nebo, 34. 1-7.
- Israel mourning for Moses, v. 8.
- Joshua as Moses' successor, v. 9.
- Moses' obituary, vv. 10-12.

4.   The Author and Date of the Book

Like the other books of the Pentateuch, Moses is identified throughout the Old and New Testaments as the author used by the Spirit of God's inspiration – see the sections on 'Author and Date' in

Leviticus and Numbers. The celebrated historian PHILIP SCHAFF sums up the matter this way:

'There is no man in the whole subsequent history of Israel, as far as we know, who could at all account for the peculiarities of the Pentateuch near so well as the great lawgiver, who is the central figure of the book. Ezra, for instance, to whom some ultra-critics assign the authorship, never was in Egypt nor in the wilderness, and lived in the reproductive period of reconstruction or restoration of the theocracy founded by Jehovah through Moses centuries before. Thus from various sides we are led to feel not only that Moses has written the Pentateuch, but also that he was the only one who could have written it: and the objections have so much the less power, as a Mosaic authorship by no means excludes either the use of earlier documents or the addition of later notes'.[274]

5.   Important Themes in the Book

A. God's oneness and uniqueness.
B. The Lord's covenant loyalty to His people – divine faithfulness.
C. The exclusivity of the true and living God against idolatry.
D. Compassion and justice in the land.
E. Obedience leading to blessing, and disobedience leading to cursing.
F. Remembering God's law.
G. God's sovereignty and grace demonstrated through Israel's history.
H. Moses' role as preacher, shepherd, and mediator.

---

[274] PHILIP SCHAFF, ed., *A Dictionary of the Bible: Including Biography, Natural History, Geography, Topography, Archæology, and Literature*, American Sunday-School Union, 1880, pg. 670.

I. Israel as an example of God's goodness on display to the nations.
J. Holiness based on a relationship with the Lord.

KALLAND's summary of Deuteronomy's portrayal of God is worth remembering:

'God in Deuteronomy is personal, eternal, omnipotent, sovereign, purposeful, loving, holy, and righteous. The knowledge of his person and will is communicated by propositional, directive, exhortative, informative, and predictive revelation. No other God exists, though cognizance is taken of the gods believed in by other nations. The most important element of subjective theology in Deuteronomy is that of the absolutely unqualified, total commitment of the people to the Lord. Nothing less is acceptable. No dissimulation, no assimilation, no syncretism with other gods or religions or religious practices are to be tolerated. The people belong to the Lord alone. He is the absolute – though benevolent – sovereign, whose people uniquely and completely belong to him'.[275]

6. The Contents of the Book

The defining power of history – Deuteronomy chapter 1 to chapter 3 verse 29

Content outline

- Introduction with reference to Sihon and Og's defeat, Deut. 1. 1-4.
- The Lord's charge to Israel to possess the land, vv. 5-8.
- Judges are appointed to ensure righteous treatment within the nation of Israel, vv. 9-18.

---

[275] KALLAND, *Expositor's Bible Commentary: Deuteronomy*, no pagination.

- Arrival at Kadesh Barnea and charge to possess the land, vv. 19-21.
- The people's requested reconnaissance mission in the land and its aftermath, vv. 22-25.
- Israel's disbelieving rebellion, vv. 26-28.
- Moses' exhortation to trust the Lord, vv. 29-33.
- The Lord's judgement against the unbelieving generation – with the promised reward for Caleb and Joshua, vv. 34-40.
- The people's remorse and ill-fated invasion attempt, coupled with the Lord's rebuke; consequently, they remain at Kadesh, vv. 41-46.

[Note: Chapter 2 to chapter 3 verse 11 comprise the thirty-eight years of wandering in the wilderness.]

- The Lord's instructions regarding Edom and Israel's journey to their territory, Deut. 2. 1-8.
- The Lord's instructions regarding Moab, Israel's journey to their territory, and reference back to previous inhabitants of their territory, vv. 9-12.
- Thirty-eight years of wandering, followed by crossing Moabite and Ammonite territory, vv. 13-23.
- The Lord defeats Sihon and gives his territory to the Israelites, vv. 24-37.
- The Lord defeats Og and gives his territory to the Israelites, Deut. 3. 1-11.
- Sihon's and Og's lands are given to Reuben, Gad, and the half tribe of Manasseh; Joshua is given encouragement based on the defeat of these kings, vv. 12-22.
- Moses asks to enter the land, God refuses and tells him to encourage Joshua in preparation for the conquest of the land, vv. 23-29.

Chapters 1 to 3 look back to Israel's recent history over the past forty years; chapter 4 then builds upon that narrative, offering Moses' exhortation to the nation. This is a wise technique, using God's works in the past to offer meaning and guidance for the present. One must not forget that the Lord is unfolding the drama of the ages, as He works out mankind's destiny for our good and for His glory, Eph. 1. 11. He wanted Israel to remember where they came from and what that taught them about God. The setting is significant; they are on the edge of the Promised Land – as opposed to in it. They tarried there because of their own past failure. As SHEARMAN explains: 'Because of unbelief and hardened hearts, they had wasted valuable years in unintentioned wanderings. Instead of *walking* in God's ways they had *wandered* and a whole generation perished in the wilderness. We either walk with God, loving His ways, or we wander aimlessly without Him; see Eph. 5. 15-16'.[276] Now a new generation had arisen, and, in keeping with His promise, the Almighty would lead them into His inheritance. But first He would remind them of His faithfulness, despite their frequent mistakes and provocations in the wilderness.

More than a pep talk

The discourse is dated 'After he had slain Sihon the king of the Amorites, which dwelt in Heshbon, and Og the king of Bashan, which dwelt at Astaroth in Edrei', Deut. 1. 4. Thus the history lesson takes place after two notable victories by the Lord. This speaks auspiciously of good things to come in the conquest, if Israel will just trust and rely on Him! Furthermore, the land belongs to God, and He wants them to live there as His tenants.[277] The right to live in it and

---

[276] A. T. SHEARMAN, 'Mar. 19th: Wilderness Wanderings, Deuteronomy 1. 1-8, 19-46', in *Day by Day through the Old Testament*, pg. 94 [italics original].

[277] The word 'possess' in verse 8 refers to this divine 'inheritance', for it implies that God already owns the land and may thus give it to whomsoever He pleases. As MERRILL unpacks it: 'That it was theirs by right and not by might is clear from the verb "take possession" (v. 8), for in context of the covenant promise the Heb. *yāraš* ("take possession of") connotes inheritance.[6] Yahweh the Great King owns all the earth, and it is his to bestow upon his peoples as he wishes. His people, therefore, were not about to take the land of other people but to receive the land as a gift from its

remain there stems from His pleasure in His people, 29. 14-28, and is rooted in His oath[278] to their ancestors, 1. 8.

Moses exults over their size, but remembers the personal strain this brought to him as a leader; consequently, the Almighty graciously appointed judges to administer justice and assist him, vv. 9-18. Three categories of leaders were established, BLOCK explains:

'Continuing his pattern of triads, Moses identifies the officials who were chosen with three expressions, vv. 13, 15: (a) "Leading men" (*rā'šîm*) refers to those who bear responsibility for the well-being of a social group; (b) "commanders" (*śārîm*) refers to military leaders within specific spheres of jurisdiction; (c) "tribal officials" (*šōṭerîm lešibtêkem*) refers to a literate group called upon to record decisions or to muster the troops . . . The vocabulary and pattern of organization suggest that Israel was structured socially as a military camp; they were "the Lord's divisions", Exod. 12. 41; lit., "the hosts of Yahweh"'.[279]

These men were to be respected, trustworthy, and wise; thereby earning the confidence of their people. As MERRILL writes:

'The necessary attributes were that they be wise, understanding, and respected, v. 13. The first of these qualifications is expressed

---

divine owner, coming into their own rightful claim as vassals who work the royal estate of the Lord their God, cf. 1. 39; 3. 20; 10. 11; Josh. 1. 15; 21. 43'.[7]
[Fn. 6: A. D. H. MAYES, *Deuteronomy*, NCBC, Eerdmans, 1979, pp. 120-21. Fn. 7: N. LOHFINK, "ירַשׁ *yāraš*," etc. *TDOT* 6, pp. 384-85.]
EUGENE H. MERRILL, *Deuteronomy*, The New American Commentary, Vol. 4, Broadman & Holman Publishers, 1994, pg. 68. See also the use of the word 'inherit' in Deuteronomy chapter 1 verse 38.
[278] 'Sware' in verse 8 translates a word meaning 'an oath' or 'promise', NKJVmg., NIV, and NET have this latter meaning; see also BROWN, DRIVER, and BRIGGS, pg. 989.
[279] BLOCK, pg. 64.

by the common Hebrew word *ḥōkmâ*, a term suggesting capability in practical matters, here ability in civil and military affairs, cf. v. 15. The juxtaposition of this word with *nābon* ("understanding"), a synonym in many passages ... might best be rendered here as a hendiadys, 'very wise' or the like. The third adjective, "respected", derives from a verb meaning "to know". That is, these leaders must be well known to the community and, having passed the test of close scrutiny, end up being respected by it'.[280]

Obviously character counts a great deal in Israelite leadership. These respected and capable men were commanded to administer true and impartial judgements towards Jews and Gentiles alike, Deut. 1. 16-17.

On to Kadesh Barnea: missed opportunities

After traversing 'the great and terrible wilderness', v. 19, the oasis of Kadesh Barnea must have been a welcome sight to the nation. They were now invited to take possession of the land. Prior to the invasion, however, the Israelites wanted intelligence regarding the land and the opposition that they would face. The parallel account in Numbers chapter 13 speaks of the spies as being sent by the Lord, Num. 13. 1-3, but this is easily harmonized with the details in Deuteronomy chapter 1. They desired more information, Moses asked God, and He mercifully acquiesced in an effort to build their faith. The sight of this fertile land with its impressive fruit was meant to give them an augmented desire for the inheritance, as well as to demonstrate the truthfulness of God's past description. They could trust the One who promised to give them the 'land flowing with milk and honey', Exod. 3. 8. Accordingly, Moses urged them to 'fear not neither be discouraged', Deut. 1. 21.[281] Sadly, they rebelled[282] instead, and paid

---

[280] MERRILL, pg. 69.
[281] These Hebrew words – *awrats* STRONG'S #6206 and *chathath* #2865 – are linked together to encourage God's people nine times in the Old Testament:

204

the price for their disloyal unbelief, vv. 34-37. Though he did not share their unbelief, Moses also missed the land, Num. 20. 12-13 – something that, circumstantially, would not have happened had they begun the conquest immediately after the spies' return, as God intended, Deut. 1. 37. Instead, they were consigned to the desert for more than thirty-eight years, 2. 14, 46.[283]

Deut. 1. 21; 31. 8; Josh. 8. 1; Jer. 30. 10; 46. 27; Ezek. 2. 6; 3. 9; 1 Chr. 22. 13; 28. 20. Moses adds 'neither be afraid' – *yarel* STRONG'S #3372 – in Deuteronomy chapter 1 verse 29. This latter word means 'to tremble', 'fear', 'be in terror', or sometimes 'reverence'. It is used to describe Adam's terror of God after his disobedience in Eden, Gen. 3. 10. It bears both senses of 'terror' and 'reverence' in Jonah chapter 1 verses 5, 10, and 16. See WILHELM GESENIUS and SAMUEL PRIDEAUX TREGELLES, *Gesenius' Hebrew and Chaldee Lexicon to the Old Testament Scriptures*, Logos Bible Software, 2003, pg. 364; WILLIAM D. MOUNCE, *Mounce's Complete Expository Dictionary of Old & New Testament Words*, Zondervan, 2006, pg. 244. Clearly, in the Lord's estimation they had no cause to tremble on the edge of the land.

[282] MERRILL explains the technical language signifying rebellion in Deuteronomy chapter 1 verse 26, saying: 'For Israel to rebel against the Lord was tantamount to covenant violation, for in the nature of such arrangements complete compliance and subservience was expected of the vassal partner. In fact, the verb used here (*mārâ*) to express rebellion, when accompanied by . . . "rebel against the mouth of Yahweh", regularly expresses violation of specific commandments of the Lord, cf. Deut. 1. 43; 9. 23; Josh. 1. 18; 1 Sam. 12. 14'. MERRILL, pg. 75.

[283] In their respective commentaries, both MERRILL and BLOCK point out the repetitive nature of the wilderness wanderings: 'The staccato and repetitive way in which the Hebrew refers to this period, "You settled in Kadesh many days, according to the days which you settled", v. 46, is designed to show the wearisome monotony of that lost era of Israel's history . . . All that can be said about the sojourn at Kadesh is that they stayed there'. MERRILL, pg. 88; 'Moses' observation that they milled around in circles for many days in the vicinity of Seir represents a classic understatement, for those days turned out to be 13,880 days. During these thirty-eight years, cf. v. 14, the Israelites made no progress whatsoever toward the fulfillment of the mission on which they had embarked when they came out of Egypt. Yahweh had one primary goal for their desert wanderings – to get rid of that rebellious

generation, vv. 14-16. For almost four decades Israel was a death camp, a walking mortuary, in which the dominant sound was the death wail. The irony is inescapable. So long as they were slaves in Egypt, Israel's population mushroomed; as soon as they were free, it shrank'. BLOCK, pg. 75.

[284] Here are two literary outlines showing the parallelism of Deuteronomy chapter 2:

'A Summons to journey northward to land beyond Edom, 2. 2-3.
B You are to pass through the territory of the children of Esau, 2. 4.
C Summons not to contend with children of Esau, 2. 5-6.
D A look backward – provision for forty years in the wilderness, 2. 7.
E Travel: "we" section – from Seir to the wilderness of Moab, 2. 8.
X Summons not to contend with Moab, 2. 9-12.
E´ Travel: "we" section – crossing the Zered Valley 2. 13-14a.
D´ A look backward – a generation of warriors dead 2:14b–16.
C´ Summons not to contend with children of Lot, Moab, and Ammon, 2. 17-21.
B´ The children of Esau dispossessed the Horites in times past, 2. 22.
A´ Summons to cross the Arnon and to battle against Sihon, 2. 23-25.
. . .

A Journey northward from Seir, 2. 2-3.
B The children of Esau in Seir fear you, so be careful, 2. 4.
C Do not contend with Edom – I have given them Mount Seir, 2. 5-6.
X The journey from Seir to the wilderness of Moab, 2. 7-8.
C´ Do not contend with Moab – I have given Ar to them, 2. 9.
B´ Moab dispossessed the Emim, 2. 10-11.
A´ The inhabitants of Seir dispossessed the Horites, 2. 12.
A The crossing of the Wadi Zered, 2. 13.
B It was thirty-eight years from Kadesh to the crossing of the Zered, 2. 14a.
C A generation of warriors has perished, 2. 14b-16.
X Summons not to contend with the children of Lot, 2. 17-22.
C´ The Avvim were displaced by the Caphtorim, 2. 23.
B´ Summons to cross over the Wadi Arnon to war against Sihon, 2. 24.
A´ YHWH will spread the fear of Israel in the land, 2. 25'. CHRISTENSEN, pp. 40-42.

The various encounters with the nations that form Canaan's eastern border demonstrate God's sovereignty over kingdoms and the merciful way that He instructed His people to conduct themselves in these meetings.

For instance, Israel first encountered Esau's descendants, the Edomites, and had a heated exchange, Num. 20. 14-21, which ended in Jacob's progeny having to bypass the territory of their distant cousins. In contrast, Deuteronomy chapter 2 looks at things from the perspective of the Lord, who raises up kingdoms and puts them down when He wills.[285] What is more, He deals with all nations and gives light to them at different times in history. Esau's line was allotted certain territory by the Almighty, Josh. 24. 4; consequently, He commanded Israel not to 'meddle'[286] with them nor with Lot's descendants, the Ammonites, Deut. 2. 9, 19.

Despite the prohibition against harming the neighbouring nations, there is much to encourage Israel in this passage, in view of their coming conquest of Canaan and its inhabitants. First of all, Moses reminds them that God already removed giants to make room for the peoples on the east side of the Jordan River, vv. 20-23.[287] Secondly, he

---

[285] GORDON McCONVILLE, 'Deuteronomy', *New Bible Commentary: 21st Century Edition*, ed. D. A. CARSON, InterVarsity Press, 1994, pg. 203.

[286] There is a martial nuance in the word, as some translations demonstrate: 'attack', JND; 'engage them in battle', NRSV; 'provoke them to war', NIV. Others are slightly less warlike, but still imply conflict: 'contend' ASV, RSV, ESV; 'provoke' NAS, NET. G. A. SMITH defines it thus: 'In its causative form the Heb. verb means *to stir up*, e.g., strife, Prov. 15. 18, etc.; here the reflex. form is to *excite oneself* against another, to *quarrel* with them. In the [Pentateuch] found only in this chapter, vv. 9, 19, 24'. SMITH, pg. 31 [brackets mine; italics original].

[287] This shows that Israel was not going to wantonly displace Canaanite peoples in some sort of imperialistic jihad. 'The earth is the Lord's and the fullness thereof', Ps. 24. 1, and He gives its territory to whomever He pleases. They acted as His instrument in judging wicked peoples, who

refers back to their dramatic victories over Sihon of the Amorites, vv. 24-37, and Og of Bashan, 3. 1-11. If the Lord displaced these fearsome historical powers, then surely He would empower Israel to vanquish their contemporary foes in the land. He already had distributed their lands to Reuben, Gad, and the half tribe of Manasseh, vv. 12-17.

A bittersweet time

The Bible records Moses' impassioned and pitiable plea to the Lord at this juncture: 'And I besought the Lord at that time, saying, O Lord God, thou hast begun to shew thy servant thy greatness, and thy mighty hand: for what God is there in heaven or in earth, that can do according to thy works, and according to thy might? I pray thee, let me go over, and see the good land that is beyond Jordan, that goodly mountain, and Lebanon', vv. 23-25. Naturally, he wants to explore the land of the inheritance firsthand, but, due to his past disobedience,[288] the Lord forbids it, Num. 20. 7-13. As MAXWELL notes: 'In this day of independence, in which self-expression and personal opinion are

---

systematically and repeatedly – over four centuries – rejected His light, Gen. 15. 16-21; Lev. 18. 25-30. In fact, they did not aggressively pursue conflict with Edom, Moab, or Ammon. Sihon fell prey to his own hubris. In refusing their overtures towards peace, he set himself up for destruction, Deut. 2. 26-30. As McCONVILLE explains: 'Israel's offer of peace to Sihon, vv. 26-29, shows that he brought his fate on himself by his own attitude. Deuteronomy's telling of the story makes a contrast between Edom, Moab and Ammon on the one hand and Sihon on the other, to emphasize Sihon's guilt. When we read that the Lord *had made his spirit stubborn and his heart obstinate*, v. 30, we are reminded of Pharaoh, Exod. 8. 15, 32. The phrase does not mean that Sihon (or Pharaoh) really had no choice. Rather, it is a way of saying that they really did oppose God in his plans for his people'. McCONVILLE, pg. 204 [italics original].

[288] MOODY'S observation on disobedience is appropriate in this situation: 'There will be no peace in any soul until it is willing to obey the voice of God'. D.L. MOODY, *Short Talks,* Moody Press, 1900, pg. 36.

highly valued, as God's children we must walk in submission to Him. Our only responsibility is to be obedient to Him, regardless of the outside pressure'.[289] God refuses to overlook Moses' serious failure, and commands him to be silent regarding his punishment; nevertheless, in grace the Lord permits him to view the land from the peak of Pisgah. It is also grace that Moses did stand in the land later, but this was on glorified ground with Christ, Matt. 17. 3.

Exhortations based on Israel's history – chapter 4

It is interesting that Moses' charge begins with a command to not add to or take away from the Lord's word, v. 2, for this exact fault had been his life's greatest mistake, Num. 20. 11-12. He went beyond the divine instructions in striking the rock and verbally abusing the Israelites and taking credit for their provision. This sin barred him from leading them into the Promised Land. Thus, as the new generation approaches the land, they are warned to strictly obey God's commandments and 'lean not unto . . . [their] own understanding', Prov. 3. 5.

Content outline of Deuteronomy chapter 4

- Moses' opening charge, vv. 1-2.
- Warning based on Israel's unfaithfulness at Baal Peor, vv. 3-4.
- Warning based on Israel's intimacy with the Lord, vv. 5-14.
- Warning against idolatry, vv. 15-19.
- Charge based on Israel's deliverance from Egypt, v. 20.
- Warning based on Moses' punishment and the Lord's holy character, vv. 21-24.
- Warning of Israel's future unfaithfulness, the captivity that follows, and the Lord's faithfulness to His covenant, vv. 25-31.

---

[289] JOHN C. MAXWELL, *The Preacher's Commentary Series, Volume 5: Deuteronomy*, Thomas Nelson, 1987, pp. 76-77.

- The Lord's uniqueness and His verbal revelation to Israel, followed by a charge to keep His statutes and commandments, vv. 32-40.
- Establishment of cities of refuge on the Jordan River's eastside, vv. 41-43.
- Summary verses closing the message, vv. 44-49.

This exhortation draws upon the Lord's character, covenant, and past dealings with Israel to warn the nation of the dangers of departing from Him. He is faithful to His promises and will continue to help them; if they rebel, however, their own history assures them that the Holy One will chasten them for it. Therefore, they must follow Him into the new land, eschewing any other allegiance such as that to false gods.

The passage also calls Israel to obey His specifically revealed will. The repetition of terms like 'statutes', 'judgments', and 'commands' makes this evident.[290] They are called to follow God's law, and must not turn aside to their own sinful patterns of behaviour.

Moses' second speech, chapters 5-28

Moses' next speech builds upon the former discourse: in chapter 4 he exhorted them to obey the statutes and judgements; beginning in chapter 5 he explains the exact content of this divinely provided legislation. The second speech divides into two halves: 1. Chapters 5

---

[290] These three terms frequently occur together in the scriptures: nineteen verses with all three words: Lev. 26. 15; Num. 27. 11; Deut. 4. 5, 14; 5. 31; 6:1, 20; 7. 11; 8. 11; 11. 1; 26. 16, 17; 30. 16; 1 Kgs. 2. 3; 6. 12; 8. 58; 9. 4; 2 Chr. 7. 17; Mal. 4. 4; plus other combinations: 'statutes & judgements': Lev. 26. 46; Deut. 5. 1; 11. 32; 12. 1; 1 Chr. 22. 13; 'statutes' and 'commands': Neh. 9. 13; 'judgements' and 'commands': Lev. 26. 15; Num. 36. 13; Deut. 1. 16; 1 Chr. 28. 7; Neh. 9. 29; Ps. 119. 66'. [TIMOTHY A. GABRIELSON, 'Law', ed. DOUGLAS MANGUM ET AL., in *Lexham Theological Wordbook*, Lexham Bible Reference Series, Lexham Press, 2014, electronic edition, no pagination.]

to 11 are mainly exhortational preaching; 2. Chapters 12 to 28 are more formal and spell out the covenant obligations of the Israelites, concluding with a section on blessing and cursing.[291] Moses' shepherd heart is manifested throughout the second speech; moreover, the Lord's love for His people is repeatedly expressed in it.[292]

The second speech begins with the call to 'Hear, O Israel',[293] Deut. 5. 1 – the first of five occurrences of this phrase in the book of Deuteronomy.[294] The Sinai covenant is rehearsed in their ears, which was made with their fathers as well as with them, v. 3. God spoke to them from the fire, and so Moses acted as their intercessor, vv. 23-27, bringing them the Lord's word and covenant. This chapter highlights the ten commandments afresh; it is legislation that forms the basis of their conduct in the inheritance that the Lord was providing for them. It begins with commands that emphasize the unique identity of the true God and His supreme claims over the idols of the land, Deut. 5. 6-11.

The Lord is described as 'jealous', v. 9, employing a Hebrew word that is exclusively used of Him in its six Old Testament

---

[291] BLOCK, pp. 153-154.

[292] As HOUSE maintains: 'Each command helps God explain how much he cares about every minute issue that affects the beloved chosen people. Each stipulation strengthens the covenant relationship between the Creator and the elect nation'. HOUSE, pg. 176; likewise, G. A. SMITH writes of the pervasive character of love in Deuteronomy: 'But nowhere else in the Pentateuch has the love of God to man such free course as in Deuteronomy; and nowhere else is man's love to God invoked, except once in Exodus chapter 20 verse 6 . . . These two, God's love to man and man's love to God, are everywhere in Deuteronomy'. SMITH, pg. xxvii.

[293] The concept of hearing divine revelation is a major theme of the book of Deuteronomy. E.g. Deut. 4. 33, 36; 5. 25, 27; 13. 11; 18. 15-16, 19; 19. 20; 21. 21; 29. 4, 19; 30. 12, 13, 17; 31. 11-13, 28, 30; 32. 1, 44; 33. 7.

[294] The others are in Deut. 6. 3-4; 9. 1; 20. 3.

occurrences.[295] The term does not mean that He is 'envious', but rather that He is zealous for His own honour and glory. He has supreme authority and worth and guards these qualities against man's sinful diminution of His person.[296] What is more, true love always contains an element of holy jealousy. The best life is the one that submits to the Lord's will and seeks an ongoing relationship with Him, John 17. 3. God does not want His children to be polluted by idolatry and the accompanying rites that corrupt their devotees; therefore, regarding such vanities He instructs them not to 'bow down to them nor serve them', v. 9. One writer relates the significance of these phrases:

'The picture which "bowing to someone and serving" evoked to the Israelite was a well-defined one. It would evoke the scene of a vassal approaching the throne of his overlord, prostrating before him and stating: "I am your servant". It was the scene of a man losing his independence, of a man forced to submission, of a man entering the new status of vassality. The prostration symbolized and effectively began the status of dependency'.[297]

The Israelites had one master, the Lord, and they were redeemed to serve and prostrate themselves to Him alone. He is merciful and loyal

---

[295] *Qana* – Strong's #7067; it occurs six times in five verses and always refers to God: Exod. 20. 5; 34. 14 [2x]; Deut. 4. 24; 5. 9; 6. 15. '[It is] used of God as not bearing any rival; the severe avenger of departure from himself' WILHELM GESENIUS and SAMUEL PRIDEAUX TREGELLES, pg. 735.
[296] W. E. VINE, MERRILL F. UNGER, and WILLIAM WHITE JR., *Vine's Complete Expository Dictionary of Old and New Testament Words*, Nelson, 1996, pp. 124-125.
[297] J. N. M. WIJNGAARDS, 'You shall not bow down to them or serve them', *Indian Journal of Theology*, Vol. 18:2-3 (April-September, 1969), pg. 185; electronic edition accessed here:
http://www.biblicalstudies.org.uk/pdf/ijt/18-2-3_180.pdf.

towards them, showing them abiding loving-kindness. In response, they ought to reciprocate His loving mercy with similar devotion.[298] The Lord's name is also not to be taken 'in vain', Deut. 5. 11. BLOCK explains that this goes beyond common profanity or scatological speech:

> 'Literally the Hebrew translates, "You shall not bear/carry the name of Yahweh your God emptily". The idiom derives from the ancient practice of branding slaves with the name of their owner . . . To bear the name of Yahweh means to claim him as one's owner and to accept the role of representing him, cf. Isa. 44. 5. At issue is Israel's status and function as the people of Yahweh. They may not claim Yahweh as their covenant Lord and then live as if they belonged to Baal . . . The consequences of misrepresenting Yahweh are declared only in the vaguest of terms: these Yahweh will not acquit (NIV "hold guiltless")'.[299]

This command tells the Israelites to honour the name by which they are called by obeying the Lord. They must possess the reality of their life in Jehovah and not merely falsely profess to be His people.

The fourth command reiterates the Sabbath, which provides rest for Israel, but also owns the supreme claims of the Lord as creator and redeemer, Exod. 20. 11; Deut. 5. 15. The other six commandments

---

[298] 'Mercy' translates the word *hesed* – Strong's #2617. MERRILL declares its importance: 'No term is more theologically significant than *hesed*, translated in the NIV here as "love" . . . It speaks of God's unmerited favour by which he elects people to covenant relationship and on the basis of which he extends all its blessings . . . Within that relationship, however, *hesed* is part of a reciprocal process, a disposition conditioned upon the love (*'āhăbâ*) and obedience of those who owe them, v. 10'. MERRILL, pg. 148. Based on its usage in Hosea, G. A. SMITH defines it as 'more than an affection; it is a relation and duty better rendered by *loyal love*'. SMITH, pg. 112 [italics original].
[299] BLOCK, pg. 163.

focus on horizontal relations between man and his fellow man, vv. 16-21. All of 'the 10 words' – as the Jews call them – set Jehovah forth as the moral lawgiver and the ultimate arbiter of truth. Ethics are derived from His character and will.[300] Interestingly, the New Testament reaffirms nine of the ten commandments for believers – all but the Sabbath are still valid moral expressions.[301] Ceremonially, the Sabbath points forward to a greater spiritual and eternal rest provided by Christ, Heb. 4. 1-11.

The horizontal commands begin with the most fundamental human relationship: parents and their children, Deut. 5. 16. 'Honour' carries the thought of 'ascribing weight to' or 'treating with respect'.[302]

---

[300] Deuteronomy chapter 5 verses 28 to 33 demonstrate that the Lord longed for this generation – and subsequent generations – of Israelites to obey Him so that they might prosper in the land. He revealed His statutes, judgements, and commandments to Moses so that they would obey and enjoy His blessings. As one author comments: 'These words reveal God's desire, which is for Israel to obey and prosper, 5. 28-29. Just as God reveals personal principles and emotions by offering commands in concrete, understandable language, so must Israel reveal what love and commitment reside in their hearts by offering total allegiance to God, 5. 30-33. Such commitment requires careful adherence to and consistent walking in faith according to God's word, 5. 32-33'. HOUSE, pg. 176.

[301] That is not to say that believers are under the law. They are neither under the law for justification nor for sanctification. Law means command plus obedience equals blessing; while disobedience brings cursing. Romans chapters 6 to 8 and Galatians chapters 3 to 5 demonstrate that believers are under grace and obey the Lord in the power of the Holy Spirit – 'walking in the Spirit' as Romans 8 and Galatians 5 describe it. Having said that, murder, adultery, idolatry, and the like are still immoral activities. The law depicts the nature of sin and therefore serves as an example for us.

[302] It also means: '[T]he way one treats a master, Mal. 1. 6, an envoy of Yahweh, Judg. 13. 7, or God himself, 1 Sam. 2. 30; Ps. 50. 15. Its opposite is represented by the verb qallēl ("to treat with contempt, to denigrate", Exod. 21. 17; Lev. 20. 9, often translated as "to curse". Echoes of this command are heard in 2 Sam. 10. 3 (= 1 Chr. 19. 3) and Mal. 1. 6'. BLOCK, fn. 28, pg. 165

Mothers and fathers are the first authority that one knows in one's life. To dishonour or disobey them establishes a pattern of behaviour that often leads to problems with other authorities – especially with God Himself. The Lord Jesus considered it a grievous sin to violate this rule and cited it as proof of the Pharisees' hypocrisy, Mark 7. 9-13. He also demonstrated that the other horizontal commands extended to one's thought life as well as one's actions, Deut. 5. 17-21; Matt. 5. 21-22, 27-30, 33-37. God's righteous standards have not diminished, and that is why people desperately need the Saviour, Rom. 8. 3-4.

The manifesto of the one true God, chapters 6-8

DANIEL BLOCK lays out the content of these chapters this way: 'While [Deuteronomy chapter] 6 [verses] 4 [to] 5 embodies the central idea, in the rest of chapters 6 through 8 Moses concretizes his understanding of unreserved love for Yahweh with a series of tests of devotion that life in the Promised Land will present'.[303] The famous 'shema'[304] – 'Hear,[305] O Israel' – calls Israel to recognize the

---

[brackets mine].

[303] BLOCK, pg. 180; brackets mine.

[304] The Hebrew verb *shema*, Strong's #8085, means 'hear' with the implication of obedience. As MERRILL says: 'It is the expression of the essence of all of God's person and purposes in sixteen words of Hebrew text', MERRILL, pg. 162. To modern observant Jews this forms the basis of their central confession, as another writer explains: 'These verses introduce the theme of heartfelt obedience to Yahweh, the God of Israel, and have become the basis for one of the most important rituals in Judaism, the reading of the Shema'. BRUCE E. WILLOUGHBY, 'A Heartfelt Love: An Exegesis of Deuteronomy 6. 4-19', in *Restoration Quarterly* 20 (1977), pp. 73-74.

[305] The concept of hearing God's word is vitally important for conversion and the subsequent life of a believer. Two historic Bible teachers unpack this with clarity and eloquence: 'There must be an individual hearing of the truth, and a reception of it for yourself in your own heart. Then, too, you must hear the truth *penitently*. You must be as that Mary, who when she

uniqueness of the true and living God and His claims on them as His people, 6. 4-5. The greatness of His person demands corresponding total commitment on the part of the saints.[306] He wants complete allegiance stemming from a person's entire being, v. 5. Furthermore, the commands were to be passed along to succeeding generations and commemorated at home, on the road, and in one's own thought patterns, vv. 7-9.[307] In other words, their lives were meant to revolve around God and His word.

---

listened to the Word, must needs go and wash the feet of Jesus with her tears, and wipe them with the hairs of her head. There must be tears for your many sins, a true confession of your guilt before God. But above all you must hear it *believingly*. The Word must not be unto you as mere sound, but as matter of fact. You must be as Lydia, whose heart the Lord opened; or as the trembling gaoler, who believed on the Lord Jesus with all his house and was baptized forthwith. You must be as the thief, who could pray, "Lord, remember me", and who could believe the precious promise given, "Today shalt thou be with me in Paradise"'. C. H. SPURGEON, 'Preaching! Man's Privilege and God's Power', in *The New Park Street Pulpit Sermons*, Vol. 6, Passmore & Alabaster, 1860, pg. 491 [italics original].

'Each time we hear the Word of God preached we are personally addressed by Him. Then always our small self is directly confronted by His great Divine Self, and every such time is an hour of decision'. ERICH SAUER, *In the Arena of Faith*, Wm Eerdmans, 1974, pp. 167-168.

[306] The doctrine of monotheism is not treated as an abstract philosophical subject in the scriptures; instead it is a practical impetus to greater obedience on the part of the Israelites. As two contemporary authors note: '[N]owhere in the Old Testament does a monotheistic claim appear an argument for peering into the nature of God's essence. The purpose of monotheistic claims is more practical: to keep Israel from adopting other pagan deities instead of – or alongside of – their worship of the one true God. Old Testament monotheism is not a psychoanalysis of God's inner being'. PHILIP RYKEN and MICHAEL LEFEBVRE, *Our Triune God: Living in the Love of the Three-in-One*, Crossway Books, Kindle Edition, pg. 64.

[307] Sadly, later rabbis extrapolated physical rules from these instructions, creating *mezuzahs* – physical boxes containing written scripture that are posted beside observant Jews' doors – and *tefillin* – also called 'phylacteries', which are small boxes containing scripture that Jews wear on their arms or

Verses 10 to 15 go on to caution Israel against forgetting God when they possessed the land and enjoyed the prosperity of that land – blessings that flowed exclusively from divine largesse. It is an all too human tendency to forget the Lord who gives us all things, Rom. 1. 21, imagining instead that we are entitled to good things or that we have earned them by our own work. Enjoying the Lord's gracious goodness must never lead to ingratitude or forgetfulness of our creator and redeemer. They are also warned anew against the insidious peril of idolatry.

The Son of man using chapter 6

Verses 13 to 16 recur in the New Testament in two key passages that describe Satan's testing of the Lord Jesus in the wilderness, Matt. 4. 7; Luke 4. 12. Christ fought off the tempter's attacks by citing the book of Deuteronomy three times. This speaks volumes regarding the importance of memorizing and wielding God's word aright to fend off temptation.[308]

In context, 'Ye shalt not tempt the Lord your God, as ye tempted him in Massah' hearkens back to a historic time when the nation put Jehovah to the test. Exodus chapter 17 verse 7 summarizes this infraction by saying: 'And he called the name of the place Massah, and Meribah, because of the chiding of the children of Israel, and because they tempted the Lord, saying, Is the Lord among us, or not?' They were thirsty in the desert. Instead of asking the Lord to meet their needs, they petulantly demanded that He do something, implying that He and His spokesman Moses sadistically wanted them to suffer an excruciating death, vv. 3, 7. This was an absurd allegation that ran

---

foreheads during prayers. The Lord Jesus condemned such practices as exhibiting self-righteousness, Matt. 23. 1-12.
[308] See Ps. 119. 9; Eph. 6. 17; Heb. 4. 12.

counter to all of God's past dealings with them.[309] They demanded that the Lord act, thereby tempting Him. This was putting things exactly backwards: they were the servants; He was the master; yet they acted as if the Almighty were a celestial genie who existed to grant their every whim.

In contrast, the Lord Jesus refused to manipulate His Father into doing something merely to gratify personal desires. He could position Himself on the temple roof and jump off. Yet the Lord Jesus refused such base conduct and faithfully acted according to His Father's will – so much so that His words and deeds were the Father's, John 5. 19, 30; 14. 24. He is Jehovah's perfect servant, and, accordingly, during His earthly ministry He never tempted His master by manipulation or making demands.

Christ used Deuteronomy chapter 6 verses 13 to 14 to meet Satan's third test, Matt. 4. 8-10. He adamantly refused to break the first commandment; no glittering reward could induce the Son of Man to worship and serve anyone besides His Father. He would take the throne of the world only in keeping with His Father's timetable, Matt. 25. 31; Acts 1. 6-7. So often in the wilderness, Israel behaved like a rebellious son. The Lord Jesus was completely different, however, loving and serving God the Father every moment of His life on earth, John 8. 29.

Deuteronomy chapter 6 ends with a renewed charge to keep the Lord's commandments and to pass along the knowledge of their historic redemption from Egypt when their children ask about such obedience, Deut. 6. 17-25. Chapter 7 begins by looking towards the future conquest of the land by destroying the seven egregiously

---

[309] As MAXWELL remarks: 'The people who had insulted God by not trusting Him wanted for nothing! The Lord gave them food, clothing, and protection. He knew their path in the wilderness and for forty years He took care of them', MAXWELL, pg. 57.

wicked Canaanite nations. The chapter's content may be outlined in this manner:

- Instructions regarding the complete destruction of the seven nations; make no unequal yoke with them, Deut. 7. 1-5.
- Israel is chosen and holy according to the Lord's loving-kindness; therefore, they must keep His commandments, vv. 6-11.
- Israel's obedience leads to blessing and not cursing, vv. 12-15.
- Certain destruction of the Canaanite nations in spite of their numbers by the Lord's power; complete eradication of their gods and everything tainted by them, vv. 16-26.

Going forth to conquer

Having established the Lord's sovereignty and reaffirmed His covenant in chapters 5 to 6, in chapter 7 Moses now sets forth their dealings with the Canaanites:[310] Israel must destroy their wicked religions, reject their immoral practices, and remain distinct from them. This passage prescribes a truly just war to rid the land of peoples that were at a terminal stage of corruption. If God had left them to their own devices they would have no doubt corrupted themselves to the point of self-destruction – their practices of child sacrifice, incest, homosexuality, and ritual prostitution evidence this sad reality. Israel was to act towards them as a divine instrument of justice.

Israel was not selected for their natural advantages, vv. 1-11, but rather because of the Lord's electing grace. He chose them 'to be a special people', v. 6; other versions bring out their privileged position in strong language: 'to be a people for Himself, a special treasure', NKJV; 'to be a people for His own possession', ASV, RSV, NAS; 'to be a

---

[310] THOMPSON, pp. 143-144.

people for a possession', JND. This sentiment is echoed concerning the New Testament people of God, the church, in several passages, Titus 2. 14; 1 Pet. 2. 9. As His people, the Lord assured Israel of victory over the numerically intimidating Canaanite nations, Deut. 7. 1-2, 14-25. Their utter destruction is graphically depicted in strong terms throughout much of the chapter: 'the hornet', v. 20; 'drive out' and 'consume', v. 22; 'deliver them' and 'destroy them with a mighty destruction until they be destroyed', v. 23; 'destroy their name from under heaven' and 'there shall no man be able to stand before thee, until thou have destroyed them', v. 24, all demonstrate that their enemies would be completely devastated.

Yet the Lord also has another side: He is just and holy, but He is simultaneously loving, merciful, and gracious. That other side appears in statements such as verse 8, which says: 'the Lord loved you', and verse 9: 'Know therefore that the Lord thy God, he is God, the faithful God, which keepeth covenant and mercy with them that love him and keep his commandments to a thousand generations'. As WIERSBE writes:

'There's no conflict between the greatness of God and the grace of God, His transcendence and His immanence; for we can love the Lord and fear the Lord with the same heart, Pss. 2. 10-12; 34. 8-9. The fear of the Lord is a major theme in Deuteronomy, 6. 2, 13, 24; 10. 20; 14. 23; 17. 19; 31. 12, but so is the love of God for us, 7. 7; 10. 15; 23. 5, as well as our love for Him, 6. 5; 10. 12; 11. 1, 13, 22; 19. 9; 30. 6, 16, 20. The immature believer with a shallow theology sees a contradiction here, but the mature believer rejoices in the balance revealed in the Word: "God is love" and "God is light", 1 John 4. 8; 1. 5'.[311]

This loving Being promises Israel that He is 'in thy midst', Deut. 7. 21 JND; this guaranteed their victory against their enemies, as long as

---

[311] WIERSBE, pg. 40.

they trusted in Him. Verses 25 to 26 caution them in the strongest possible way against adopting the idols of their foes. As the *English Standard Version* renders verse 26: 'And you shall not bring an abominable thing into your house and become devoted to destruction like it. You shall utterly detest and abhor it, for it is devoted to destruction'.[312]

CHRISTENSEN notices another chiastic pattern of literary parallelism between chapter 7 verse 12 to chapter 11 verse 25:

'A When you obey, you will be blessed above all the peoples, 7. 12-26.
B Remember the lessons from the wanderings in the wilderness, 8. 1-20.
C As you enter the land remember your past rebellion, 9. 1-29.
X At that time YHWH spoke the Ten Words, 10. 1-7.
C´ At that time the Levites were set apart and the people spared, 10. 8-11.
B´ Love God and remember what he did for you in the wilderness, 10. 12-11. 9.
A´ The Promised Land – if you love God you will possess it, 11. 10-25'.[313]

This structure highlights the importance of obedience to the Lord, which inevitably leads to blessing. It also reminded them of their historical mistakes that cost them much blessing. The Holy Spirit uses history to teach and exhort His people for their future possession of the inheritance. Chapter 8 especially calls on Israel to remember, as SHEARMAN observes:

---

[312] G. A. SMITH explains some of the key Hebrew terms in verse 26: '*utterly detest . . . utterly abhor.* The latter verb is that of the noun *tō'ebah, abomination* . . . the former verb, *shikkeṣ,* with its noun, is also used with respect to what is ritually forbidden or unclean . . . e.g. Lev. 11. 10-13, 20, 23, 41-42', SMITH, pp. 116-117.
[313] CHRISTENSEN, pg. 158.

'Remember the pathway, v. 2.
Never forget God's provision, vv. 10-13.
Always remember God's power, vv. 14-18'.[314]

The chapter accentuates the wilderness wanderings as a testing experience for Israel, vv. 2, 16. The Lord used this desert period: 'to humble thee, *and* to prove thee, to know what *was* in thine heart, whether thou wouldest keep his commandments, or no. And he humbled thee, and suffered thee to hunger, and fed thee with manna, which thou knewest not, neither did thy fathers know; that he might make thee know that man doth not live by bread only, but by every *word* that proceedeth out of the mouth of the Lord doth man live', vv. 2-3. At the same time, it demonstrates the Lord's fatherly care and incomparable provision for them. 'Manna' means 'What is it?'; this is ironic, for they survived for almost four decades by eating something nutritious, yet personally unknown to them. He goes on to say: 'Thy raiment waxed not old upon thee, neither did thy foot swell, these forty years', v. 4. God provides for His people, Matt. 6. 31-34. MACKINTOSH expounds this truth beautifully:

'*They were shut up to God*. This is the one grand reality. Faith owns nothing real, nothing solid, nothing true, but the one true, living, eternal God. Nature might cast a longing look at the granaries of Egypt, and see something tangible, something substantial there: faith looks up to heaven and finds *all* its springs there. Thus it was with the camp in the desert, and thus it is with the Church in the world. There was not a single exigency, not a single contingency, not a single need of any sort whatsoever, for which the Divine Presence was not an all-sufficient answer. The

---

[314] A. T. SHEARMAN, 'Mar. 24th: A Good Memory, Deuteronomy 8. 1-20', in *Day by Day through the Old Testament*, ed. C. E. HOCKING and M. HORLOCK, Day by Day Series, Precious Seed, 1982, pg. 99. The wording is slightly altered to suit this context.

nations of the uncircumcised might look on and marvel; they might, in the bewilderment of blind unbelief, raise many a question as to how such a host could ever be fed, clothed, and kept in order. Most certainly they had no eyes to *see* how it could be done. They knew not Jehovah, the Lord God of the Hebrews; and therefore to tell them that He was going to undertake for that vast assembly would indeed seem like idle tales'.[315]

The Lord Jesus quoted this passage to meet Satan's first temptation.[316] Unlike Israel who often failed in their dependence on God in the wilderness, Exod. 16. 2-3, the Son of Man trusted His Father implicitly, and could not be induced – even under extreme circumstances – to act independently of His Father or question His perfect provision. Christ's food was His Father's will, which was spelled out in 'every word that proceedeth out of the mouth of God', Matt. 4. 4, and He would obey even though it meant tremendous mental, physical, and spiritual suffering, Phil. 2. 8.

Once more the Israelites are instructed not to forget the Lord who blesses them when they eventually come into the goodness of the land, Deut. 8. 11-20. At first glance, this may seem incongruous – how could they forget the One who did so much for them? Yet personal experience ought to teach every believer that we are capable of putting the Almighty out of mind similarly – especially in times of prosperity. For that reason, the word of God and physical reminders like baptism and the Lord's Supper are vital to remind us of what the Lord has done for us. As the hymn says: 'We'll praise Him for all that is past and trust Him for all that's to come'.[317]

---

[315] C. H. MACKINTOSH, *Genesis to Deuteronomy: Notes on the Pentateuch*, Loizeaux Brothers, 1972, pg. 433 [italics original].
[316] See Deut. 8. 3; Matt. 4. 4; Luke 4. 4.
[317] JOSEPH HART, 'How good is the God we adore'.

Content outline of chapter 9

- Facing the giants through the power of the consuming fire, vv. 1-3.
- God is not giving them the land because of their own righteousness, but rather because of the Canaanites' wickedness, vv. 4-6.
- Israel's rebellious character is revealed: they are stiff-necked, vv. 7-14.
- Moses' intercession for Israel and Aaron at Horeb in the matter of the golden calf, vv. 15-21.
- Further rebellion at Taberah, Massah, and Kibroth Hattaavah, vv. 22-24.
- The substance of Moses' intercession: The Lord must remember the covenant with the Patriarchs and defend His own reputation, vv. 25-29.

A chiastic breakdown accentuates Israel's historic rebellion:

'A Moses tells the people that YHWH will dispossess nations in the land, 9. 1-3.

B YHWH is not giving them the land because of their righteousness, 9. 4-5.

C As a stiff-necked people Israel provoked YHWH to anger, 9. 6-7.

D While Moses was on the mountain, the people acted corruptly, 9. 8-12.

E YHWH decided to destroy his stiff-necked people, 9. 13-14.

E´ Moses went down, saw the golden calf, and shattered the tablets, 9. 15-17.

D´ Moses prayed for the people and for Aaron on Mount Horeb, 9. 18-20.

C´ Moses crushed the golden calf the people had made, 9. 21.

B´ The people of Israel were rebellious from the first, 9. 22-25.

A′ Moses interceded for the people of Israel in times past, 9. 26-29′.[318]

Structurally, Deuteronomy chapter 9 is set in contrast to chapter 6 verse 4 to chapter 7 verse 11; thus the commandment to love God with the entirety of one's being is contrasted with Israel's frequent rebellions in this latter passage.[319] For the second time in this book, the Almighty's holiness is emphasized by the description 'a consuming fire', Deut. 9. 3; 4. 24; cf. Heb. 12. 29. The Lord was not giving Israel the land because of their moral rectitude or faithfulness. For example, chapter 9 verse 6 calls them 'a stiff necked people' – a term emphasizing their recalcitrance.[320] Moses uses positive and negative exhortations to remind the Israelites of their past sins, and their present need to obey the Lord, Deut. 9. 7-8. THOMPSON summarizes God's motivation in providing Canaan for Israel:

'Two factors operated, the righteousness of Yahweh and the unrighteousness of the people of Canaan. What the future might hold for Israel was in God's hands. Since she had been chosen to fulfil Yahweh's purpose, the fulfilment of his purpose would require a victory. However, Yahweh was sovereign and he might choose even the ungodly nations to fulfil his purposes at times, cf. Assyria in Isa. 10. 5, 13, 15; Babylon, Jer. 25. 9; 27. 6; Persia, Isa. 44. 28; 45. 1-6. The two reasons given here for the conquest of Canaan are the *wickedness of these nations*, cf. Gen. 15. 16, and

---

[318] CHRISTENSEN, pg. 179.
[319] CHRISTENSEN, pg. 178.
[320] 'The image is that of a draft animal that is unsubmissive to the rein or yoke and refuses to bend its neck to draw the load', NETmg.; The NKJVmg. has 'stubborn or rebellious'. G. A. SMITH compares this metaphor to Isaiah chapter 48 verse 4, saying: '*thou art obstinate, thy neck is an iron sinew*: the figure is of an animal refusing to turn in the direction his rider desires', SMITH, pg. 126 [italics original].

that he may confirm the word which the Lord swore to your fathers'.[321]

Throughout their repeated revolts, Moses faithfully acted as their intercessor before the Lord. On one occasion he even had to plead for his brother Aaron, Exod. 32. 11-14; Deut. 9. 20! If the people's high priest was carried away into idolatry, what standing could the people claim for themselves? As one commentator notes: 'How completely devoid of merit, therefore, and how dependent on the mercy of God was a people whose very High Priest had to be saved from death. The incident is mentioned here not necessarily in chronological order but because of the point that it makes in the context of a discussion on Israel's rebellion'.[322] CHRISTENSEN concurs that Israel was only there because of the Almighty's loving-kindness: 'The long history of Israel's perfidy underscores that they would not be standing in the plains of Moab to renew their covenant but for the grace of God'.[323]

Chapter 10 offers God's response to their waywardness: He reaffirmed the covenant and laid up its documents – 'two tablets of stone', v. 1 – in the ark of the covenant. Once again divine faithfulness and grace shine through the gloom of human unfaithfulness. He appointed a priesthood and their servants the Levites to maintain the covenant documents' location in the congregation, vv. 8-9, and continued the priestly line by appointing Aaron's son as his successor when the first high priest died, v. 6. Verses 10 to 11 assure Israel that Moses' intercession on Sinai was successful and that the Lord would not destroy them. Instead, He promised to bring them into the land; by His grace, the second generation would succeed where the first failed.

---

[321] THOMPSON, pp. 155-156 [italics original].
[322] THOMPSON, pg. 159.
[323] CHRISTENSEN, pg. 187.

The remainder of the chapter explains God's expectations of them with unparalleled clarity:

'And now, Israel, what doth the Lord thy God require of thee, but to fear the Lord thy God, to walk in all his ways, and to love him, and to serve the Lord thy God with all thy heart and with all thy soul, To keep the commandments of the Lord, and his statutes, which I command thee this day for thy good? Behold, the heaven and the heaven of heavens is the Lord's thy God, the earth also, with all that therein is. Only the Lord had a delight in thy fathers to love them, and he chose their seed after them, even you above all people, as it is this day. Circumcise therefore the foreskin of your heart, and be no more stiffnecked. For the Lord your God is God of gods, and Lord of lords, a great God, a mighty, and a terrible, which regardeth not persons, nor taketh reward: He doth execute the judgment of the fatherless and widow, and loveth the stranger, in giving him food and raiment. Love ye therefore the stranger: for ye were strangers in the land of Egypt. Thou shalt fear the Lord thy God; him shalt thou serve, and to him shalt thou cleave, and swear by his name. He is thy praise, and he is thy God, that hath done for thee these great and terrible things, which thine eyes have seen. Thy fathers went down into Egypt with threescore and ten persons; and now the Lord thy God hath made thee as the stars of heaven for multitude', vv. 12-22.

These verses recount God's wonderful characteristics of steadfast faithfulness, sovereign power, and impartial justice, while carefully applying them to His people. Because the Lord is that way, so should His people comport themselves with love, fairness, and mercy towards others. The end of the chapter particularly echoes God's promise to make Abraham's descendants into a great nation, v. 22; Gen. 15. 5.

The eleventh chapter begins with a familiar expression that appears elsewhere in this passage and throughout the book of Deuteronomy for a total of nine times: 'love the Lord your God', vv. 1, 13, 22.[324] The frequency of this language demonstrates the importance that God placed on His people's love. The central purpose of their lives was to love the One who first loved them; in like manner, modern believers are to love the Lord above anything or anyone else, Matt. 10. 37; 1 John 4. 12-19. Israel's love for the Lord should be demonstrated in their obedience to His revealed will, Deut. 11. 1 – a principle that His New Testament people must also follow, John 14. 15.

In this chapter, Israel is given two incentives for possessing the land:

1. They are reminded of God's former punishment in Egypt and the wilderness against those who rebelled against His word; unlike the previous generation of rebels, they should obey Him, Deut. 11. 2-7.
2. The land is 'flowing with milk and honey', v. 9 – i.e., it is prosperous and fruitful; it is truly worth possessing and they should therefore long to take it.

But this beautiful land also functions as a spiritual barometer, gauging their loyalty to their Lord. Unlike Egypt, which was a low maintenance land of fertility, revolving around the regularity of the Nile's flooding, v. 10, Israel depended on the 'early and latter rains', v. 14. In fact God described it as a territory that He directly superintended, vv. 11-12; if they obeyed His word, then the rains would come and the earth's fecundity would be assured. If they turned to idols, however, He would chasten them by withholding the rain and thus cause a famine, vv. 13-17. The land's prosperity was directly tied to their allegiance to the Lord. So when one sees a famine in scripture, such as in Elijah's time, 1 Kgs. 17-18, one knows that Israel has departed from the Lord. Repentance brings about rain and blessing, 1 Kgs. 18. 39-46.

---

[324] Its other occurrences are in Deut. 6. 5; 13. 3; 19. 9; 30. 6, 16, and 20.

After defining afresh their future territory contingent on their obedience, Deut. 11. 22-25, Moses then presents the blessings and cursings for obedience or disobedience to God's law, vv. 26-32. When Israel conquered the land, they would publicly confess these things on Mounts Ebal and Gerizim surrounding Shechem.

Spiritual places and practices in the land, chapters 12 to 18

From considering the land itself, this section of the book of Deuteronomy focuses on the Israelites' religious life within their physical inheritance. The thematic breakdown of these chapters appears below:

Chapter 12: The sanctuary and the sacred usage of blood.
Chapter 13: Testing prophets and judging idolatrous cities.
Chapter 14: Rejection of paganism in personal mourning behaviour and diet; care for the Levites.
Chapter 15: The sabbatical year and proper treatment of the poor and servants.
Chapter 16: The Feasts of Jehovah and justice administered by just judges.
Chapter 17: Judgement of pure offerings, against idolaters, the upholding of the law, and God's king as a man of one book.
Chapter 18: Levites, priests, and prophets – especially the Messiah, vv. 15-22.

A contemporary Bible student sees Deuteronomy chapter 12 to chapter 16 verse 17 as a distinct section, which he calls 'The God Who Deserves and Defines Worship';[325] he goes on to connect this section of the book with Exodus, Leviticus, and Numbers:

'By now Moses' comments have linked his current situation to Israel's history in Egypt, at Sinai and in the desert. They have also

---

[325] HOUSE, pg. 182.

reminded readers of Exodus [chapter] 20, Leviticus [chapters] 1 [through] 7 and Leviticus [chapters] 18 [through] 20 and have always kept the first commandment in the foreground. In Deuteronomy chapter 14 [verse] 1 [to chapter] 16 [verse] 17 he speaks of religious observances mentioned in Exodus, Leviticus and Numbers. Each topic, whether clean and unclean food, 14. 1-21; cf. Lev. 11. 1-23, tithes, 14. 22-29; cf. Num. 18. 21-29, debt cancellation, 15. 1-11; cf. Lev. 25. 8-38, freeing indentured servants, 15. 12-18; cf. Lev. 25. 38-55, redeeming the firstborn, 15. 19-23; cf. Exod. 13. 1-16 or celebrating national festivals, 16. 1-17; cf. Lev. 23. 4-8; Num. 28. 16-29. 40, is addressed to highlight Israel's status as God's people, 14. 1-3; cf. Exod. 19. 5-6. Yahweh has chosen Israel to honor God among the nations by being different than other peoples. The goal is for them to stand out from, not be absorbed by, the cultural setting to which they are going. Historically speaking, their relationship to Yahweh sets them apart, and it will be this covenantal agreement that does so in the distant future'.[326]

Obviously there is a great deal of interconnectivity within the books of the Pentateuch. These books emphasize the Lord's uniqueness and His special relationship with His people.

Sacred real estate

The pagan religions that surrounded Israel often worshiped their deities at multiple high places, shrines, and temples. Canaan had no shortage of places where false gods' names were placed, Deut. 12. 2-3. They were not to engage in syncretism – mixing pagan rites and shrines with the worship of the Lord, v. 4. Jehovah promised to choose a specific place for His sanctuary – a place where He would place His authority by putting His name there, vv. 12-28. R. P. AMOS outlines the distinctiveness of this place:

---

[326] HOUSE, pg. 184 [brackets mine].

'A. It was the place of God's choosing, not man's convenience or popular desire

B. It was the gathering center for His people to assemble in a God-appointed design

C. It was God's habitation (living place) – His house. Thus it is designed foremost for the desires of God and not man's needs and wants

D. It was where one came to offer and give to God, not to get something from Him

E. It was where God put His Name (Lord – Jehovah). Since He put His Name there, only He has authority there, never man's traditions (When one comes "in the name of the law", he means the authority of law)'.[327]

In the era of the conquest through the early monarchy, the tabernacle was the sanctuary, and it resided in different geographical locations. From Solomon's time until Christ's crucifixion, the temple in Jerusalem became 'the place', 1 Kgs. 8. 29. The Lord Jesus opened up a new spiritual aspect to worshipping God, John 4. 21-24; His work made the old temple obsolete. In this age, the true sanctuary is open to the believer in Christ, Heb. 9. 6-15; 10. 19-25. GOODING discusses the difference between the Lord's heavenly and earthly sanctuaries:

'Unlike the old covenant's earthly sanctuary, his tabernacle is not man-made; it is not a part of this creation, 9. 11. Moses' man-made sanctuary was at best only a copy of the true one, 9. 24. Christ has entered into heaven itself, 9. 24. He ministers in the greater and more perfect tabernacle, 9. 11, the real thing. Compared with this greater and more perfect tabernacle, all the

---

[327] R. P. AMOS, 'Feed My Sheep – Chronicles of the Church 1: The Place: Where God's People Come', electronic edition accessed here: http://sheepfood.com/fms/Church%201%20place.pdf.

gold and silver and jewels of Moses' tabernacle were but the toys and tinsel of a child'.[328]

VINE comments further:

'The first ten verses of this chapter [Hebrews chapter 9] have presented the picture of the earthly tabernacle and its offerings, and their incompleteness to effect what was necessary for the perfecting of the worshipper. Now comes a striking antithesis. The background in the first part of the chapter serves to set forth by way of contrast the glories and perfections of Christ, His offering, His heavenly sanctuary, His mediatorship of the new covenant. All serves to present the perfections of His priesthood, connecting it with His incarnation, His death and His appearing a second time'.[329]

In the early days of the first-century church the major controversy between Judaism and Christianity centred around Jesus' name.[330] That is because His name provides the authority and identity for His people's salvation, worship, and practice in this world and in the coming age. His name and the works done in it affirm His deity, humanity, saviourhood, and Lordship, Acts 2. 32-36.

In the present church age, where two or three gather together in His name the Lord is in their midst, Matt. 18. 20.[331] The place where He

---

[328] DAVID GOODING, An Unshakeable Kingdom: The Letter to the Hebrews for Today, Myrtlefield Expositions, Myrtlefield House, 2013, pg. 173.

[329] W. E. VINE, Collected Writings of W.E. Vine: Hebrews, Thomas Nelson, 1997, electronic edition, Logos, no pagination.

[330] See Acts 2. 21, 38; 3. 6, 16; 4. 7, 10, 12, 17, 18, 30; 5. 28, 40-41.

[331] SHEARMAN exults: 'Here He deigned to dwell among them. How much more blessed we are today. Whenever we gather to His Name, Jesus has promised to be with us, Matt. 18. 20. No place can contain the greatness of God. Yet how often we feel the warmth of His presence as we gather. What a privilege'! A. T. SHEARMAN, 'Mar. 26th: The Chosen Place, Deuteronomy 12. 1-

has chosen to put His name is not limited to a certain geographical locality; instead, He is present in the gatherings of His people in jungles, prisons, homes, schools, a thousand rented halls and other types of buildings. R. P. AMOS describes its varied function in the New Testament, saying it is:

'A place of assembling for offering and sacrificing to God, 1 Pet. 2. 5, 9
A place of separation from all other names, 1 Cor. 1. 10-31
A place of learning to fear the Lord, 1 Tim. 5. 20, 2 Cor. 6. 16; 7. 1
A place of sacrificing the best to God, 1 Pet. 4. 11
A place of remembrance, 1 Cor. 11. 17-34
A place of observing and obeying God's traditions (ordinances), 1 Cor. 11. 2; 2 Thess. 2. 15
A place of worship, John 4. 20-24, 1 Cor. 14. 23-25
A place of judging matters among God's people – God's supreme court on earth, Matt. 18. 15-22
A place of proclaiming God's Word, 2 Tim. 4. 2
A place of liberty for the priesthood of all believers to minister unto the Lord, 1 Cor. 14'.[332]

32', in *Day by Day through the Old Testament*, ed. C. E. HOCKING and M. HORLOCK, Day by Day Series, Precious Seed, 1982, pg. 101. SPURGEON shared his enthusiasm for this truth: 'Does not this make our meetings delightful – Christ in the midst of us? Does not this make our meetings important? How one ought to strain a point to be there! If we have met with Christ aforetime we shall not bear to be away'. C. H. SPURGEON, 'The Lord With Two Or Three', *The Metropolitan Tabernacle Pulpit Sermons*, Vol. 30, Passmore & Alabaster, 1884, pg. 47.
[332] R. P. AMOS, 'Feed My Sheep – Chronicles of the Church 1: The Place: Where God's People Come', electronic edition accessed here: http://sheepfood.com/fms/Church%201%20place.pdf.

After establishing the chosen place and the authoritative name, the Israelites were not to tolerate rival 'names' in the land. A person's apparent ecstatic spiritual gift, Deut. 13. 1-5, close family relationship, vv. 6-11, or city of origin, vv. 12-18, must be disregarded if they promote apostasy from the true faith in Jehovah. This sin knows no respect of persons; anyone who entices others to adore idols must suffer the death penalty – regardless of who they are or seem to be. The Lord only permits this sin to occur to test his people's hearts, v. 3, because He wants them to have loyal, loving hearts.[333]

The Israelites' loyalty to the Lord was to extend to all areas of life, including their personal mourning practices – eschewing cutting their flesh, for example, 14. 1 – and their daily food, vv. 3-21. They were also taught to tithe their produce and to use the proceeds to care for God's special tribe for holy ministration, the Levites, vv. 22-29. This raised Israel's daily work to a higher level of God-inspired service; the church is given similar instructions, Phil. 4. 14-19; Col. 3. 23-24.

Vulnerable members of society like widows, orphans, and strangers were also to be cared for from the tithes, Deut. 14. 29; cf. Jas. 1. 27; 1 Tim. 5. 3-16. The succeeding chapter also weds their faith in Jehovah with religiously-inspired good works providing for the poor and alienated in their land. This is seen in:

1. the year of release every seventh year, Deut. 15. 1-11; and
2. their ethical compensation of indentured servants, vv. 12-18.

---

[333] For the New Testament equivalent of this principle, see 1 Cor. 11. 19; 1 John 4. 1-3; 1 Thess. 5. 19-21.

Their devotion to the Lord in agricultural life was further exemplified in their giving of the firstborn animals to Him, vv. 19-23, as well as the harvest festivals known as the feasts of Jehovah, 16. 1-17.[334] Dispersed throughout the first, third, and seventh months, these holidays commemorate God's redemptive plan for Israel – and by extension the entire earth – from Egypt through to Christ's millennial reign. Three times a year all Israelite males had to attend such celebrations with their gifts for the Lord in hand, vv. 16-17. Purity and justice were the operating principles of God's land for He set up righteous judges,[335] vv. 18-20, and forbad idolatrous practices like wooden images or sacred pillars, vv. 21-22.

Ceremonial and ethical abominations and leadership's response, chapters 17-18

BLOCK outlines the literary structure of Deuteronomy chapter 17 verses 2-12:

'In verses 2 [to] 3 Moses prescribes the response to violations of the principle of "righteousness, only righteousness" as stated in 16. 20. This section divides into two panels of identical length [verses] 2 [to] 7 and [verses] 8 [to] 12, 31 followed by a summary conclusion, v. 13. Each panel opens with a complex clause setting the context, vv. 2-4a; [verse] 8a, is followed by a lengthy prescribed response, vv. 4b-7a; vv. 8b-12a, and concludes with a declaration of the goal, v. 7b; v. 12b. The symmetry of structure and the verbal links suggest that verses 2 [to] 7 and 8 [to] 12 have been intentionally composed to develop a common point – how to deal with unrighteous behavior. The first involves relatively clean

---

[334] For a fuller discussion of the significance of these feasts, see the author's discussion of Leviticus chapters 16 and 23 in the 'Leviticus' section of this volume.

[335] HOUSE defines the theme of Deuteronomy 16. 18 to 18. 22 as 'The God Who Defines Effective Leadership', HOUSE, pg. 184.

cases; the second involves the procedure for cases insoluble by ordinary means of investigation'.[336]

He divides the rest of chapter 17 into two parts concerning Israel's future monarchy:

'1. The anticipation of a king in Israel, vv. 14-15;
2. The prescribed conduct of Israel's future king, vv. 16-20'.[337]

The first section offers evidence of the singularly just standards of Israelite jurisprudence. For instance, two or three witnesses were required to condemn someone in a capital case, v. 6; likewise, these witnesses must personally participate in the convicted criminal's execution, v. 7. Chapter 19 verses 15 to 21 add further witness requirements, such as capital punishment for perjury.[338] These instructions faithfully carried out would help avert false testimony and wrongful conviction. In the trials of the Lord Jesus, they were especially violated, Matt. 26. 57-68. Verses 8 to 13 establish a supreme court, composed of Levites and the high priest; their

---

[336] BLOCK, pg. 405 [brackets mine].
[337] BLOCK, pp. 416-417.
[338] 'False' witnesses in Deuteronomy chapter 19 verse 16 is rendered in more shocking ways by different translations: 'malicious', NASB, RSV, NRSV, ESV, NIV; 'unrighteous' ASV, JND. THOMPSON comments on the Hebrew text: 'The case of the malicious witness (lit. "witness of violence", i.e. his testimony would lead to violence) is now discussed. When such a witness declares that the accused is guilty of wrongdoing (lit. "turning aside", i.e. religious or moral, apostasy, defection or misconduct), the two parties to the dispute were called to appear *before Yahweh* to answer the priests and judges who were in office at the time. The tribunal at the central sanctuary seems to be in view here, cf. 17. 8-13. After careful enquiry the judges (probably the whole "bench" of priests and judges) give the verdict. If the witness is false he must suffer the punishment intended for the accused. In that way evil would be "burnt out" (*purged*) from Israel and false witness discouraged'. THOMPSON, pg. 239.

decisions were binding, and rejecting their authority carried the death penalty.

The rest of the chapter looks forward to an as-yet-future circumstance: the recognition of a king. Israel's motivation for this request is troubling, for it proceeds from a desire to be 'like all the nations', v. 14 NKJV. This always bodes poorly for the people of God – especially when their ancient near eastern neighbours are as depraved as were the Edomites, Ammonites, Moabites, and the like. WIERSBE notes the danger:

'Imitating the world instead of trusting the Lord has always been the great temptation of God's people, and each time they've succumbed, they've suffered. During their wilderness journey, Israel compared everything that happened with what they had experienced in Egypt, and at Kadesh-Barnea they even wanted to choose a leader and go back to Egypt!, 14. 1-5. But the church today is equally guilty of unbelief. When church leaders adopt the methods and measurements of the world, then the church has taken a giant step toward becoming like the world and losing its divine distinctives. Instead of trusting the Word of God and prayer, Acts 6. 4, we depend on following the world's wisdom, imitating the world's methods, and catering to the world's appetites, giving people what they want instead of what they need. Believers today need to take to heart God's reminder to Israel: "I am the Lord your God, who has separated you from the peoples", Num. 20. 24, NKJV'.[339]

The king was not to:

1. be a foreigner, v. 15;
2. multiply horses or return to Egypt to multiply horses, v. 16;
3. multiply wives or silver and gold, v. 17.

---

[339] WIERSBE, pg. 118.

He was to:

1. copy the law, v. 18;
2. read the law, v. 19;
3. obey and walk according to the law, v. 19.

Verse 20 summarizes the result of this observance of God's law: 'That his heart be not lifted up above his brethren, and that he turn not aside from the commandment, to the right hand, or to the left: to the end that he may prolong his days in his kingdom, he, and his children, in the midst of Israel'.

Priests and Levites – righteousness at work

The Levites' lives and those of their Aaronic members, the priests, are intermittently woven throughout chapters 17 to 19. We have already seen their role as the supreme court, 17. 8-13; chapter 18 goes on to establish the provision for their needs by the Israelites in the land, vv. 1-8. Chapter 19 provides 'the cities of refuge', which were administered by the Levites, Num. 35. 9-34 – though that is not mentioned in this passage.[340] Their existence and service was an ongoing picture of the Lord's righteousness at work in the midst of Israel.

Voices from beyond: the false and the true, chapter 18 verses 9-22

Canaanite civilization was saturated in the occult – something that Israel was to resolutely reject as an abomination to the Lord, Deut. 18. 9-14. Spiritists, mediums, and soothsayers were false voices. But Jehovah would speak through His special Moses-like prophet – yet one who is greater than Moses, vv. 15-19; cf. Acts 3. 22-23.

---

[340] See also Exodus chapter 21 verses 12 to 14 and Joshua chapter 20. See also my comments on Numbers chapter 35 in the 'Numbers' section of this volume.

MACKINTOSH captures the special nature of this promise and the ongoing blessing that flows from it:

'We can be at no loss to know who this Prophet is, namely, our adorable Lord and Saviour Jesus Christ. In the third chapter of Acts, Peter so applies the words of Moses. "He shall send Jesus Christ, which before was preached unto you; whom the heaven must receive until the times of restitution of all things, which God hath spoken by the mouth of all His holy prophets since the world began. For Moses truly said unto the fathers, 'A Prophet shall the Lord your God raise up unto you of your brethren, like unto me; him shall ye hear in all things whatsoever he shall say unto you. And it shall come to pass that every soul which will not hear that Prophet shall be destroyed from among the people", ver. 20-23'.

How precious the privilege of hearing the voice of such a Prophet! It is the voice of God speaking through the lips of the Man Christ Jesus – speaking, not in thunder, not with flaming fire, nor the lightning's flash, but in that still small voice of love and mercy which falls in soothing power on the broken heart and contrite spirit, which distils like the gentle dew of heaven upon the thirsty ground. This voice we have in the holy Scriptures – that precious revelation which comes so constantly and so powerfully before us in our studies on this blessed book of Deuteronomy. We must never forget this. The voice of Scripture is the voice of Christ, and the voice of Christ is the voice of God.

We want no more. If any one presumes to come with a fresh revelation, with some new truth not contained in the divine volume, we must judge him and his communication by the standard of Scripture and reject them utterly. "Thou shalt not be afraid of him." False prophets come with great pretensions, high-sounding words, and sanctimonious bearing. Moreover, they seek to surround themselves with a sort of dignity, weight, and impressiveness which are apt to impose on the ignorant. But they cannot stand the searching power of the Word of God. Some simple clause of holy Scripture will strip them of all their imposing surroundings, and cut up by the roots their wonderful revelations. Those who know the voice of the true Prophet will not listen to any other: those who have heard the voice of the good Shepherd will not listen to the voice of a stranger. Reader, see that you listen *only* to the voice of Jesus'.[341]

This passage also sets forth the stringent criteria for a true prophet of the Lord in Israel: He must be accurate 100 percent of the time; otherwise, he is discredited and must be disregarded, Deut. 18. 22. False prophecy is so grave a sin that its exponents are subject to the death penalty, v. 20.

Bloodshed: unrighteous and righteous, chapters 19 to 21

In the broader context of the book of Deuteronomy chapters 16 to 21 concern important leadership matters, as this chiastic parallel structure shows:

'A Laws concerning judges and officials in your towns, 16. 18 – 17. 13
B Law of the king, 17. 14-20
X Law of the Levitical priests – provisions for the clergy, 18. 1-8
B´ Law of the prophets, 18. 9-22
A´ Laws concerning the courts – judicial and military matters, 19. 1 – 21. 9'.[342]

Some outline chapter 19 around issues relating to homicide:

'1. Dealing with homicide, vv. 1-13;
2. Prevention of homicide, v. 14;

---

341 MACKINTOSH, pp. 851-852 [italics original].
342 CHRISTENSEN, pg. 417.

3. Dealing with the accusation of homicide, vv. 15-21'.[343]

This subject carries over into chapters 20 to 21, as CHRISTENSEN points out:

'A Laws on manslaughter and the cities of asylum, 19. 1-10
B The case of intentional murder – no asylum, 19. 11-13
X Laws on encroachment and witnesses in court, 19. 14-21
B′ Intentional killing – warfare and military deferments, 20. 1-20
A′ Law on unsolved murder – role of elders and judges 21. 1-9'.[344]

In keeping with the theme of violence against one's life, Deuteronomy chapter 19 verse 14 upholds property rights, prohibiting the removal of one's neighbour's 'landmark'. Such boundaries were established to safeguard one's livelihood and to maintain one's God-given inheritance. People may be killed in an instant by violent action, or they may be slowly deprived of their sustenance and succumb to a pauper's death. Proverbs chapter 23 verse 10 commands: 'Remove not the old landmark; And enter not into the fields of the fatherless'.[345] Elsewhere the Lord angrily condemns this infraction: 'The princes of Judah are like those who remove a landmark; I will pour out my wrath on them like water', Hos. 5. 10 NKJV. Taking advantage of the weak or vulnerable often leads to worse crimes. For example, Ahab's lust for Naboth's vineyard led the wicked king to arrange his murder; afterwards, he unlawfully took possession of his neighbour's inheritance, 1 Kgs. 21.

Along with the teaching regarding witnesses in judicial cases, this chapter sets the famous 'lex talionis' – better known as 'an eye for an

---

[343] KAUFMANN, quoted in MAXWELL. MAXWELL goes on to write: 'Obviously, the laws about both asylum and witnesses have a common concern – that innocent blood not be shed, either by the avenger of blood or, indirectly, by the witness who perjures himself against the defendant'. MAXWELL, pg. 222.
[344] CHRISTENSEN, pg. 417.
[345] See also Proverbs chapter 22. 28.

eye and a tooth for a tooth', Matt. 5. 38, or 'the law of retaliation' – as the governing principle of the land.[346] Some people mistakenly think this is evidence of the cruelty of life in ancient Israel. In actuality it set guidelines for judges limiting the severity of the castigation; it was a way of saying that the punishment ought to fit the crime. As MAXWELL explains: 'This law also served as a restraint in cases where the disciplinarian might be inclined to be excessive in administering punishment. Jesus did not deny the validity of this principle for the courtroom, but He denied its use in personal relationships, Matt. 5.

---

[346] Christ's commentary on this principle is unpacked well in the following two quotations: 'The law, as an administration of public justice, was meant to punish wrongdoers and protect the community. We tend to see the law as institutionalized cruelty and revenge. But it was actually meant to prohibit such vicious responses to criminal behavior. The "eye for an eye" principle forbade disproportionate penalties. While it prescribed a just punishment, it also proscribed anything more than an eye for an eye. It did not allow for vigilante justice or personal revenge, even though that's how many in Jesus's day understood the commandment. The Jewish leaders were misapplying a public law code and turning it into their personal right for retaliation. Jesus was right – and true to the biblical passage – to correct this misappropriation of the text. Throughout the Sermon on the Mount, and especially in Matthew [chapter] 5, Jesus tries to impress upon his audience the real meaning of Scripture. He does not want to correct Scripture. He wants to bring its full weight to bear on the human heart'. Donald Macleod, 'Jesus and Scripture', in *The Trustworthiness of God: Perspectives on the Nature of Scripture*, ed. Paul Helm and Carl Trueman, Eerdmans, 2002, pg. 73. 'Jesus wants more of Scripture in our lives, not less . . . Jesus doesn't want us to keep the little commandments in Scripture and miss the big stuff, but neither does he allow us to overlook the smallest parts so long as we get the big picture right. He expects obedience to the spirit of the law and to the letter. Our Messiah sees himself as an expositor of Scripture, but never a corrector of Scripture. He fulfills it, but never falsifies it. He turns away wrong interpretations of Scripture, but insists there is nothing wrong with Scripture, down to the crossing of t's and dotting of i's'. KEVIN DEYOUNG, *Taking God at His Word*, Crossway, 2012, electronic edition, Kindle Locations 1250-1268.

38-42'.[347] KALLAND amplifies this teaching in these words: 'Jesus spoke to individuals about violence against themselves personally. One must not take the law into his own hands, returning evil for evil. Such action should be referred to the officials responsible before God to adjudicate and to punish offenders'.[348] Finally, THOMPSON concludes about this legislation: 'Far from encouraging vengeance it limits vengeance and stands as a guide for a judge as he fixes a penalty suited to the crime. The principle was thus not licence or vengeance, but a guarantee of justice'.[349] The *lex talionis* teaching is parallel to the cities of refuge earlier in the chapter:

'A The six cities of refuge in the Promised Land, 19. 1-10
B Intentional murderers – "Purge the guilt of innocent blood", 19. 11-13
X The inviolability of boundary markers, 19. 14
B′ Laws about witnesses – "Purge the evil from your midst", 19. 15-19
A′ *Lex talionis* is intended as a deterrent to false witness, 19. 20-21'.[350]

Onward Jewish soldiers, marching as to war – chapters 20 to 23

BLOCK divides chapter 20 into three parts, all with a martial theme:

'1. Encouraging troops for battle, vv. 1-9;
2. Instructions for battle, vv. 10-18;
3. Instructions for siege warfare, vv. 19-20'.[351]

---

[347] MAXWELL, pp. 222-223.
[348] KALLAND, *Deuteronomy*, electronic edition, no pagination.
[349] THOMPSON, pg. 239.
[350] CHRISTENSEN, pg. 427.
[351] BLOCK, pg. 467.

He points out that three other passages in this section also deal with warfare, Deut. 21. 10-14; 23. 9-14; and 24. 5, setting forth moral obligations for treating captives, laying siege to cities, treating fearful or otherwise distracted soldiers.[352] He also sees five distinct sections in chapter 21:

1. verses 1-9;
2. verses 10-14;
3. verses 15-17;
4. verses 18-21; and
5. verses 22-23.

As he further comments: 'These sections are held together by variations of the land grant formula that frame the chapter, vv. 1, 23; each one opens with a conditional clause, ("If, when"), followed by a prescribed response; there is a common concern to separate life and death . . . and there is an overall chiastic arrangement, with instructions on the rights of the firstborn, vv. 15-17, being the center of gravity'.[353] The chiastic structure that he mentions looks like this:

'A Death and Defilement, vv. 1-9;
B Basic Family Relationships: Husband and Wife, vv. 10-14;
C The Rights of the Firstborn, vv. 15-17;
B' Basic Family Relationships: Parents and Child, vv. 18-21;
A' Death and Defilement, vv. 22-23'.[354]

A murder mystery and the sanctity of human life – chapter 21

The idea of the intrinsic value of human life is sprinkled throughout this part of Deuteronomy. The elders and priests played a vital role in ensuring that the land is purified from bloodshed. This is seen in the

---

[352] BLOCK, pg. 467.
[353] BLOCK, pg. 487.
[354] BLOCK, pg. 488.

case of an unsolved murder. The elders of the nearest town were to call on these authorities to attest that their community was not covering up a homicide. A costly offering of a heifer was offered by breaking its neck at the scene of the crime. Furthermore, a solemn oath was sworn before Jehovah and the elders washed their hands ceremonially and called on Him to make atonement for them, vv. 7-9. The entire procedure declared that every person's life has value. They are God's creatures and may not be written off as unimportant. Although human authorities are sometimes unable to arrive at the identity of the guilty party, the Judge of all the earth will one day reveal and punish 'the secrets of men', Rom. 2. 16. Until then, He demonstrates in passages like Deuteronomy chapter 21 verses 1 to 9 that every life is valuable in His sight.

The Almighty's compassion for the value of human life is also seen in two cases connected with family situations:

1. of marriage to women enslaved after a battle;
2. of a polygamous union,[355] where there are children by two wives.

The case of a captive woman takes into consideration her natural feelings – especially her bereavement, vv. 10-14. The Lord safeguards the firstborn rights of the unloved wife's progeny, making sure that the husband's preference does not supersede the proper rights of the oldest child, vv. 15-17.[356]

---

[355] Polygamy was never God's best for mankind, but it was permitted in the Old Testament. His original and best intention for humanity was a monogamous marriage, Gen. 2. 21-24.
[356] There are echoes of the experiences of Leah and Rachel throughout this injunction, see Gen. 29. 31 – 30. 24.

Another scenario envisions a rebellious son who refuses to submit to his parents, vv. 18-21 – a violation of the command to 'honour thy father and mother', 5. 16.

Preachers often point out that the Old Testament has no recorded instance of parents carrying out this drastic procedure; yet the perfectly obedient Son of God died in the place of many rebellious sons and daughters! Interestingly, the last two verses teach Israel not to leave executed criminals hanging on trees overnight, because such a one is under God's curse, v. 23. This fairly obscure instruction is cited in Galatians chapter 3 verse 13 as explanatory for Christ's vicariously sacrificial death on behalf of the condemned.[357] The hymn writer wondered at the condescension: 'blesser yet a curse once made',[358] and every believer responds: 'Amen, this is amazing grace'!

Seeing the divine in everyday experience

Consideration for human well-being must permeate the everyday lives of God's people. This mindset extends to the property of our neighbour, Deut. 22. 1-4, and the safe construction of one's own house, v. 8. The attitude of the Lord's people also emphasized purposeful stewardship of animals, vv. 6-7, and discernment expressed in common things like the type of clothing one wears, vv. 5, 11-12, and how and with what one sows his field, vv. 9-10.

---

[357] As OWEN writes: 'To see him who is the wisdom of God, and the power of God, always beloved of the Father; to see him, I say, fear, and tremble, and bow, and sweat, and pray, and die; to see him lifted up upon the cross, the earth trembling under him, as if unable to bear his weight; and the heavens darkened over him, as if shut against his cry; and himself hanging between both, as if refused by both; and all this because our sins did meet upon him; – this of all things doth most abundantly manifest the severity of God's vindictive justice. Here, or nowhere, is it to be learned'. JOHN OWEN, 'Of Communion With God', in *The Works of John Owen, Volume 2*, ed. WILLIAM H. GOOLD. T & T Clark, 1862, pg. 85.
[358] Hymn 'Lord of Glory we adore thee'.

Although these latter instructions concern relatively mundane, physical things, God was cultivating in their minds critical, God-ward thinking. He was to be central to everything that the Israelites did in life.

Purity among God's people – chapter 22 verses 13 to 30

Verses 13 to 30 discuss sexual matters relating to the marriage bond's purity. This section deals with:

1. a husband making a false accusation of impurity against his new bride, vv. 13-19;
2. a husband making a true accusation of impurity against his new bride, vv. 20-21;
3. adultery, v. 22;
4. sexual misconduct involving a betrothed woman, vv. 23-29;
5. sexual misconduct involving a virgin, vv. 28-29;
6. incest by taking one's father's wife, v. 30; cf. 1 Cor. 5.

The first situation demands that the husband pay a penalty to the bride's parents and that he may not divorce her. The second results in the impure woman's execution by stoning. The third demands capital punishment for both parties. The fourth case depends on the woman's culpability: 1. If the attack occurs in the city and she is compliant, both she and the man are executed, vv. 23-24; 2. If it occurs in the country and she is innocent then only the man is executed, vv. 25-27. In the fifth situation, the man must pay a penalty of fifty shekels to the parents and marry her without the possibility of divorce,[359] v. 29. The sixth situation is prohibited, but no specific penalty is here defined; elsewhere it says that this crime carried the death penalty, Lev. 20. 11; see also Deut. 27. 20.

---

[359] It seems that her willingness also comes into play. If she is unwilling, there is no scripture that forces her to marry him or anyone else.

WENHAM and MCCONVILLE note the literary structure of this passage:

'a. Offenses of married women: 13–22
1) Offense in father's house ("if", "gate of city"): [vv.] 13-19
2) Offense in father's house ("if not"): [vv.] 20-21
3) Adultery ("if," "caught in the act"): [v.] 22
b. Offenses by unmarried girls: [vv.] 23-28
1) Betrothed girl in city ("if," "gate of city"): [vv.] 23-24
2) Betrothed girl in field ("if not"): [vv.] 25–27
3) Unbetrothed girl ("if," "caught in the act"): [vv.] 28–29
The laws are also arranged in chiastic order according to the punishment of each.
A.   19 - damages of 100 shekels to girl's father; no divorce
B.   21 - woman executed
C.   22 - man and woman executed
C'. 24 - man and woman executed
B'. 25 - man executed
A'. 29 - damages of 50 shekels to girl's father; no divorce'.[360]

The sanctity of the Lord's assembly – chapter 23 verses 1 to 8

Six times in the first eight verses of chapter 23 the phrase 'the assembly of the Lord' appears, vv. 1, 2, 3, 8; it occurs twice in both verses 2 and 3. The related concept of 'the camp' is found later in the chapter, vv. 9-20. This portion of Deuteronomy accentuates the exclusive nature of holiness. God's holy being is separate from those who oppose Him, vv. 1-8, and from anything defiling, 9-20. Those who were excluded included:

1. eunuchs, v. 1;
2. illegitimate children, v. 2;
3. Ammonites, v. 3;
4. Moabites, vv. 3-6;

---

360 G. J. WENHAM and J. G. MCCONVILLE, quoted in HALL, pp. 334-335.

5. Edomites and Egyptians prior to the third generation, vv. 7-8.

Eunuchs were excluded possibly because of heathen associations with emasculation, cf. Lev. 21. 17-20. Illegitimacy destabilizes society and so was naturally frowned upon. Historically, the Ammonites and Moabites opposed Israel during the wilderness journey. The latter nation even hired the celebrated mercenary-prophet Balaam to curse Israel, but because of His great love for Israel, the Lord turned this into abundant blessing for His people, v. 5.[361] Edomites and Egyptians had roles in Israel's history that were less adversarial and were therefore excluded for fewer generations than Ammonites or Moabites.[362]

Verses 9 to 14 likewise portray the camp as a holy place because of the Lord's presence, for they detail matters of personal ceremonial cleanliness from warfare and bodily functions. His presence in their midst affected their lifestyle, but it also assured them of His protection. Verse 14 shows that Israel's behaviour was to imitate Jehovah in protecting others as well as keeping themselves pure, as HALL points out:

'There seems to be a deliberate catchword connection with the previous law and verse 14. God was in the camp to protect Israel (נצל, nṣl). Likewise the Israelite was to care for the slave who had **taken refuge** (נצל) within Israel. This wordplay agrees with a common theme in Deuteronomy: Israel was to imitate God, see on 10. 17-19. Although the motivation for the generous act here was not given, elsewhere Israel was to recall her slavery in Egypt as a reason for gratitude toward God and kind treatment of others, 10.

---

[361] For more on this incident from Numbers chapters 22 to 25 and 31, see my comments in the 'Numbers' section of this volume.
[362] Sometimes divine grace admitted a Moabitess sooner than ten generations, Ruth 4. 10-21.

19; 15. 15; 23. 7; 24. 17-18. The grace God extended to her was to be extended to others'.[363]

While runaway slaves were afforded shelter, no quarter was to be given for ritual prostitutes, vv. 17-18. Ancient false religion – as well as certain modern religions like certain Hindu temples – used heterosexual female harlots and sodomites[364] for the 'adoration' of their idols. Neither the participants in these perverse ceremonies nor their financial proceeds were to be brought into the Lord's house or practised among His people. Contrary to modern belief, He cares a great deal about people's personal sexual and religious practices, 1 Cor. 6. 9-11.

Deuteronomy chapter 23 ends with several practical matters, including not charging interest towards fellow Israelites, and treating their property responsibly, vv. 19-20, 24-25. The latter two verses form an interesting background to the disciples' activity in Mark chapter 2 verses 23-28. As in Leviticus chapter 27 and Numbers chapter 30, Israelites were to fulfil their vows, Deut. 23. 21-23.

---

[363] HALL, 350 [boldface original]; he further comments in fn. 20 on pg. 350 in his book: 'This was the precise point of Jesus' parable about the unforgiving servant, Matt. 18. 21-35. Jesus was saturated with the theology of Deuteronomy'.

[364] As the NKJV margin indicates, both of these classes of perverts are designated by the same Hebrew word. In the case of the woman, the female ending is added to the word: *qadesh* becomes *qadeshah*. These words occur eleven times in nine Old Testament verses, including interesting references to Tamar, Gen. 38. 21 [two times], 22; besides its two appearances in Deut. 23. 18, it occurs elsewhere in 1 Kgs. 14. 24; 15. 12; 22. 7; 2 Kgs. 23. 7; Job 36. 14; Hosea 4. 14. It may also be rendered 'temple-prostitute'. BROWN, DRIVER, and BRIGGS, pg. 873.

Righteous living in Israel

Deuteronomy chapter 24 verses 1 to 4 concern the sadly relevant and contemporary scourge of society that is called divorce. Of course, it is a large subject in the Bible – for Christ's direct commentary on this passage see Matthew chapter 19 verses 3 to 12; suffice it to say that this chapter teaches that it was reality in Israel, and that remarriage was permissible under certain circumstances. If a man found 'uncleanness' in his wife, he could give her 'a bill of divorcement', v. 1.[365] MCCONVILLE summarizes it this way:

'This law takes for granted the practice of divorce in Israel, in spite of the Lord's hatred of it, recorded elsewhere, Mal. 2. 16. (Notice, however, the two exceptions to the man's right to a divorce; 22. 19, 29). This law makes no attempt to justify the practice in general. The reason for the man's wish to divorce (*he finds something indecent about her*) is not clear; it may be some ritual impurity, or a failure to bear children, or sexual immodesty. It is not, in any case, said to be an adequate reason for divorce. The point of the law is merely to prevent a return to the first husband after a second marriage of the divorced woman has ended. (Jeremiah [chapter] 3 [verses] 1 [to] 5 presupposes this point). The aim may have been to make divorce so solemn and final that it would not be entered upon lightly'.[366]

Since the Bible is God's progressive revelation to man, one must study all of the scriptural passages on this subject – especially New

---

[365] The *New English Translation* has this translation note in the margin: '*Heb* "nakedness of a thing". The Hebrew phrase . . . (*'ervat davar*) refers here to some gross sexual impropriety . . . Though the term usually has to do only with indecent exposure of the genitals, it can also include such behavior as adultery, cf. Lev. 18. 6-18; 20. 11, 17, 20-21; Ezek. 22. 10; 23. 29; Hos. 2. 10'.
[366] MCCONVILLE, 'Deuteronomy', in D. A. CARSON ET AL., eds., *New Bible Commentary*, pg. 221 [italics original; brackets mine].

Testament portions like Romans chapter 7 verses 1 to 6 and 1 Corinthians chapter 7 verses 10 to 17.

The remainder of the chapter discusses miscellaneous statutes safeguarding individual rights, happiness, and the general well-being of one's neighbour. They include:

1. A newly married husband's exemption from military service for the sake of his wife, Deut. 24. 5.
2. Not taking a millstone as collateral because it is the means of the borrower's livelihood, v. 6; verses 10 to 13 give further instructions on humanely receiving a pledge for a loan, with the emphasis on the debtor's human rights.
3. Kidnapping is forbidden and carries the death penalty, v. 7.
4. Conduct during an outbreak of leprosy: heed the priests and remember Miriam's example, vv. 8-9; cf. Lev. 13-14.
5. Paying fair and timely wages to poor labourers, Deut. 24. 14-15; cf. Jas. 5. 1-7.
6. Only the criminal is to be executed – not his children, Deut. 24. 16.
7. The rights of widows, orphans, and strangers are safeguarded and provision is made for their sustenance based on Israel's status as those redeemed from Egypt's slavery, vv. 17-22; Ruth 2. 2-23; Titus 2. 14.

Chapter 25 continues assorted injunctions that are loosely connected, all promoting righteousness in daily life in Israel. The first three verses delineate proper court procedure and penalty for a case between two Israelites. It envisions a case where the punishment is flogging. To guard against cruelty and the undue humiliation of the guilty party, the number is set at forty lashes; this provides historical background for Paul's sufferings at the hands of rabbinic Judaism, 2

Cor. 11. 24.[367] The Lord is merciful and always remembers that this guilty person is one of His people, as BLOCK explains: 'While it is unclear what constitutes excessive public degradation, the identification of the convicted person as "your brother" suggests that even though justice was to be administered by objective standards, floggings were never to be carried out heartlessly. After all, even guilty persons are members of the community'.[368]

'Thou shalt not muzzle the ox when he treadeth out the corn', Deut. 25. 4, seems like a mundane though important principle showing compassion towards livestock; nevertheless, the Holy Spirit uses it to establish the greater truth of God's provision for His servants through His people, 1 Cor. 9. 8-11. Likewise, Deuteronomy chapter 25 verses 5 to 20 establish case law that figures prominently in later biblical stories, Ruth 3-4; Matt. 22. 23-33. This 'levirate marriage'[369] not only provided a husband for an eligible widow, but, more importantly, it ensured the continuation of an Israelite man's line and name in the inheritance given by the Lord. The importance of preserving a man's line is seen in the shame that befalls the brother-in-law who dared to refuse this obligation, Deut. 24. 7-10. If he persisted in his intransigence in the face of the widow's entreaties and the elder's intercession, then his house would perpetually bear an ignominious name, v. 10. He cared not for his brother's name, so the Lord would punish him in connection with his own name. Concern for a man's physical line is further seen in the serious punishment meted out to a woman who assaulted a man in the genitals, vv. 11-12.

---

[367] The 'minus one' in this verse stems from rabbinic tradition that prescribes thirty-nine stripes to be even more merciful than Deuteronomy's standard. See COLIN G. KRUSE, *2 Corinthians: An Introduction and Commentary*. Tyndale New Testament Commentaries, Vol. 8, InterVarsity Press, 1987, pg. 190.

[368] BLOCK, pg. 579.

[369] 'Levirate' is from the Latin word for 'brother-in-law', since he is the one who marries his brother's wife to raise up seed in his brother's name.

The Lord demanded just weights and balances in business dealings, vv. 13-16. Economic injustice is harmful to human life and is therefore rejected as a grave type of sin; God calls it 'an abomination', v. 16. Proverbs chapter 16 verse 11 asserts: 'Honest weights and scales are the Lord's; All the weights in the bag are His work'. Other Old Testament passages also deplore trickery with commercial weights and measures, Prov. 11. 1; 20. 10, 23; Mic. 6. 11.

The passage ends with a stern denunciation of the Amalekites who harassed Israel at a particularly vulnerable time in their history, vv. 17-18; Exod. 17. 8-16. Not only was it cruel to attack the stragglers and the weak, it also demonstrated their fundamental lack of the fear of God, Deut. 24. 18. Verse 19 looks forward to the happy time when Israel will have 'rest from their enemies' and they are in the land of their inheritance, v. 19. The Lord solemnly enjoins them to 'blot out the remembrance of Amalek from under heaven', v. 19. Amalek was an implacable foe who perennially fought the Lord and His people; thus, they were to be utterly destroyed – something that was still ongoing in the early monarchical period in Israel, 1 Sam. 15. 2-33; 2 Sam. 1. 1-16. To be blotted out by divine wrath is the most serious type of judgement; how much better it is to have one's transgressions blotted out, Isa. 43. 25, and to know that one will never be blotted out of the book of life, Rev. 3. 5. This promise is open to whoever repents and believes on the Lord Jesus Christ for salvation, Acts 3. 19.

Gratitude and worship in the land – chapter 26

After centuries of promise and anticipation, chapter 26 now considers the blessed time of consummation when Israel are in their inheritance, enjoying the fruit of the land. It is the unfortunate human tendency to rejoice in the blessings and forget the blesser. Knowing this fact, the Almighty instructs them to bring of the firstfruits of their produce and offer thanksgiving to Him who gave it to them. While doing this, they were to remember their unlikely path to prosperity:

their father was 'a Syrian ready to perish', v. 5. The 'Syrian'[370] whom they mentioned was the patriarch Jacob – later renamed 'Israel'; his mother and two wives hailed from the region known as 'Aram', Gen. 28. 5. When they confessed that he was 'ready to perish' they were noting the naturally perilous circumstances that he faced. The Hebrew word also may mean 'wandering'; thus many versions refer to their ancestor as 'a wandering Aramaen'.[371] From this uncertain, nomadic existence, the Lord led his family down into Egypt, where He formed them into a nation.

Verse 5 marks the historic transition from the initial 'few' to 'a nation, great, mighty, and populous'. This dramatic change led to Egyptian oppression, but when Israel cried to the Lord, He heard and delivered them, vv. 6-8. He brought them out of slavery and into the bountiful 'land, flowing with milk and honey', vv. 8-9. How wonderful then that they concluded their confession in this manner: 'And now, behold, I have brought the firstfruits of the land, which thou, O Lord, hast given me', v. 10. Before enjoying the fruit, they first gave God His portion; thereby expressing their thankfulness for His faithful generosity. Their joy in the present flowed from His work in the past. Just as believers today must never forget their once lost condition,

---

[370] Rendered by many 'Aramean', JND, NAS, ESV, RSV, NET, HCSB, NLT, NRSV, LEB.

[371] RSV, NAS, NRSV, ESV, NET, NLT, HCSB, LEB all have 'a wandering Aramean'. '"Wandering" is one possible interpretation of a verb that means "to perish, to be lost" [BENEDIKT OTZEN, "אָבַד, ʾābhadh," TDOT, 2. 20]. A more literal translation is, "A perishing Aramean was my father". "Wandering" points to Jacob's rootless and landless existence as compared with Israel settled firmly in the land. "Perishing", the preferred translation, points to Jacob's precarious existence because of the famine that drove him from Canaan into Egypt, Gen. 42. 1-2; 43. 1-2; 47. 4. The recitation at the time of harvest was to call attention to the sharp contrast between Israel's experience in the land and Jacob's. The rich bounty of the land was proof of God's blessing and his faithfulness to his promises to Jacob, Gen. 46. 3-6'''. HALL, pp. 388–389.

which was graciously changed to a status of blessed sonship and justification through Christ's sacrificial death, resurrection, and ascension. Paul never forgot where he came from, and neither should we, 1 Tim. 1. 15; Gal. 2. 20.

Tithing in the third year

In addition to giving the Lord the firstfruits, the Israelites were also commanded to bring their tithe in the third year. This ten percent portion of their crop was used to provide for needy groups that the Almighty wanted to support: Levites, widows, orphans, and strangers, Deut. 26. 12-14. The fulfilment of this gift was also accompanied by a confession of the Lord as the source of blessing and giver of this fecund land: 'Look down from thy holy habitation, from heaven, and bless thy people Israel, and the land which thou hast given us, as thou swarest unto our fathers, a land that floweth with milk and honey', v. 15.

The chapter ends with the reaffirmation of the Lord's covenant with Israel and the blessed position where it placed them. It also reminds them of their responsibility to obey God's commands, statutes, and judgements, vv. 16-18. The end result of such obedience is that He will bless them to the fullest extent, as He says: 'And to make thee high above all nations which he hath made, in praise, and in name, and in honour; and that thou mayest be an holy people unto the Lord thy God, as he hath spoken', v. 19.

Blessing and cursings in the land – chapters 27 and 28

The Lord was giving the land to Israel; consequently, it must operate according to His principles. When Israel entered it their first activities must revolve around God's word and His worship. Accordingly, pillars with the law inscribed on them and an altar were their first constructed things in the land. BLOCK explains the covenantal aspect of these instructions:

256

'The ritual prescribed in verses 11 [to] 13 functions as a verbal equivalent to the sprinkling of the blood on the people in Exodus [chapter] 24 [verse] 8, binding the Israelites once more to the covenant made at Sinai and renewed on the Plains of Moab under the supervision of Moses. However, this time Mounts Ebal and Gerizim are present not only as witnesses to the blessings and curses, but as the repository to the Torah itself (the inscribed pillars of uncut stones taken from the region), and the land of Canaan (now Israel) is also engaged as a vital partner in the covenantal relationship'.[372]

Afterwards, blessings and cursings would follow, corresponding to their response to God's will as revealed in His law. CRAIGIE points out that there was a natural connection to the Lord's character and between the prosperous events that went along with obedience and the imprecations that accompanied rebellion:

'There are two themes running through both the blessings and the cursings which are significant for a proper understanding of the nature of God as it is expressed in Deuteronomy; God is the Lord of history *and* of the world of nature. He controls other nations *and* the course of nature, whether it be health, the fruitfulness of the land, or any other part of the created order. In other words, God has total control of all the factors that might affect the future well-being of Israel. If his people were obedient, he had the power to grant blessing: he controlled the affairs of nations and could therefore give Israel peace; and he could give them health, long life, and bountiful crops as the Lord of his created world. But if Israel were disobedient, there was no sphere of life in which Israel could escape God; the strength of their army or the richness of the land would be of no avail when the living relationship with God was broken. The tragic element is

---

[372] BLOCK, pg. 631 [brackets mine].

introduced by the knowledge the reader has of the subsequent history of Israel. The blessing of God is at first realized, but then a decline sets in so that the curses dominate that history, until at last the history of the nation is terminated with the curse of exile from the Promised Land, 28. 36. In the light of Israel's history, the emphasis given to the curses loses something of its character and function as a *warning*, and comes to be seen rather as a prophetic anticipation of the course of Israel's history. But the sad story is not written to enable us to pass judgment on the men of ancient Israel. It serves rather as a paradigm of the nature of man. Granted the highest possible privilege, an intimate relationship with God, man nevertheless goes his own way, forgetful of that high calling, until he brings upon himself the curse of God. The curse of God is not something inflicted with vindictive pleasure; rather, it appears to be the inevitable outcome of life that is lived regardless of God, by rejecting a relationship with God whose essence is love'.[373]

Content outline of chapters 27 to 28

- Israelites are commanded to set up pillars with the law written on it on the west side of the Jordan river; they are also to erect them on Mount Ebal, and offer peace offerings on an altar of natural, unhewn stones. They then enjoin Israel to obey the Lord's commandments, Deut. 27. 1-10.
- Arrangement for blessings from Mount Gerizim and cursings from Mount Ebal by specified tribes on each mountain, vv. 11-26.
- Blessings as the results of obedience, Deut. 28. 1-14.
- Cursings as the results of disobedience, vv. 15-68.

---

[373] PETER C. CRAIGIE, *New International Commentary on the Old Testament: Deuteronomy*, Eerdmans, 1994, pg. 44 [italics original].

The place of this covenant ratification is significant. Surrounding the city of Shechem, Mounts Ebal and Gerizim are a place of decision in the scriptures. The Hebrew authorities GESENIUS and TREGELLES define Shechem's name as 'the shoulder, or rather . . . *the hinder part of both shoulder-blades,* or *the upper part of the back next below the neck'.*[374] It is the middle of the back, metaphorically speaking, and therefore topographically presents a natural contrast between two mountains. One author cites its geographical centrality in these words: '[It] was marked out by nature to play an important part in the history of its day. It was situated in a fertile valley between Mounts Ebal and Gerizim, which formed a natural link between the coastal plain and the Jordan valley. Many of the trade-routes converged on Shechem, which, standing at one of the crossroads of Palestine, dominated a considerable area of the surrounding countryside'.[375]

Abraham erected his first altar there, Gen. 12. 6, and Gideon's son Abimelech launched his campaign to rule as Israel's unofficial king at Shechem, Judg. 9. 1-4. Later, in King Rehoboam's day, the nation would divide into ten and two tribes at this same place, 1 Kgs. 12. 1-23. In the New Testament, the Lord Jesus offered a sinful woman the chance to change her life at Shechem, which by then was called 'Sychar', John 4. 5-42. Clearly, this was the place of choice in Israel; by posting the law there, God was offering them the choice of obedience or disobedience, blessing or cursing, Deut. 27. 4-13.

The sins listed in chapter 27 verses 15 to 26 revisit sins that are condemned elsewhere in the Pentateuch and result in divine cursing; they include:

---

[374] GESENIUS and TREGELLES, pg. 822.
[375] ARTHUR E. CUNDALL, *Judges and Ruth: An Introduction and Commentary,* ed. Leon Morris, Tyndale Old Testament Commentaries, Vol. 7, InterVarsity Press, 1968, pp. 122-123 [italics original; brackets mine].

1. Idolatry, Deut. 27. 15; a violation of the second commandment, 5. 8-10.
2. Dishonouring parents, 27. 16; a violation of the fifth commandment, 5. 16.
3. Removing one's neighbour's landmark, 27. 17; falls under the broader category of covetousness – the tenth commandment, 5. 21.
4. Making the blind wander off the road, 27. 18; obviously, this is not loving one's neighbour as oneself, Lev. 19. 14.
5. Perverting justice due to 'the stranger, the fatherless, and the widow', Deut. 27. 19 – a vulnerable group who are frequently grouped together, 10. 18.
6. Incest with one's stepmother, 27. 20; a twofold sin of dishonouring one's father and also of adultery, breaking the fifth and seventh commandments, 5. 16, 18.
7. Bestiality, Deut. 27. 21; Exod. 22. 19; Lev. 18. 23.
8. Incest with one's sister, Deut. 27. 22, or mother-in-law, v. 23; Lev. 18. 9, 17.
9. Stealthy attacks on one's neighbour, Deut. 27. 24, and contract killing or receiving a payment to orchestrate someone's death, v. 25; a violation of the sixth commandment against murder, 5. 17; Exod. 23. 7.
10. A catch-all commandment to confirm God's law, Deut. 27. 26.

Twelve times the tribes of Israel were to cry out 'amen' in response to each of these twelve pronouncements.[376] They were agreeing with God's holy standards from the outset of their career in the inheritance that He was giving to them, vv. 15-26.

---

[376] Since I combined a few from the same category into the same group, my list has 10 sins; it should be noted, however, the list in the text comes to 12 distinct infractions.

Chapter 28 graphically describes the life of blessing versus the life of cursing, depending on Israel's response to the Lord's law. Their blessings would include:

1. Being exalted above the nations, Deut. 28. 1.
2. Fruitfulness in bodily offspring, and agricultural work, including their cattle's offspring, and their crops; sufficient rain, vv. 4-5, 11-12.
3. Victory over enemies, v. 7, and Israel's establishment in their eyes as God's people, causing the nations to fear, vv. 9-10; exaltation, v. 13.
4. General material prosperity, v. 8; they would lend and not borrow, v. 12.

They are warned once more not to turn away from the commandments – 'to the right hand or the left', v. 14 – and they are cautioned against idolatry. The curses of verses 15 to 68 are basically the exact opposite of the blessings, and are a disgusting catalogue of human depravity's fruits. These are drastic consequences listed that accurately describe the disobedient life, including:

1. Cursing in city or country, v. 16.
2. Cursed in personal fruitfulness of progeny or in one's livestock and crops, vv. 17-18, 30-33, 38-42; no rain, vv. 23-24.
3. Cursing, rebuke, confusion, and ruin in all of their undertakings, v. 20; Madness, blindness, confusion, resulting in oppression and despoilment, vv. 28-29, 35.
4. Various types of plagues and diseases, vv. 21-22, 27, 34, 58-63.
5. Defeat at the hands of their enemies, vv. 25-26, 48-57.
6. Foreign captivity and their name becoming a byword for ruin, vv. 36-37, 46; serving idols, 64-68.
7. Borrowing not lending, and abasement rather than exaltation, vv. 43-44.

Various reminders of divine mercy and goodness are dispersed throughout this tragic picture of the devastation that attends a life of sin and insubordination against the Lord. For instance, Deuteronomy chapter 28 verses 45 and 47 maintain: 'Moreover all these curses shall come upon thee, and shall pursue thee, and overtake thee, till thou be destroyed; because thou hearkenedst not unto the voice of the Lord thy God, to keep his commandments and his statutes which he commanded thee . . . Because thou servedst not the Lord thy God with joyfulness, and with gladness of heart, for the abundance of all things'. That is to say, these awful judgements were the natural outcomes of their own wicked choices. The Lord preferred to bless them so that they might have joy and gladness, but they eschewed such preferments in favour of iniquity and the wrath that it inevitably brings. Likewise, another quotation shows that He wanted them to identify themselves as His people: 'If thou wilt not observe to do all the words of this law that are written in this book, that thou mayest fear this glorious and fearful name, THE LORD THY GOD', v. 58. Finally, verses 63 and 68 make the point definitively that the cursings would result from their own fallen wills: 'And it shall come to pass, that as the Lord rejoiced over you to do you good, and to multiply you; so the Lord will rejoice over you to destroy you, and to bring you to nought; and ye shall be plucked from off the land whither thou goest to possess it . . . And the Lord shall bring thee into Egypt again with ships, by the way whereof I spake unto thee, Thou shalt see it no more again: and there ye shall be sold unto your enemies for bondmen and bondwomen, and no man shall buy you'.

Applying the covenant to a new generation – chapters 29 to 30

Having rehearsed the blessings and cursings of obedience or disobedience to the covenant, Moses now calls this conquest generation to recognize this agreement over them. WIERSBE sets the stage:

'The word "covenant" is used seven times in this chapter; in fact, this chapter is the Book of Deuteronomy in miniature. Moses reviewed the past, vv. 1-8, called the people to obey God's Law, vv. 9-15, and warned them what would happen if they disobeyed, vv. 16-29. As we read and study Moses' farewell address, we may get weary of these repeated themes, but they are the essence of God's covenant with His people. While the priests and Levites had a copy of the Law of Moses and could refer to it, 17. 18; 28. 58; 29. 20, 27; 31. 26, the common people had to depend on their memories, and therefore repetition was important . . . The covenant declared in Deuteronomy wasn't different from the covenant given at Mount Sinai. Rather, it was an explanation and application of that covenant to the new generation and their new situation in the Promised Land. If what Moses taught in Deuteronomy had been a separate covenant, he would have offered blood sacrifices to seal the covenant as he did at Sinai, Exod. 24. 3-8; Heb. 9. 18-22. Many of the people who accepted the covenant at Sinai had perished in the wilderness, but there was still a "nation of Israel" that was accountable to the Lord to obey that covenant, Deut. 4-5'.[377]

Chapters 29 and 30 are divided by HOUSE in this way:

'1. The covenant determines Israel's future, Deut. 29. 1-18;
2. A personal, accessible, and understandable covenant, vv. 9-15; 30. 11-14;
3. The Covenant awakens Israel to obey the true God and not serve idols, 29. 16-18;
4. Infidelity brings wrath, 29. 19-29;
5. God's revelation is based on grace, and Israel's response to this grace should be based on gratitude fuelled by love, 30. 15-20.

---

[377] WIERSBE, pp. 171-172.

6. God's gift of land is a physical symbol of divine grace, just as the promise of presence is the main spiritual blessing God offers, 30. 17-18. Lack of loving obedience on Israel's part is the only way the physical and spiritual blessings may be forfeited. Otherwise love and life are inseparable, 30. 19-20'.[378]

There are important themes that are revisited throughout these chapters:

1. The Lord's historic redemptive work in Egypt, 29. 2-3, his guidance and provision in the wilderness, vv. 5-6, and the victories that He gave over Sihon and Og, vv. 7-8, are all rehearsed to encourage Israel for their present and future trust of Him, vv. 9-13.
2. The Lord's covenant is representative for all of the believers in Israel – for that and subsequent generations, vv. 14-15.
3. Unfaithfulness will surely lead to dire judgements, vv. 16-30.
4. Yet repentance will surely bring about restoration and fulfilment of the Lord's blessings, 30. 1-10; cf. 1 Kgs. 8. 33-53.

A New Testament connection – the accessibility of God's revelation, chapter 30 verses 11 to 14 and Romans chapter 10 verses 6 to 8

Moses comments on the clarity and nearness of God's revelation to Israel, saying that it is not 'hidden from thee', v. 11[379] – others translate it 'not too mysterious for you' NKJV; others say 'not too hard for you', ESV or 'not too difficult for you' NAS, NET. They do not have to make an arduous trip across the sea or an impossible journey to heaven, vv. 12-13. Instead, it is 'very near you, in your mouth and

---

[378] HOUSE, pp. 192-193.
[379] Compare Isaiah chapter 48 verse 16: 'Come ye near unto me, hear ye this; I have not spoken in secret from the beginning; From the time that it was, there am I: And now the Lord GOD, and his Spirit, hath sent me'.

in your heart, that you may do it', v. 14 NKJV. Paul cites these verses in Romans chapter 10 verses 6 to 8, establishing the proximity of the gospel to Israel – and, by extension, to Gentiles as well, vv. 12-13.

There is a key difference between the original text in Deuteronomy and the quotation in Romans: Moses says 'that thou mayest do it', Deut. 30. 14; Paul omits this and refers instead to 'the word of faith, which we preach', Rom. 10. 8. This seems to equate the law and faith, yet this is too facile a comparison. Paul is equating the accessibility of the word, not the principle of law-keeping with the principle of faith; elsewhere he shows that they are opposing concepts, e.g., Rom. 10. 3-6; Gal. 3. 10-14. Thankfully, the apostle quotes this passage to demonstrate that the living Word has come down from heaven to show us the Father and bring salvation as a free gift! Men must cease from their futile works-righteousness systems and embrace God's grace through His only begotten Son, the Lord Jesus Christ, Rom. 10. 9-13.

Deuteronomy chapter 30 verses 15 to 20 present a rousing summation to Moses' second speech. Heaven and earth are called to witness this momentous covenant, which speaks of the most serious issues in the universe: 'life and good, death and evil', v. 15. In contrast to the modern spirit of toleration and relativistic beliefs which present an endless array of choices, the Lord brings it down to two simple issues: obedience and life or disobedience and death. The first pathway presents a walk with God – a living relationship – that results in blessing; the second offers the only alternative: temporal cursing that eventually leads to the eternal perdition of 'the second death', Rev. 2. 11; 20. 6, 14. But this second scenario is not what the Lord desires for them. He leaves the prospect of a living relationship with Himself ringing in their ears in Moses' final sentence: 'That thou mayest love the Lord thy God, and that thou mayest obey his voice, and that thou mayest cleave unto him: for he is thy life, and the length of thy days: that thou mayest dwell in the land which the Lord sware unto thy fathers, to Abraham, to Isaac, and to Jacob, to give them', Deut. 30. 20.

Moses' farewell remarks to the nation – chapters 31 to 32

Deuteronomy chapters 31 to 32 leave behind Moses' legacy for the nation of Israel:

1. His successor, Joshua, Deut. 31. 1-8, 23.
2. The Law – i.e., the book of Deuteronomy, vv. 9-13, 24-29 – every seven years (in the year of release) they were to read the entire Law aloud, cf. Neh. 8. 3.
3. His song, Deut. 31. 19-22, 24 – 32. 47.[380]

One author describes this section's theme as 'The God whose word gives life'.[381] BLOCK outlines these chapters in this way:

'A. The Appointment of Joshua as Moses' Successor, 31. 1-8;
B. The Torah, 31. 9-13;
A. The Appointment of Joshua as Moses' Successor, 31. 14-15;
C. The National Anthem, 31. 16-22;
A. The Appointment of Joshua, 31. 23;
B. The Torah, 31. 24-27;
C. The National Anthem, 31. 28 – 32. 44;

---

[380] A modern commentator likens Moses' activities to the modern church's duty: 'How could Moses encourage his beloved people to stay true to their Lord who had done so much for them? Moses did what God commanded him: he appointed Joshua to be his successor; he gave the people the Book of the Law and told them how to use it; and he sang them a song of warning. What Moses did to help prevent apostasy in Israel needs to be done to prevent apostasy in the church today, for the church's record isn't much better than that of Israel . . . We have three responsibilities before the Lord: to honor godly leaders, to hear the Word of God, and to heed the warnings God gives us'. WIERSBE, pp. 177-178.
[381] HOUSE, pg. 193.

B. The Torah, 32. 45-47.

. . . In essence, chapters 31 – 32 function as "a textual witness or memorial", a perpetual reminder of the covenant renewed on the Plains of Moab, of Yahweh's enduring commitment to them, and of the response required of them. Its memorial status is reinforced by the root *'d* ("witness"), which occurs repeatedly, 31. 2, 19, 21, 26, 27, 28; 32. 46 . . . Remarkably, Moses has no interest in erecting memorials to himself; the only legacy that concerns him is a people who never forget Yahweh's covenant with Israel'.[382]

Moses declares that at 120 years of age he can no longer 'go out and come in among them', Deut. 31. 2; a parallel passage exposes his heart for Israel's well-being, saying: 'Let the Lord, the God of the spirits of all flesh, set a man over the congregation, who may go out before them and go in before them, who may lead them out and bring them in, that the congregation of the Lord may not be like sheep which have no shepherd', Num. 27. 15-17 NKJV. Solomon also used the same expression when he petitioned God for wisdom in ruling over the nation, 2 Chr. 1. 10; it is a sort of shorthand expression for 'leadership'.[383]

Even though Joshua was Moses' designated successor, the Lord Himself would lead the invasion and give them victory, Deut. 31. 3-6. Consequently, He tells them not to fear[384] because He would do to the

---

[382] BLOCK, pg. 721.

[383] Other more dynamic equivalence – i.e., semiparaphrastic – versions translate it as: 'am no longer able to lead you', NIV, NLT; 'act as your leader' HCSB.

[384] The military strategist, BARON CARL VON CLAUSEWITZ opines: 'War is the province of danger, and therefore courage above all things is the first quality of a warrior'. BARON CARL VON CLAUSEWITZ, *On War*, Wilder Publications, 2008, pg. 60.

Canaanites exactly what He did to Sihon and Og.[385] His past victories assure them of future success. What is more, their confidence is to be in the Lord and not in any mere man, Ps. 118. 8-9. Even Joshua is directed to have courage emanating from his faith in God, Deut. 31. 8; an allusion to this verse appears in Hebrews chapter 13 verse 5.

Despite His promises and the resources that He gave them for future victory, the Lord foresaw their eventual defection and predicted it, Deut. 31. 16-18. Accordingly, He directed Moses to leave them a song as a witness against them in that future day, vv. 19-22. WIERSBE breaks down the song thus:

1. 'The character of God', vv. 1-4;
2. 'The kindness of God to His people', vv. 5-14;
3. 'The faithfulness of God to chasten His people', vv. 15-25;
4. 'The vengeance of God against His adversaries', vv. 26-43.

He summarizes the song's theme this way: 'The song traces God's dealings with Israel and is a concise review of the nation's history, from their wilderness sojourn to the judgments in the end times. It has both historic and prophetic aspects'.[386] It begins with Moses

---

[385] The memory of the defeat of these kings is frequently used to encourage Israel in Deuteronomy. See Deut. 1. 4; 2. 24, 26, 30-32; 3. 1-4, 6, 10-11, 13; 4. 46-47; 29. 7; 31. 4.
[386] The preceding outline and this quote are both found in WIERSBE, pg. 182. Another teacher outlines it like this:
'A. The Exordium: A Call to Acknowledge the Perfections of Yahweh, vv. 1-4;
B. The Recollection: A Call to Acknowledge the Imperfections of Yahweh's People, vv. 5-18;
Stanza I: The Thesis Statement, vv. 5-6;
Stanza II: A Call to Remember Yahweh's Grace, vv. 7-14;
Stanza III: Trampling Underfoot the Grace of Yahweh, vv. 15-18;
C. The Confession: A Call to Recognize the Justice of Yahweh, vv. 19-35;
Stanza I: Yahweh's Justice in Dealing with His Own People, vv. 19-25;
Stanza II: Yahweh's Justice in Dealing with Israel's Enemies, vv. 26-35;

calling on heaven and earth to bear witness; this poetic description reminds Israel that their doings are observed within the greater universe. Moses' first speech also invokes this witness, 4. 26; see also 30. 19; 31. 28.

It begins with a beautiful description of God's character, drawing on the authority of His name[387] and His intrinsic attributes, vv. 3-4. As PARMENTER declares:

'God's love, goodness and patience to Israel, in spite of their falling into every kind of sin, inspired its people to ascribe greatness to their God. He is ineffable in holiness, infinite in wisdom, mysterious in trinity, boundless in His attributes of omnipotence, omniscience and omnipresence. His eternal supremacy and redeeming grace call upon the hearts of all who know Him to, "ascribe ... greatness unto our God". God chose us in Christ before the foundation of the world, and made us sons by adoption, and placed us in the Beloved. He has also redeemed us and forgiven all our sins. In the riches of His grace God has linked us with Christ eternally as His Body, setting us in the place of highest dignity. Christ in His love for us will bring us to the

---

D. The Gospel: A Call to Treasure the Compassion of Yahweh, vv. 36-42;
E. The Coda: A Call to Celebrate the Deliverance of Yahweh, v. 43'. BLOCK, pp. 746-747.
[387] Concerning His name, MACKINTOSH remarks: 'Here lies the solid, the imperishable foundation of everything. Come what may, the name of our God shall stand forever. No power of earth or hell can possibly countervail the divine purpose, or hinder the outshining of the divine glory. What sweet rest this gives the heart in the midst of this dark, sorrowful, sin-stricken world, and in the face of the apparently successful schemes of the enemy! Our refuge, our resource, our sweet relief and solace, are found in the name of the Lord our God, the God and Father of our Lord Jesus Christ'. MACKINTOSH, pg. 898.

269

nearest place of affection as His Bride. How can we not "ascribe greatness to our God?"'[388]

In light of verse 4, SPURGEON cautions: 'Reject every philosophy that does not ascribe greatness to God, for there is a worm at the root of it, there is some cancer at its heart and it yet shall be destroyed. That and that alone shall stand which ascribes "greatness unto our God"'.[389]

In verse 5 'the perverse and crooked generation' reappears in an allusion by Paul, Phil. 2. 14, who desired better behaviour from the church than Israel in the Old Testament era. Deuteronomy chapter 32 verse 6 references God's role as Father, Redeemer, and Creator and is denouncing their rebellion as absurd. Like thirteen times before in this book,[390] verse 7 calls them to 'remember'; the Lord obviously wants His people to keep in mind the history of His work for them – in the church age the same principle stands, 2 Pet. 1. 12-15.

Israel's preciousness in the Lord's sight is evidenced by Him calling them 'the apple of his eye', Deut. 32. 10. This intimate term is rendered 'the pupil of the eye' by other translations, NKJVmg., NAS, NET, and indicates a tender and much protected part of one's anatomy. Their security further appears in God's metaphorical description of an eagle protecting His young, v. 11. In spite of His protection and rich provision for them, they merely became engorged and ungrateful in response to His goodness, vv. 12-15. He calls them by the affectionate name 'Jeshurun'; two Hebrew authorities describe it as 'a tender and loving appellation of the

---

[388] ERIC PARMENTER, 'February 13th: Ascribe Greatness to God, Deuteronomy 32. 1-4', in *Day by Day in Prayer*, ed. IVAN STEEDS, Day by Day Series, Precious Seed, 1997, pg. 60.
[389] C. H. SPURGEON, 'The Great Supreme', in *The Metropolitan Tabernacle Pulpit Sermons*, Vol. 7, Passmore & Alabaster, 1861, pg. 156.
[390] For the other references, see Deut. 5. 15; 7. 18; 8. 2, 18; 9. 7; 15. 15; 16. 3, 12; 24. 9, 18, 22; 25. 17.

people of Israel'.[391] Tragically, despite His kindness, they responded with malice. The song goes on to say that they 'lightly esteemed' their Rock, v. 15.[392] Being turned from the truth, they inevitably turned to idols – in actuality, 'demons', vv. 16-17 NKJV; cf. 1 Cor. 10. 20.[393]

Israel's future apostasy would bring about severe discipline from God, Deut. 32. 19-38. Their substitute gods – in actuality mere vanities – would be powerless to help them. Thus, they would remember that there is only one true and living God – Jehovah who

---

[391] GESENIUS and TREGELLES, pg. 376. It occurs four times in the Old Testament: Deut. 32. 15; 33. 5, 26; Isa. 44. 2.

[392] As HALL exegetes this verse: 'She renounced God and treated him disdainfully'. He goes on to unpack the nuance of the Hebrew that 'lightly esteemed' translates: 'This is the same verb used for the son who dishonored the father, Mic. 7. 6, and for God treating Nineveh with contempt, Nahum 3. 6'. HALL, pg. 474.

MACKINTOSH notices the parallel among believers in this age, writing: 'Surrounded on all hands by the rich and varied mercies of God, we are apt to make use of them to nourish a spirit of self-complacency. We make use of the gifts to shut out the Giver. In a word, we, too, like Israel, wax fat and kick – we forget God. We lose the sweet and precious sense of His presence and of His perfect sufficiency, and turn to other objects, as Israel did to false gods. How often do we forget the Rock that begat us, the God that formed us, the Lord that redeemed us!' MACKINTOSH, pg. 900.

[393] SPURGEON excoriates the wickedness of departing from God and His word in these powerful sentences: 'Moses multiplies expressions to show the folly of Israel's idolatry. Only think of "new gods that came newly up", as if that which is new could be a god! The same thing may be said of the "new truth" of which we hear so much nowadays. That which is new cannot be true. Certainly, there is nothing new in theology but that which is utterly false. The idols, which the Israelites worshipped, were not only new gods, but they were strange gods, which their fathers feared not. Worse than that, they were demons: "they sacrificed unto devils, not to God". How low had even the chosen people sunk'! C. H. SPURGEON, 'Man's Extremity, God's Opportunity', in *The Metropolitan Tabernacle Pulpit Sermons*, Vol. 47, Passmore & Alabaster, 1901, pg. 119.

will take vengeance[394] on all of His adversaries, vv. 34-42. Verse 43 ends this sobering song with a ray of triumphant gospel hope: 'Rejoice, O ye nations, with his people: For he will avenge the blood of his servants,[395] And will render vengeance to his adversaries, And will be merciful unto his land, and to his people'. As Moses reminded Israel, heeding God's word is the essence of life. To ignore it is to court spiritual and temporal disaster in this world and in the age to come.

The chapter concludes with a bittersweet charge for Moses to ascend Mount Nebo, where he will view the Promised Land into which he is not permitted to lead Israel because of his sin at Meribah Kadesh, vv. 48-52. Before recording the fulfilment of this in chapter 34, there is first a parting blessing that Moses leaves with the nation in chapter 33.

Blessed are the people whose God is the Lord – chapter 33

In a modern world that is obsessed with human titles that aggrandize man and his accomplishments, it is refreshing to read of Moses, one of the greatest leaders in history, described simply – yet wonderfully – as 'the man of God', Deut. 33. 1; see also the superscription of Psalm 90, which the Holy Spirit used him to pen. His blessing begins and ends on positive notes, emphasizing God's law and rule, vv. 2-5. This glorious poem takes in the twelve tribes' destinies – Simeon is omitted, but they were linked with Judah in their inheritance, Josh. 19. 1, 9. HOUSE notes the importance of this passage in the Pentateuch:

'The Pentateuch concludes its discussion of God's relationship to Israel the same way it began its description of God's relationship

---

[394] 'Vengeance is mine', Deut. 32. 35, is cited twice in the New Testament: Rom. 12. 19; Heb. 10. 30.
[395] It seems that Revelation chapter 19 verse 2 is quoting this verse.

272

to the human race: it speaks of God blessing them, Gen. 1. 26-31. At the same time it continues to stress the written word's ability to interpret the past, to guide the present and to predict the future. It also presents Moses himself as a unique blessing to God's people'.[396]

This theme of blessing makes Deuteronomy chapter 33's tone much more sweet than the parting prophecy of Israel's great ancestor and namesake, Jacob, regarding his offspring, Gen. 49. 1-28. Although it is an interesting and fruitful study to compare and contrast that chapter with this one, this volume's scope does not permit it. The reader should carefully examine both passages. The blessings of the tribes according to Moses are summarized below:

1. Reuben, Deut. 33. 6 – Life and not death; numerical blessing.
2. Judah, v. 7 – safe return from and sufficiency in battle; victory over enemies.
3. Levi, vv. 8-11 – Instead of looking at Moses' failure at Massah, the Lord looks at the other side of things: because of their identity as the priestly tribe, Levi was criticized by the people. Yet they remained loyal to God, above family considerations, vv. 8-9. They also provided guidance – e.g., 'urim and thummim', v. 8 – teaching and leading worship, v. 10, for Israel. Bless his property and labour, and smite his enemies, v. 11.
4. Benjamin – Jacob's youngest son is described as 'beloved', v. 12, and has the beautiful picture of dwelling 'between his shoulders'. MERRILL explains this lovely phrase:

'The anthropomorphism here is suggestive of the most tender compassion and solid security at the same time. The phrase speaks not of carrying on the back but of being held close to the breast or bosom . . . The Hebrew noun *ĥêq* expresses the idea

---

[396] HOUSE, pg. 195.

more explicitly, frequently occurring as a picture of parental love and protection, cf. Num. 11. 12; Ruth 4. 16; 2 Sam. 12. 3; Isa. 40. 11. The most touching example of all, however, is that of John, who reclined on Jesus' bosom (Gr. *kolmos*), a sign of the closest fellowship, John 13. 23'.[397]

5. Joseph, vv. 13-17 – Joseph's sons Ephraim and Manasseh were often treated as separate tribes due to their large size; here, however, they are united. The picture presents tremendous agricultural and earthly fruitfulness, vv. 13-16. He is described as 'a firstborn bull', v. 17.[398] There is also a sidelong glance back to Joseph's exaltation in Egypt by God's providence, v. 16, and the promise of future victory, v. 17.

6. Zebulun and Issachar, vv. 18-19 – The sixth and fifth tribes are listed out of birth order to honour the former tribe. They are described as prospering from sand and sea, v. 19. This may refer to trade interests by these tribes; or they may have controlled territory along the Mediterranean that was later taken over by Asher.[399]

7. Gad, vv. 20-21 – These verses seem to refer to their part in the conquest of the eastern land on the banks of the Jordan – Sihon and Og's kingdoms. Their greatness is also demonstrated by their inclusion on the extrabiblical Moabite stone.[400]

8. Dan, v. 22 – A lion cub is an image of power in the scripture; it is used to describe Judah, Gen. 49. 9. They conquered 'Laish', Judg. 18. 27-31.

---

[397] MERRILL, pp. 440-441.
[398] BLOCK defines it thus: 'Hebrew *re'ēm* refers to the European and Middle Eastern branch of bovines known as aurochs, now extinct . . . Job 39. 9-10 characterizes them as wild and impossible to domesticate. In Balaam's oracles, God himself is a "wild ox", whose horns protect Israel as he brings them out of Egypt, Num. 23. 22; 24. 8'. BLOCK, fn. 40, pg. 795.
[399] HALL, pg. 493.
[400] HALL, pg. 493.

9. Naphtali, v. 23 – Given divine favour and blessing, they are apportioned land 'in the west and the south'.
10. Asher, vv. 24-25 – They dwelt in a fertile part of Israel bordering the Mediterranean Sea and known for its olive trees – hence, the comment about bathing 'his foot in oil', v. 24.[401] Verse 25 indicates a firmness of step and a successful walk.

The remaining verses of the blessing speak of Israel as a whole, vv. 26-29. The Phoenician storm god Baal was often pictured riding on a cloud in ancient literature.[402] But here the true God is shown to be the one who makes His chariot out of clouds, v. 26; Pss. 68. 4, 33; 104. 3. He is the real power in the universe, and He uses His might to protect Israel. He is their 'refuge',[403] Deut. 33. 27; Ps. 90. 1. In a beautiful fatherly metaphor, He promises that His everlasting arms would undergird them. A seventeenth-century preacher reminds us of the tenderness and security of this image, saying:

'Let the load be never so heavy that God lays on, if he put under his everlasting arms, all is in love, Gen. 49. 23, 24 . . . It is no matter how heavy the burden is, if God gives a shoulder to bear it: all is in love; it is no matter how bitter the cup is, if God give

---

[401] HALL, pg. 495.
[402] KOOWON KIM, 'Rider on the Clouds', ed. JOHN D. BARRY ET AL., The Lexham Bible Dictionary, Lexham Press, 2014, electronic edition, no pagination. See also MERRILL, pg. 447.
[403] Occurring nine times in nine Old Testament verses, this is the first usage of the Hebrew word me'ō·nāh – Strong's #4585; it frequently refers to an animal's den – especially lions. Its other appearances are Job 37. 8; 38. 40; Ps. 76. 2; 104. 22; S. of S. 4. 8; Jer. 21. 13; Amos 3. 4; Nahum 2. 12. See BROWN, DRIVER, and BRIGGS, pg. 733 and GESENIUS and TREGELLES, pg. 492.

courage to drink it off; it is no matter how hot the furnace is, if God gives power to walk in the midst of it: all is in love'.[404]

Moses assures them that such a powerful God 'shall thrust out the enemy from before thee; And shall say, Destroy them', Deut. 33. 27. He is their 'sword' and 'shield', and promises to subdue their enemies, v. 29 KJVmg., and destroy 'the high places' where they worshipped their idols, v. 29. Verse 28 predicts their solitary enjoyment of prosperity in the land, and the beginning of the next verse calls them 'happy'.[405] All in all, chapter 33 is a comprehensive blessing of the greatest magnitude.

Moses' exit and legacy – chapter 34

Content outline

- Moses' final moments viewing the land, his death, and Israel's mourning, Deut. 34. 1-8;
- Moses' successor Joshua, v. 9;
- Moses' epitaph, vv. 10-12.

Picking up where Deuteronomy chapter 32 verses 48 to 52 left off, this final section records the culmination of the life of one of the great heroes of the faith: Moses, the Lord's 'servant', 34. 5, and an incomparable 'prophet' who enjoyed 'face to face', v. 10, intimacy with the Almighty, Exod. 33. 11. He left an eminent successor, Joshua, who had been marked out by Moses' own hands, v. 9. Nonetheless,

---

[404] THOMAS BROOKS, 'The Mute Christian Under The Smarting Rod', in *The Complete Works of Thomas Brooks, Volume 1*, ed. ALEXANDER BALLOCH GROSART, James Nisbet and Co., 1866, pg. 344.

[405] *Ashri* – Strong's # 835 – appears forty-four times in the Old Testament and is defined as 'blessed!, happy!, a heightened state of happiness and joy, implying very favorable circumstances, often resulting from the kind acts of God'. MOUNCE, pg. 901. It is the famous word 'blessed' in Psalm chapter 1 verse 1.

Moses was used to work signs and wonders against the great superpower of the time – Egypt – in a manner seldom seen throughout history, vv. 10-12.[406] Tragically, he only saw the land at this time; he was not permitted to lead them into it. On New Testament ground, however, Moses enjoyed a glorified conversation with the Lord Jesus on another mount within the land, Luke 9. 28-30!

Sceptics have tried to undermine the scriptures by pointing out that Moses could not write his own obituary and epitaph, but this fails to consider two things:

1. The omniscient Spirit of God could obviously use him beforehand to pen these things.
2. The Spirit of God could use another amanuensis and it would still be God's word, 23. 16; 2 Pet. 1. 21.

No matter who physically wrote this chapter, the words are the Lord's!

---

[406] Rather than everyday occurrences, signs and wonders are concentrated at certain epochs, the days of Moses; Elijah and Elisha; Christ and his apostles; and the future tribulation period. Otherwise, they are almost absent from the pages of the Bible.

Bibliography for Deuteronomy

ALBERT BARNES, *Notes on the Old Testament: Exodus to Ruth*, ed. F. C. Cook and J. M. Fuller, John Murray, 1879.

DANIEL I. BLOCK, *The NIV Application Commentary: Deuteronomy*, ed. Terry Muck, Zondervan, 2012.

C. A. COATES, *Outline Of Deuteronomy*, Stow Hill Bible and Tract Depot, n.d.

CHARLES R. ERDMAN, *The Book Of Deuteronomy: An Exposition*, Fleming Revell, 1953.

GARY HARLAN HALL, *Deuteronomy*, The College Press NIV Commentary, College Press Publishing Co., 2000.

WILLIAM MACDONALD, *Believer's Bible Commentary: Old and New Testaments,* ed. Arthur Farstad, Thomas Nelson, 1995.

C. H. MACKINTOSH, *Genesis to Deuteronomy: Notes on the Pentateuch,* Loizeaux Brothers, 1972.

EUGENE H. MERRILL, *Deuteronomy*, The New American Commentary, Vol. 4, Broadman & Holman Publishers, 1994.

GORDON MCCONVILLE, 'Deuteronomy', in D. A. CARSON, R. T. FRANCE, J. A. MOTYER, and G. J. WENHAM, eds., *New Bible Commentary: 21st Century Edition*, 4th ed., Inter-Varsity Press, 1994.

J. A. THOMPSON, *Deuteronomy: An Introduction and Commentary*, Tyndale Old Testament Commentaries, Vol. 5, InterVarsity Press, 1974.

WARREN W. WIERSBE, *Be Equipped*, 'Be' Commentary Series, Chariot Victor Publishers, 1999.